Can Finance Save The World?

Regaining Control Over Money To Serve The Common Good

Bertrand Badré

Forewords By Emmanuel Macron (President Of The French Republic) Gordon Brown (Former Prime Minister Of The United Kingdom)

16

EasyRead Large

ISBN: 9781525268182

RHYW

Copyright Page from the Original Book

Can Finance Save the World?

Berrett-Koehler Publishers, Inc.
1333 Broadway, Suite 1000
Oakland, CA 94612-1921
Tel: (510) 817-2277, Fax: (510) 817-2278
www.bkconnection.com

Ordering information for print editions
Quantity sales. Special discounts are available on quantity purchases by corporations, associations, and others. For details, contact the "Special Sales Department" at the Berrett-Koehler address above.
Individual sales. Berrett-Koehler publications are available through most bookstores. They can also be ordered directly from Berrett-Koehler: Tel: (800) 929-2929; Fax: (802) 864-7626; www.bkconnection.com
Orders for college textbook/course adoption use. Please contact Berrett-Koehler: Tel: (800) 929-2929; Fax: (802) 864-7626.
Orders by U.S. trade bookstores and wholesalers. Please contact Ingram Publisher Services, Tel: (800) 509-4887; Fax: (800) 838-1149; E-mail: customer .service@ingrampublisherservices.com; or visit www.ingrampublisherservices.com/ Ordering for details about electronic ordering.

First Edition
Paperback print edition ISBN 978-1-5230-9421-9
PDF e-book ISBN 978-1-5230-9422-6
IDPF e-book ISBN 978-1-5230-9423-3

2017-1

Book producer and text designer: BookMatters, Berkeley, CA

Copyeditor: Mike Mollett

Proofreader: Janet Reed Blake

Indexer: Leonard Rosenbaum

Cover designer: The Book Designers

TABLE OF CONTENTS

Praise for Can Finance Save the World?

"Agree or disagree, Bertrand Badré has written a hugely important book on the future of finance. He provides a compelling vision for ethical global finance that makes current political debates seem petty and thoughtless."

—Lawrence H. Summers, Charles W. Eliot University Professor, Harvard University

"Bertrand Badré knows as well as anyone what gave rise to the disenchantment with the world of finance. His aim in this important and provocative book is to point to a new world in which finance is no longer a threat but becomes a handmaiden to order, stability, confidence, growth, and greater equality."

—Ezra Suleiman, Professor of Politics and IBM Professor of International Studies, Princeton University

"Bertrand has definitely witnessed the financial crisis from the inside and has drawn important lessons. More importantly, this book shows that things can actually be done, walking the talk rather than just talking the talk."

—Ricardo Ernst, PhD, Baratta Chair in Global Business and Professor of Operations and

Global Logistics, McDonough School of Business, Georgetown University

"A wake-up call. An expert's valuable overview of the need to support the nascent revolution in finance to improve lives."

—Sir Ronald Cohen, Chair, Global Social Impact Investment Steering Group, and cofounder of Apax Partners

"This book is a must-read for anyone interested in understanding why finance has become such a powerful force for our times. Can finance save the world? Maybe, but it could also cripple it. Badré's insights reflect the rare combination of a keen intellect and a wealth of hands-on experience in the world of international finance."

—Masood Ahmed, President, Center for Global Development

"This book is a powerful call to action for global leaders to reinvent the way that the public, private, and social sectors collaborate and describes the important and unexpected role that finance can play in uniting stakeholders across political and socioeconomic boundaries."

—Dominic Barton, Global Managing Partner, McKinsey & Company

"Everyone says we need more public investment. Everyone says the public and private sectors must work together. Nobody has told us how—until Badré spelled it out practically and providentially in this book."

—Adam S. Posen, President, Peterson Institute for International Economics

"Colorful, confronting, and compelling! Bertrand Badré presents the case for reshaping the international financial architecture and mobilizing global financial flows as drivers of inclusive growth. This book is a call to action for all of us—as we continue to grapple with the legacies of the global financial crisis."

—Angel Gurría, Secretary-General, Organisation for Economic Co-operation and Development

"Bertrand Badré makes a convincing argument for how financial institutions—and particularly multilateral development banks—can help humanity conquer some of its greatest challenges, from climate change to the quest for building more equitable societies. His book is a valuable contribution to the debate about development finance."

—Luis Alberto Moreno, President, Inter-American Development Bank

"Bertrand Badré's creative and insightful book on international finance paints a holistic picture of the practical and ethical dimensions of this very important social tool."

—John D. Negroponte, former US Permanent Representative to the United Nations and former Deputy Secretary of State

"Building on the seminal idea that finance, like any human activity, is here to serve the common good, Bertrand Badré outlines in this easy-to-read book a number of avenues that humankind can and should explore and embrace to address the challenges it faces today, using finance as a tool, not an end. An inspiring and practical invitation to choose the right path at the crossroad the world finds itself at."

—Hubert Joly, Chairman and CEO, Best Buy

"It has been a long-held belief of mine that leveraging the private sector much more efficiently as well as being innovative in how we use capital are two of the essential keys to unlocking development. Bertrand Badré carries these as central themes throughout his well-argued book. What is even more impressive is Bertrand's bold move to implement what has long been discussed in theory into real life and concrete action. This is why I am really proud to support him and Blue like an Orange."

—Olivier Goudet, CEO, JAB Group, and Chairman, Anheuser-Busch InBev

"Bertrand Badré offers a holistic view of finance. Like technology, it is neither good nor bad in itself. But an intelligent partnership between private financial institutions, international organizations, governments, and the philanthropic sector can produce fabulous results. To help us understand how these partnerships can be crafted and the crucial role 'domesticated' financial institutions can play, he draws on his deep experience in both the public and the private sectors. A must-read for the development finance community."

—Kemal Dervis, Director of Global Economy and Development, Brookings Institution, and former head of the United Nations Development Programme

"In these times of uncertainty and increasing nationalism, Badré makes a powerful case for the inherently global nature of finance and its capacity to be used as a tool for good."

—Agustín Guillermo Carstens Carstens, Governor, Banco de México

"Drawing on deep expertise, wide-ranging practical experience, and the vantage point of a thoughtful insider, Bertrand Badré provides important insights on how society can—and should—regain control of a bipolar finance system to deliver better and more sustainable outcomes for more people around the world."

—Mohamed El-Erian, Chief Economic Advisor, Allianz; former CEO, PIMCO; and author of *The Only Game in Town*

"Bertrand Badré and I worked on promoting the G20 infrastructure agenda during the Australian presidency. The ideas we pushed are the ones that are at the heart of *Can Finance Save the World?* Ideas are essential, but this book is about trying and doing. A true call for action."

—Honorable Joe Hockey, Australian Ambassador to the United States, former Treasurer of Australia, and former Chair, G20

"A blueprint for forceful, collective action. Against a rising tide of economic nationalism, Badré lays the course to address an unprecedented range of global threats—climate change, pandemics, inadequate access to infrastructure and water, and refugee crises. With his new venture, Blue like an Orange, Badré is also practicing what he preaches, reimagining finance as an equalizing force for the vulnerable among us."

—Antonio Weiss, Senior Fellow, Harvard Kennedy School

"This book is refreshingly different. Written by someone with a deep understanding of both the flaws and the possibilities of the financial system, it presents a level-headed analysis of what went wrong. However, it goes much further and offers a constructive view of what can be achieved if we move beyond the postmortem and remember what tremendous potential finance can bring to economic and social development. Indeed, it argues for the right kind of innovation in our financial system as an indispensable ingredient to solve many of today's global problems and create a more equitable world."

—Klaus Schwab, Executive Chairman, World Economic Forum

"Postcrisis financial reform efforts have focused on how to make the global system safer so that 'it can't happen again.' Bertrand Badré instead addresses the forward-looking challenge of making finance effectively serve broader interests of social and environmental progress, in addition to promoting growth."

—John Lipsky, Senior Fellow, Johns Hopkins School of Advanced International Studies, and former First Deputy Managing Director, International Monetary Fund

"Bertrand Badré played a key role in providing the analysis of the role of finance in achieving the sustainable development goals. We all agreed that the way forward was not going to be 'business as usual.' This is why this book is so helpful, important, and timely as it serves as a how-to guide to inspire action among a multistakeholder society."

—Charlotte Petri Gornitzka, Chair, Development Assistance Committee, Organisation for Economic Co-operation and Development

"Bertrand lays out an ambitious, but I believe completely doable, path for the public and private financial markets to take to achieve our common human objectives. And he makes a forceful argument for why it is in the best and self-interest of the financial sector to feel responsible for helping achieve the goals the world has set and to help eliminate the growing cancer of increasing inequality."

—Ray Chambers, UN Secretary-General's Special Envoy for Health in Agenda 2030 and for Malaria and former Chairman, Wesray Capital Corporation

"To build an inclusive world, Bertrand lays out ideas on how finance can be used as a force for good and inclusion. Such inclusion will significantly help reduce the societal unease that is leading to political crisis in many countries by allowing humanity to address some of its most pressing problems, including global warming, pandemics, and inequality."

—Paul Desmarais III, Senior Vice President, Power Financial Corporation, and Executive Chairman, Portag3 Ventures and Sagard Holdings

"This book is a passionate call for leadership and joint action. As Badré reminds us, finance is not a blind and uncontrollable force. It is not good or bad in itself but as good as we use it—and, going forward, we will indeed have to use this tool a lot and as wisely as we can to master the global challenges that we all face together."

—Dr. Werner Hoyer, President, European Investment Bank

"Bertrand's critical expertise, acquired through his work at the heart of the financial system over three decades, is brought to the fore in this outstanding work. We all have a stake in ensuring that the international finance system succeeds and serves society, not the other way around."

—Mark Carney, Governor, Bank of England, and Chairman, G20 Financial Stability Board

FOREWORD

Emmanuel Macron

Hasty and definitive judgments about finance are frequently heard. For some, finance is the enemy of the people, dispossessing them of their sovereignty. For others, finance is a tangible expression of human greed; it is merely an instrument of domination, making it possible to create value without effort and to accumulate wealth without producing. For still others, finance has become a religion before which our societies should prostrate themselves. These caricatures miss the mark. They do not recognize that finance encompasses diverse realities. They do not make it possible to understand that finance is only a means to serve human ends. We must use finance—not serve it.

At its core, finance does not constrain us: it obliges us. It is this reality that Bertrand Badré, with whom I have considered these questions regularly for years, highlights in this beautiful work. Throughout his professional career, Badré has been a privileged witness to world-changing events, such as the acceleration of trade, the progressive integration of our economies, the emergence of new challenges, notably environmental ones, and the advent of new risks, especially threats to security.

The reflections he shares here are a call for determined action.

Indeed, recent history shows that we have made the collective choice of inaction. The decades of prosperity after the Second World War, based on the Bretton Woods Agreement, the Marshall Plan, and the beginnings of the European construction, forged a stable and organized financial system. This cycle broke with the suspension of the gold convertibility of the dollar, and then the first energy crisis. After this shock and the ensuing stagflation, the conservative and neoliberal revolution of the 1980s ushered in a new period of our economic history. Growth and considerable progress were achieved. But by unleashing the movement of capital, by drastically reducing regulation, and by expanding public and private debt, governments finally relinquished their power to make finance serve their greater goals, or to use finance as a tool for action. In 2007 the financial crisis suddenly lifted the veil on this pernicious system. The political and social disorders that it engendered and the fractures that it accentuated were the violent outcome. However, it would be a grave error to conclude that this crisis discredited finance itself. I believe this is a misconception. The crucial lesson of this crisis is the urgent need to regain control of the global financial system. In particular, we must address three global challenges.

The first challenge is the environment. I am convinced that the necessary ecological transition will first be an economic transition. At a time when the president of the United States seems to have abandoned this battle, France and the European Union must understand that their responsibility is all the greater. To succeed we have to accelerate the mobilization of private and public actors, politicians, and civil society. Success will also require massive use of global savings in order to transform our productive model and create the conditions for environmental innovation. Finally, it is important to reorganize our financial system so that it can better integrate the ecological imperative. Finance is the arena in which progress can be made, such as accounting for the long term, valuing externalities (in particular, the price of carbon), and holding economic actors accountable. In this matter, France recognizes its role and is on the front line. The financial center of Paris is in the process of adopting a strategy and rules of the game to turn it into an international leader in green finance. I will encourage this movement in favor of a useful finance.

The second challenge is innovation. We are no longer in an economy of catch-up priorities and big projects, as was the case some 30 years ago. Our course is no longer toward the imitation of products imagined abroad; it is found in innovation in the developed countries and in all the countries of the world. The strength and power of the emerging model resides in the alliance that companies are able to seal with millions of users. The result is a formidably decentralized, more horizontal economy, in which it is a question of constant investment to create employment and encourage our businesses to grow. The digital revolution is revealing itself to be at the heart of financial cycles. The released energy thus appears to be without limits; the effects are colossal and can cause alarm. They must, however, benefit all. In this battle, we must put finance to the task. Investment needs to exceed the capacity of governments. Cooperation between the public and private sectors requires new approaches and new tools. It is not enough merely to better regulate! We must also innovate in the financial field, in order to allow all the territories and all the actors to benefit from the waves of progress. And such crucial innovation is now unfolding in a renewed framework. Bertrand Badré recalls an exchange with Sir Ronald Cohen: "The 19th century was the age of rewards; the 20th century was that of risk/reward; the 21st century looks like the age of risk/reward/impact." Investment is at the heart of the economic policy I lead in France. It is more broadly a major challenge for Europe as a whole, which must invest more and better to accelerate the digital revolution and boldly enter the new economy.

The third challenge is development. The needs are immense, but they have never been more urgent. Climate change, the rise of migration, and the unprecedented risks associated with pandemics require us to act quickly and to mobilize the necessary resources. Again, public institutions alone will not be able to cope with this global challenge. The money exists, but it is poorly allocated. It is important to reinvent forms of international cooperation, to renew our multilateral tools by adapting them to the new demands, and to encourage private institutions to take risks for the general interest—to invest most heavily where needs are greatest.

Environment, innovation, and development—these three global challenges are at the heart of a new paradigm that we must imagine and build after 10 years of crisis. Together, they demonstrate that we cannot do so without finance, albeit useful and responsible finance. To refuse to put the financial system at our service would be to give up action and prepare the conditions for our collective failure. Of course, this book provides neither all the answers nor all the solutions. But it allows us to confront the fatalists, the adherents of decline, and all those who imagine or imply that we are disarmed. Yes, finance can help save the world. It is up to us to claim it for ourselves.

FOREWORD

Gordon Brown

Few have done more to expose the challenges globalization throws at us than Bertrand Badré. And few have come up with more positive proposals for how to manage globalization in the interests of those who need our help most than he has done—first in his capacity as Chief Financial Officer of the World Bank and then as the inspirational architect of the "From Billions to Trillions" proposals, which were agreed at the Addis Ababa Conference as a means of financing the Sustainable Development Goals. He now challenges us with his plan for managing international finance and as the author of this new book, which introduces us to new thinking about globalization, he suggests how it can be made to work for the poorest of the world.

Dean Acheson spoke about his role as a US diplomat and later Secretary of State in evolving the new institutions of the post-1945 world and said it felt like being "present at the creation." Then the task was to create multilateral institutions for what was still a world of detached nation states. Now in a new generation—the post-millennium interdependent world where we need global solutions to global problems—Badré and other leading economists are present at the creation, or at least at attempts at the creation, of a new more relevant global architecture for this still young century.

New thinking at the turn of the century influenced the introduction of the path-breaking Millennium Development Goals, which were kicked off in 1999 when the then UN Secretary General, Kofi Annan, called for a "global compact of shared values." In a visionary speech, Annan argued that "the spread of markets [was outpacing] the ability of societies and political systems to adjust to them." His warning, that globalization was fragile and "vulnerable to backlash from ... protectionism, populism, nationalism, ethnic chauvinism, fanaticism and terrorism" as extremists exploited discontent, led him to propose new ways of dealing with poverty, malnutrition, disease, illiteracy, and inequality.[1]

And the process he initiated that was formally launched with the commitment to the MDGs in 2000 had to be rethought, adapted, and streamlined in the wake of the global financial crisis of 2008, and as we came to understand the urgency of co-ordinating global efforts to deal with climate change. This evolution in the world's thinking is charted by Badré in his book.

Finance is, as he says, a good servant but a poor master and the global financial recession exposed the reality that while we had global banks and financial institutions, they were inadequately supervised by purely national regulatory systems. But the crisis asked even more profound questions: it challenged the very idea of self-adjusting financial markets and was so all encompassing that it forced world leaders to agree to the biggest rescue operation ever attempted.

To underpin the recovery of the world economy, one trillion dollars in grants, loans, and trade support guarantees was made available, but as Badré suggests a lot more has to be done to turn a rescue operation into an exercise in repairing the world's financial system. Even after the welcome strengthening of the global Financial Stability Board no one can be sure that we have done enough to protect ourselves against the next financial crisis.

And in our journey from Copenhagen's failed climate change summit of December 2009 to the success recorded at Paris in December 2015, new thinking has had to be developed to reduce global carbon emissions. Some of the results of these efforts are contained in the Sustainable Development Goals agreed on unanimously by the United Nations in September 2015 after the Addis Ababa Conference in which Bertrand Badré played such a large part. The new SDGs now see economic growth, social justice, and environmental sustainability not as antithetical to each other but as complimentary objectives. But the question remains as to how we can realize them in difficult financial times and to what extent we can enhance the multilateral co ordination necessary to do so.

For although we all agree that the world is more interconnected and interdependent, our collective ability to tackle urgent issues has been weakened as a result of trade protectionism and cuts in international economic support and aid. As Georg Kell, the former head of the UN Global Compact, has recently argued, the case has again to be made for multilateralism. Perhaps in every generation we have to make anew the arguments for co ordinated multilateral action. At no time is this more true than now and reinventing multilateralism is what Badré seeks to achieve in his set of essays: they set out to develop better ways of mobilizing finance for public good, so that instead of finance being a threat to the stability of the global economy, it can become the key that unlocks economic and social problems.

The new thinking which stresses the urgency of enhanced global co-operation is underpinned by Badré's analysis of what globalization means and how it can be better managed. Globalization can be described in many ways: some see it as an economic phenomenon only; some as a cultural phenomenon—that we eat the same global foods, we watch the same global TV programs, and so on; and others see it simply as a new phase in the evolution of capitalist economies and the development of markets.

If, however, we start by identifying the seismic shifts we have recently witnessed in the international economy, we can come closer to understanding the discontents that arise from it and the challenges that those of us who believe in enhanced global co-operation have to surmount.

Of course, we have seen a revolution in communications since the 1980s empowering us to connect instantaneously across borders, but two other big changes have swept the world since the 1980s—the move from what were primarily national flows of capital to global flows, and from the national sourcing of goods and services to their global sourcing. These shifts have had a dramatic effect on the industrial and occupational structure of modern economies. Industrial change has reduced the share of mining and manufacturing in modern economies from the peak of 40 percent of all jobs reached at the height of the British industrial revolution. According to Professor Tyler Cowan: "In the United States the proportion of the work force engaged in manufacturing peaked at about 25–27 percent in the 1970s. In Sweden manufacturing employment peaked at about 33 percent of the work force in the mid-1960s, and for Germany manufacturing employment rose as high as 40 percent in the 1970s. South Korea managed a manufacturing share of employment of 28 percent in 1989."

But in emerging markets like Brazil and India, manufacturing has barely exceeded 15 percent of employment, and writers like Dani Rodrik talk of "premature deindustrialization."[2] The figures suggest that the old model of modernization through export-led manufacturing growth is becoming a less crucial path out of poverty for developing economies; fading questions about what kind of economic future lies ahead for today's low-income countries.

Occupational change has been if anything more dramatic creating a polarized labor force, as many traditional skilled jobs from typists, secretaries, clerks, administrators, to draughtsman and boilermakers have declined in importance and the labor force has become divided between an elite of highly educated professionals who can command high salaries (at least for now) and a mass of unskilled and semi-skilled whose bargaining position is weak, whose job security is limited, and for whose children opportunities appear to be poor.

This is not just the kind of problem that is unique to the advanced economies. In country after country, the gap between the promise of globalization and people's day-to-day experiences of insecurity, joblessness, and stalled living standards is so stark that we are almost certainly likely to see more Arab Springs, more Occupy movements, and more "take back control" protests.

What is the fall out? Globalization creates the need for co-operation but also awakens in people the need to belong. For while the logic is economic integration, the emotional response is to demand that we "bring control back home"—a slogan that has become commonplace in protectionist movements in many continents. Such discontent demands a political response. In recognition of both the importance of identity and the imperative of co-operation nation states must strike the right balance between the national autonomy people desire and the border sharing we need. It is indeed a balancing act: too much integration and people feel their culture and identity are at risk. Too little integration and their prosperity is at risk.

So the policy imperatives are two-fold: as a world economy to show we can manage globalization well by co-ordinating polices where appropriate; and as individual nation states to get the balance right between autonomy and integration. To quote a recent article by the NYU academic Jonathan Haidt: "The great question for Western nations after 2016 may be this: How do we reap the gains of global co operation in trade, culture, education, human rights, and environmental protection while respecting—rather than diluting or crushing—the world's many local, national, and other 'parochial' identities, each with its own traditions and moral order? In what kind of world can globalists and nationalists live together in peace?"[3]

Across Europe and beyond countries are now having to respond to nationalist and protectionist pressures and show they have struck the right balance. Much has been written of how national government should help those who feel they have lost out from global change with training, employment, and income support policies. Much less has however been written about how we can finesse the international architecture. Here Badré's work can help as he shows us in his essays where and how global co-operation can be enhanced to best effect. It is not a choice between whether we have open and closed societies: the real choice is between those like Badré who want to lead, manage, and tame what should always be an open global economy; and those who oppose intervention—either because they favor a neo-liberal global free-for-all or are globalists who wish to shelter, insulate, and protect themselves against change.

Badré's focus on how we can strengthen global co operation through the repair and reform of the global financial system and how we can raise the funds necessary to finance the SDGs leads him to make innovative proposals. His work that started in the 1990s with innovative initiatives in global health has now been extended to proposals for financing other public goods including infrastructure and global education. A further set of proposals revolve around a new role in infrastructure and other areas for public–private partnerships.

When Kofi Annan spoke of a global compact in 1999, he called on businesses, both on their own and together, to "embrace, support and enact a set of core values in the areas of human rights, labour standards, and environmental practices" and to "use these universal values as the cement binding together your global corporations, since they are values people all over the world will recognize as their own." He added: "unless those values are really seen to be taking hold, I fear we may find it increasingly difficult to make a persuasive case for the open global market." He might have referred not only to human rights, labor standards and environmental practices but also to how business approaches issues of democracy and the rule of law. Since then the UN global compact led by Secretary General Ban Ki-moon and stewarded by Georg Kell has expanded our ideas of what is possible. As Kell has put it: "A growing number of companies across all continents have started the journey of reconciling societal priorities with corporate missions, strategies and operations based on universal principals ... [In] an era of transparency, the societal and environmental implications of investor behaviour can no longer be externalized. They must be accounted for and priced. Doing well and doing good can happen together."[4]

How the public sector can aid private–public co operation is explored in Badré's essays below, as it is by the work of Klaus Schwab at the World Economic Forum and in the new thinking that has arisen from Larry Summers's contention that the world has to break free from what he calls "secular stagnation." We have to take into account the new institutions now in the process of being born—like the BRICS Bank (Brazil, Russia, India, China, and South Africa), the Asian Infrastructure Investment Bank, and the Silk Road Fund. The challenge now is bringing our thinking on these new initiatives together in a more concerted and co-ordinated way and, in encouraging wider debate about the future of the Bretton Woods institutions, investigate whether we can find a consensus on the new international architecture needed to cope with wave after crushing wave of global change. Right across the world in the immediate aftermath of 1945 there was a ferment of new ideas and initiatives: we need the same explosion of new thinking now.

INTRODUCTION

Finance at the Crossroads

Left, right, backward, forward.... The crossroads facing us and the decision we make collectively has never been so important. It's about finance and how we make use of it, and the direction we take will either save our world or lead us on the road to ruin.

Everyone has a view on what *finance* means. In my experience, this is usually taken as a reference to Wall Street or the City of London or sometimes to Bank X or the chief executive officer (CEO) of Hedge Fund Y when they happen to make the headlines. Actually, I am referring to a much broader perspective. By *finance* I mean the financial tools used by the players in the international finance ecosystem (such as banks, investors, pension funds, institutions, and lenders). And, yes, I mean *tools* and not companies or specific institutions. Far from the magic and mirrors it has come to seem in recent years, finance has never been anything but a tool, an instrument manufactured by humans to be of use, to aid survival, and to act within the environment. In this case, the tool of finance is first and foremost a mechanism for the mobilization and allocation of resources to benefit the economy.

Do we save the world or ruin it?

Over the past several decades, we have, perhaps subconsciously, been creating a new, extremely powerful force, potentially one of the strongest humanmade forces on earth. It has been quietly humming in the background of people's lives, and we have been oblivious to what was building up. The 1920s and 1930s are rapidly vanishing from living memory, leaving only bumps in the road (some quite serious) of "localized" financial crises acting as sirens but seemingly falling on deaf ears. The financial crises of 2007–2009 were the price we all paid for not keeping up with regular health checks on a system that had quietly continued to grow to a scale few understood. This lack of understanding contrasted starkly with the strength of finance and the extent to which it governs all of our lives. Almost everything we do is underpinned by the structure that hitherto most had ignored, either by choice or ignorance.

The decisions we make now, the actions we take now and implement with full vigor and accountability, will directly influence our future. It is about regaining control and not just being the witness to a chain of events imposed on us. If we let finance continue on the path that led us to the financial crisis—serving the elite and feeding the speculators profiting from harnessing the power of finance in narrow and self-serving ways—then we are certain to drive up the level of discord. People will continue to feel increasingly disenfranchised. The recent resurgence in nationalism and protectionism will accelerate, and political disharmony will be inevitable. This story does not end well. Pulling down our respective shutters has not served us well in the past; there is no basis, beyond short-termism, to believe it would be any different now. A return to the depression of the 1930s would be only too real. Those were dark times in our history. We cannot underestimate the power of this new incredible force we have created.

We are facing a crossroads.

We barely survived a massive crisis. What comes next is not yet written. We are facing a crossroads. We have to be the ones who choose. "We" comprises each and every one of us. If it is just the so-called elites, then it will not succeed and will lead to resentment and a greater risk of more of the same issues recurring. This is not easy, as it requires hearing the voices of those who have been ignored in the past. How can this be achieved? It requires an ongoing, sustained commitment from every element. This means accountable government, civil society organizations, multilateral efforts, nongovernmental organizations (NGOs). The list goes on, but it is critical to have everyone's voices heard.

When I participated in G20 (Group of 20) meetings, I did so representing the World Bank Group. This meant that a group that is, by definition, narrow in its participants had someone who sought to represent the views of our clients, emerging market countries, including small island states, that would not have otherwise necessarily had a direct voice at the table. When I participated in the Financial Stability Board discussions (as a representative of the World Bank group including its private sector arm, the International Finance Corporation (IFC) and its investments in hundreds of financial institutions), I could bring to the table an informed voice reflecting this wide exposure. These are just two examples, but this is how we have to build forums where all our voices can be heard.

We can and we must choose a direction. We must be proactive and committed in the decision making, and that responsibility lies with each of us. Finance can save the world. It is a strong force that belongs to us and serves us. Finance is not the master and should not be allowed to be manipulated by the elites. Finance exists for the common good.

By using finance as our servant, we have the ability to hit reset. We can reposition its use. Finance is for everyone, and we need to use it accordingly. We need to set the agenda for financial inclusion and give access to everyone. Empowering people in the right way will reenergize the level of trust in the tool and enable all of us to assert our rightful authority over it.

We have to strengthen our multilateral approach. This is, however, not obvious for all, as we are reminded by an Op-Ed in the *Wall Street Journal* on May 30, 2017: "The world is not a 'global community' but an arena where nations, non-governmental actors, and business engage and compete for advantage. We bring to this forum unmatched military, political, economic, cultural, and moral strength. Rather than deny this elemental nature of international affairs, we embrace it."[1] I do not subscribe to this vision, as will become clear in the following pages. I believe that, despite territorial tensions, countries have to work together in a revamped manner. It is not easy or quick, but by walking down the path together in a cohesive, collaborative, and respectful way, we will have stronger outcomes. In times of difficulty, it is, of course, much easier to narrow our focus, adopt a nationalistic approach, seek higher levels of protectionism, all under the banner of helping ourselves first. This does not work anymore. Globalization and the deep level of interconnectedness we have are real and irreversible. Taking a narrow approach is destined to fail because complete sovereign control, in financial terms, is a myth. By contrast, moving ahead with multilateralism, albeit revamped, will be to the benefit of all of us. This is even more the case with finance, a fungible commodity that is blind to international boundaries.

Now is the time to regain control over money to serve the common good.

Using finance will help us build a truly sustainable framework for development. It is inconceivable that development should be only short term in its outlook and unequal in its distribution. The immense power that we can unleash with finance is much more far-reaching that most people believe. We can drive growth through sustainable development. The goals outlined by the United Nations (UN) and endorsed by all nations are broad, but they set the compass in the right direction. This can be achieved only if the necessary financial resources are mobilized in a revised manner. We will not achieve sustainable development without a new sustainable approach to finance. Each of us needs to take ownership and change the way we think about and use finance. Whether we manage or invest money or are stakeholders in other ways (don't forget, ultimately it is almost always our money), we have a duty to make our voices heard. Invest responsibly in a clear and credible way, not just by paying lip service or seeking out the most benign hurdles to step over.

The decision before us as to which direction to choose is serious and must be accorded the appropriate level of respect and consideration. We should not make the mistake of thinking that our role is to be one of a passive actor or, even worse, a willing victim. Finance can be a force for good. It is a force that will not go away. We ignore our responsibilities at our peril. Taking back the power over finance means we can then undertake the changes that are needed to serve the common good. Regaining trust in the system after everything we have been through recently, and living with some of the undesirable consequences of that, is part and parcel of the new approach we have to adopt. Finance can save the world, but only if it gets the guidance it desperately deserves.

It all started in 2000 as a dream.

Was the year 2000 just a dream? Perhaps. From May 1968, when I was born, until the dawn of the new millennium, imagination still held sway. Like many, I had hoped that there was a bit of magic at work, a mix of technology and a new and improved human race, with just a soupçon of the "end of history," per the famous phrase of Francis Fukuyama after the fall of the Berlin Wall. Then, as 2000 approached, we felt the anticipation of the Y2K (year 2000) bug, Europe's adoption of a single currency, and the ambition to remove the boundaries between nations to create a unified, limitless human race.

When that fateful hour arrived, we counted down the seconds separating us from the new age. We kissed our loved ones and shouted out our hopes for the New Year amid champagne and fireworks. We expected it to be magical. The hopeful feelings lasted throughout the year, culminating in September in New York at the UN headquarters with the largest gathering of heads of state and government the world had ever seen: the Millennium Summit, where humankind enthusiastically set goals for itself to accelerate the pace of development.

All did not go as planned.

More than 15 years later, and the world has changed so much. Yet the film doesn't quite match what that September 2000 trailer in New York promised.

Who would have thought in 2000 that a financial system thought to be synonymous with peace, prosperity, and progress would lead the world so close to the brink of disaster? The many crises of the 1990s seemed behind us. After years of turbulence, we hoped that the "Great Moderation" was bearing serious fruit. Who would have thought that Europe would be so close to crumbling, to failing, at the conclusion of a major humanitarian drama? Who would have thought that Kodak could go bankrupt, that the World Trade Center could fall? Who would have thought that China could in a generation overtake the United States as the top world economic power? Who would have thought that these same powers, and others, could one day sign the Paris climate accord together? Who would ever have thought that, as bright as the euro's future looks on the European continent, 52 percent of the British population would choose to withdraw from the construction of Europe?

Unleashing finance led us to a disaster.

All of this is to say that the years since 2000 have turned out to be tumultuous. We have all felt the splintering and fracturing that is still playing out, and we have yet to learn what these ruptures will make of us in the end. Our financial, economic, political, geopolitical, environmental, social, and cultural worlds are all changing.

The 2007–2008 financial crisis and the deep worldwide economic recession that followed have made finance the enemy in the eyes of many global citizens. Many current tensions throughout the world, starting with the hints of populism and nationalism, are an echo of the great disillusionment that has overtaken those who believed, since 1944 and the Bretton Woods Agreement, that the financial system would bring us economic development and guarantee international cooperation.

In the United States as in Europe and around the world, we can sense a deep-seated fear among populations who feel they may have been passed up by a movement they no longer understand, or perhaps they never did. The directions in which globalization and a united Europe are headed have never been so uncertain, never so weakly embodied by its leaders, and all the while, geopolitical tensions are rising around the world. Think of the thunderclap that was Brexit, the crises in Ukraine, the Sahel, the Sea of China, oil-rich countries, and the Middle East, the upswing in terrorist attacks around the globe, from San Bernardino to Lahore, Orlando, Copenhagen, Brussels, Paris, Nice, Istanbul, Ankara, Beirut, Tunis, Sousse, Bamako, Ouagadougou, Bagdad, Sana, London, and on and on. Advanced economies and emerging economies are regularly tempted to use strong-arm tactics to shape monetary policy, and some people are coming to realize that global economic growth might be entering a lasting era of stagnation, embodied in the unprecedented number of bonds with prices at low if not negative interest rates in a number of developed nations.

A lack of confidence now dominates.

Yet the world has never been so well equipped to deal with these threats! Humanity has never been so wealthy, so productive, so avid, so invested. But this amazing abundance is far from being equally split. Bit by bit, balance is actually getting harder to achieve, given the risks inherent in the management of big data and the Uberization of the economy—not to mention the climate threat and the acceleration of the rate of pandemics—in a world that is so well connected. The path globalization has taken is sometimes terrifying. To countries like the United States or France that have had so much influence over the shape of previous stages of globalization, this threat is even more dizzying. Our communities tremble at the idea of being passed by.

Faced with numerous uncertainties, humankind is also faced with an unprecedented crisis of confidence.

Confidence—in our future, in our colleagues, in ourselves—is exactly what we need at a time like this to meet the crucial challenges we can no longer avoid: the elimination of poverty, the preservation of peace and our climate, the reorganization of a digital civilization, the fight against pandemics. All these require, more than ever, our cooperation, our willingness, and our courage to get the work done.

Nonetheless, humanity has committed to sustainable development and shared prosperity.

As recently as 2015, we saw that humankind can still experience bursts of confidence and audacity: three successive international conferences, in Addis Ababa, New York, and Paris, gave us a yearlong opportunity to come to an agreement on the decisive roadmap for the coming years with respect to development funding, the sustainable development of our planet, and the fight against climate change. All nation states have chosen and agreed on a roadmap for our planet. We do not have to invent anew. The roadmap is there for us to implement.

We are at the crossroads. The choice is ours.

We have to take these declarations of principle seriously. They are not just pieces of paper. They demonstrate our utmost desire, as a human race, for unity to overcome division. If only hope will continue to keep us above the cynicism and fatalism we have come to expect! And if we take these declarations seriously, we have to commit the necessary resources and financial tools.

We should not be naïve and underestimate these commitments or treat hope like a toy. These immense but necessary ambitions can become reality only if we manage to mobilize all our centripetal strength against the innumerable and often brutal centrifugal forces tearing us apart. By joining forces at all levels, we can defeat the forces of dispersion. Our lovely promises will come true only through united efforts between and within nations, and cooperation between public and private actors and the community at large. We must walk the same road together if we are to open up dialogue between multilateral international institutions and the various advanced, emerging, and developing economies, if we are to rebuild the connections in Europe, and in the 50 United States, and across the Pacific and Atlantic Oceans. And we must come together to make the G20, the group of the 20 largest economies of the world, more than just a yearly gathering of heads of state with little to say and even less to do.

Such mobilization is possible, I am convinced, having had the chance to participate in numerous summits, projects, meetings, and working groups during this period. But I also know that following that road of the declarations is not going to be easy.

Where do I come from?

I have found myself in the position of a privileged witness and an actor, in the United States and in Europe, in some of these major changes that have happened in the world since 2000, in times both exciting and dramatic.

I have seen finance firsthand as a problem.

I was an investment banker for Lazard in New York when the dotcom bubble burst. I saw the September 11 attacks from my window. I worked in Paris alongside Michel Camdessus, managing director of the International Monetary Fund (IMF) from 1987 through 2000, and Jacques Chirac, then president of France, who led with Gordon Brown two of the major financial innovations for development in recent decades.[2] During the 2007–2008 financial crisis, I watched the collapse of a whole system from the inside, as a senior executive first for Crédit Agricole and then for Société Générale. Finally, at the World Bank, I was involved, to varying degrees, from Washington, DC in the three international summits in 2015 that may make it a historic year for decisions made in the name of humankind.

It was not destiny but rather chance encounters and assignments that led me to these experiences—which I joke makes me more like Forrest Gump than anyone else. I always thought that after finishing my degree, I would spend my whole career with the same government agency (the Ministry of Finance) or the same company. Life thought otherwise.

My meeting with Michel Camdessus, when I was the treasurer for the Semaines sociales de France,[3] turned out to be decisive, allowing me to work in multiple roles on the problems related to development. As a banker, and therefore thought to be an expert in international "liquidity," coincidence led me to work on the question of water with Michel Camdessus from 2000 until 2003 as part of President Chirac's team for the preparations of the G8 summit in Évian, France. Initially knowing little about the subject, I found myself reflecting on funding for water infrastructure and cowriting a book on the topic.[4] In turn, I also was the reporter for a working group on international funding innovations to relieve poverty, and I collaborated on the drafting of a report about ideas for new growth in the French economy.[5]

As chief financial officer of two of the largest global banks, occupied by the day-to-day management of the financial crisis, I never thought I could find the time again to reflect on these matters when, in 2012, I was asked to join the World Bank as managing director, with a broad financial mandate. I immediately accepted this opportunity to put the convictions I had gained from my experience into action: to make use of one of the best financial laboratories in the world to attempt to innovate for the public good, to demonstrate how finance might also contribute positively to the global market, rather than being reduced to the destructive force so cruelly unleashed in 2007.

In hindsight I appreciate how much these apparently unrelated, seemingly disconnected experiences actually make sense. They offered me a relatively complete view of the international financial system. Through various public and private sectors, at both the national and international levels, I was able to take stock from successive and diverse perspectives: as a civil servant with the Ministry of Finance, as an investment banker on Wall Street and in the City of London, as a commercial banker who was regulated, and later as a regulator and leader of a multilateral development bank. These viewpoints have given me an understanding of the limits of the system, as well as the potential for reinvention it harbors.

I want to promote finance as a solution. And I have started.

Working through the World Bank was, in this sense, a synthesis of all my past positions. In addition to seeing the potential for financial innovation, I was able to observe the system of international governance from up close, the many frustrations it created, as well as its profound utility. It is imperfect, and yet indispensable! My experiences revealed an exceptionally diverse world in which the elites are so alike and yet so different, with a common language overlaying so many singular life experiences. This commonality can help. It also sends a serious signal outside, which can raise widespread and legitimate questions about an aloof and disconnected global elite.

Finance is an amazing renewable energy that needs to be controlled.

The numerous professional trips I took also fed this vision. From the Salomon Islands to each of the BRICS nations (Brazil, Russia, India, China, and South Africa), I visited nearly one hundred countries, rich and poor. I was able to engage with people of all kinds and from all places, some ordinary, some extraordinary.

From these precious experiences and the many ideas they led me to consider, I learned a number of lessons that may be helpful to share today, at this crucial moment, with globalization and humanity at a crossroads. If I have but one conviction to share, it is that the mobilization of every source of energy is vital to combat the disruptive forces that threaten our world today. Such mobilization is, indeed, possible, as I have been able to prove several times over. I also know from experience that we are far from our goal—it is so much easier to play devil's advocate, to rest firmly on our preexisting interests and positions! The way we will be able to get all humanity working together is to share a clear vision of our future, to get a compass, and to have legitimate leadership to guide us and concrete means of cooperation.

Finance is a tool to serve the common good.

The financial catastrophe that occurred in 2007–2008 must not cause us to make mistakes: finance is not the enemy, for the simple reason that, in and of itself, it has no quality of being good or bad. It is only a blind mechanical force that, poorly used or unsupervised, could take a turn for the worse (as we saw with the subprime crisis), or, used well and properly maintained, can offer us something better:

prosperity shared by all without harm to our planet (as seen with the development of the green bonds). Let us not forget that old saying "Money is a poor master, but a good servant." The same tool, used well or poorly according to the will of the actors, can lead to the creation or destruction of value. The same finance that took us to the brink of ruin can also lead us to the enrichment of billions of people. It remains a marvelous tool that allows us to work on projections and imagine and prepare for the future, managing risks, space, and time, and to unite humankind to build together, for everyone.

Our love for money has faltered, but perhaps all we need is a second honeymoon, a chance to find the feelings that led to its creation once more. To be proactive on purpose, isn't it time we rekindled our love for finance?

It is the hand that must control the tool and not the tool the hand.

We won't accomplish anything by repeating our past mistakes. Although the temptation is real, we must find a better, more enduring foundation for reinventing finance by thinking harder about concrete and effective responses to the problems of the real world, beginning with those in development. By reconstructing the financial system, increasing the number of real innovations that lead to this extraordinarily inventive tool, we have the capacity to redesign in depth an inclusive globalization that benefits most people.

I offer this book not as yet another attempt by a "converted banker" to distract you from the difficult truths by pulling the same old tired tricks out of the magician's hat. Not at all! Having spent three years at the heart of one of the greatest financial laboratories in the world, having had the chance to participate in large-scale financial projects that were both generous and ingenious, I have acquired a clear conviction that financial innovation *can* accomplish great things in the service of the common good, and that multilateral institutions have a key role to play, thanks to their credit, the quality of their human resources, and their mission. But they certainly won't do it alone, and they won't do it simply "as is"! Change is needed, and at scale. If change does not occur, temptation will remain to allow finance to play its own game. Remember the (in)famous words of Chuck Prince, former chairman and CEO of Citigroup, as reported in the *Financial Times* in July 2007: "As long as the music is playing, you've got to get up and dance." I don't think we can afford to let the same thing happen again.

Regaining control over money requires a collective effort.

Obviously, regulators, more than anyone else, have a crucial role to play in finding an appropriate, holistic setup for a system that has little by little been limiting itself solely to the banking system. Financial players, starting with institutional investors, also have to play a critical role in directing their resources toward sustainable projects. Multinational companies are beginning to participate in the movement themselves, to respond to the growing concerns of their current clients and their future stakeholders. In this new financial coalition, for which I have high hopes, international organizations, forums, and development groups will play a key role as catalysts. Civil society will also have the responsibility to weigh in on this interplay, to support it, and to push it forward. Through these united efforts, leveraged by and through the tool of finance, we can change the game; we can carry out this revolution that will have us looking back on 2015 as the year we made history together.

Throughout this book, I take the reader through a brief history of some key steps and discussions that have taken place at different places around the world. Part 1 touches upon critical moments and gives context to the main thesis of the book: finance, when controlled, can be the best servant to each of us, not just for an elite few but for everyone.

The recent financial crisis triggered perhaps the greatest and most sustained criticism of how finance has been manipulated to create a complete distortion of wealth and power. The evaporation of trust has resulted in debates about the very nature of money and the role it plays in society. These are the aspects I cover in Part 2, where I call for a return to basics and discuss how changes have begun.

Part 3 addresses the renewed international cooperation and how we all need to take seriously the commitments made in 2015, not just treat them as good words to be lost to history. Along with this, we need to take stock of the ongoing changes in the financial world. The business model of the banks is changing; their role is also being modified, particularly against the backdrop of a more prominent position being taken by institutional investors. In the public sector, various elements are also increasing the pressure on the multilateral banks, forcing them to adapt to a different world of greater public finance constraints and driving them to redefine their role.

The separate pressures on the private and public sectors are precisely what are causing both sides to rethink how they must work with one another. This discussion is compounded by the low or negative interest rate environment and the ever-present search for yield, expectations of a new generation (the so-called millennials), massive disruptions brought about by technological revolution, and the lack of trust in the system following the financial crisis. All of these elements are helping to foster a new framework within which to discuss the role of finance. How do we make best use of all the available resources in order to mobilize finance to lead to greater, sustainable development?

Part 4 discusses how this cooperation can be achieved through a new way of joining forces, at scale, because of the environment we have found ourselves in and our new set of expectations. What is discussed is not revolutionary, but it is far-reaching in its potential impact. Working together by its very nature will require a resetting of incentives and drivers of actions at every level, not just in how our financial institutions are regulated or through the reform of international organizations.

As is often the case, it is obviously easier said than done since there is no single point of decision. That is why the following pages might sometimes come across as being naïve or vague. On the one hand, this is true, but there is no easy prescription. Rather, it is a call for action based on what I and others have been able to do over the past few years. It is not and cannot be the so-called elites speaking to the elites, but it must include everyone, each of us making a difference. It is about what we want our banks, pension funds, the people who manage our assets, our governments, the international organizations that act on our behalf, and the NGOs to do with the resources we have granted them, whether through the taxes we pay or through entrusting them with our savings or gifts.

Finance can make a difference if pressure is applied throughout the system, not to different silos but across the board as a unified force. We have an opportunity to shape a genuinely new framework that would replace the one that began in the 1970s but that finally collapsed with the financial crisis.

Tangibly, this means reinforcing core values that should affect products, markets, and behaviors. These must be taught and monitored as well as regulated and supervised. The core values must include ethics, accountability, intelligibility, and they must be ingrained into how people operate every single day. I also try to make sense of the various innovations at play everywhere, such as green finance, which are still not central but are gaining momentum.

In discussing how to renew international cooperation, I remind the reader of the universal nature of finance and money and why this requires, more than anything else, a concerted approach. However, international cooperation should not just be a place for regulation. It should also be a place where we collectively decide to work better together and use finance in a useful manner for all. We have created institutions and forums of all kinds since 1944, such as the UN, the Bretton Woods institutions (the IMF and the World Bank), and the various *G* s (Groups, including the G7, G8, G20, G24, and G77). They are not always as effective as one would expect; reform is needed as well as continual evolution. Nonetheless, they are what we have today, and we can make good use of them; it is time to shake the tree and demonstrate that we can do something like mobilizing the various resources to address the infrastructure gap.

A critical question before us is how to finance the sustainable development of our planet. We have agreed on a set of objectives. However, to achieve them we need to shift the financial paradigm and mobilize the different kinds of finance and actors that are required. This is what I have called "the billions to trillions" roadmap: the needs are in the trillions, but public aid is in the billions. How we bridge this gap is key. I review what in particular the multilateral organizations should be doing and how to better leverage these platforms. I talk about the importance of a renewed way for the public and private sectors to work together, going beyond the traditional public–private partnership (PPP) approach. I discuss how this can work, notwithstanding the differences and suspicions between the public and private sectors. I conclude by highlighting specific areas—such as education, pandemics, or road safety, to name but a few—where this approach can continue to be implemented.

Finance can become the great servant.

Although finance was certainly part of the problem, today it can be part of the solution, too. We are poised to make good on our great ambitions for development and climate change that we set in 2015. Our top priority, for all of us in the public, private, and civil sectors, is first to accept our challenge (it would be too easy to call it impossible and give up), then to roll up our sleeves, all together now, and to put back the pieces before us in the best possible configuration.

Hope could well become a credible option for us to achieve this undertaking. It can move us off this trajectory toward fragmentation and reorient us more positively toward unification and progress. With a reset finance, we have a chance to truly achieve our goals for sustainable development. What comes next has not yet been written: we are standing at the brink of the best of times, or the worst. This informed and practical account can help global decision makers lead us in a positive direction, and can help all of us push them, and the system, in an appropriate direction.

As Saint-Exupéry says, "Your task is not to foresee the future, but to enable it."[6]

It would be to our advantage to acknowledge that the euphoric predictions that preceded the crisis have not come true. As the queen of England famously asked economists in 2008, "Why did nobody notice it?" Now is the time to enable that future to come true. There is still time to change course and be serious about the eradication of poverty or to address the issue of climate change—but we need to move now, decisively.

PART ONE

Despite Being Led Nearly to Ruin, How We Can Still React

Part 1 addresses how, notwithstanding the best of intentions, we were almost led to ruin and how, despite this truly precarious journey, we were still somehow unable to react. It looks at the period since 2000 and forms the foundation for understanding why we are where we are today, whether or not we have real choices, and what those choices might be. Part 1 examines the alternatives we are facing and assesses the crossroads at which we find ourselves.

I discuss how the financial crisis not only interrupted the plans we made for the new millennium but also undermined them, potentially causing massive disruption. This experience drives our need to ensure that we regain control over the most powerful tool, finance. By asserting our rightful ownership over it, we can reorient our direction back to achieving and delivering on the millennium undertakings. The undertakings that were made as we crossed into the new millennium set out a path of sorts, with guardrails for us to move within. I look at how after we were shunted sharply off course by the financial crisis, we were then buffeted by understandable reactions, leading to a rise in populism and to the arrival at a point of inflection, a key decision point.

In Chapter 1, I recall the hopes we had at the turn of the millennium, and what actually unfolded. I look at the developments of emerging markets, the digital revolution, increasing levels of urbanization, the growing role of the private sector, and evolution in our governance. Chapter 2 focuses on the financial crisis and how we let the financial genie out of the bottle and how it led us toward catastrophe. Chapter 3 looks at the loss of trust in the system (the most valuable form of capital we have) and the very real challenges and difficulties we have in restoring that trust. Chapter 4 assesses the efforts of the 2015 initiatives that sought to find a shared purpose for the nations of the world. Chapter 5 discusses the headwinds we have faced and the ensuing geopolitical issues, all of which make our efforts more important. Chapter 6 continues the discussion with a look at the political unrest that has swept across many countries. Chapter 7, the final chapter of Part 1, focuses on the challenge before us. It is a transition to Parts 2, 3, and 4 and questions whether we can rise to meet the expectations and regain our rightful control over finance in order to better serve the common good. I talk about what the right path could be and the benefits that could be realized from making the right decisions, the brave decisions.

CHAPTER 1

High Hopes from the Millennium Summit

The queen raised the right question: why did nobody notice it? Many thought that we had found the recipe for everlasting and shared prosperity. We believed that with the progress of finance we had found the way to propel the world if not to save it. To understand what happened, we need to think back a few years and remind ourselves what it was like to be at the dawn of the third millennium. And then we must try to answer the question: what went wrong? This is the objective of the first five chapters. Chapter 1 focuses on the years before the financial crisis and questions why it did not turn out according to the plan set up in New York in September 2000. It describes the environment that allowed the crisis to happen and against which finance needs to be rethought. Finance and its reform cannot be condensed in isolation.

The dawn of the third millennium filled us with great hope. The last decade of the 20th century had left everyone feeling a bit lost, vacillating between the highs of the fall of the Berlin Wall and the Soviet Empire, and the lows of the Gulf War and the debate in many nations about globalization that seemed "delightful" to some and "horrific" to others. Development, public aid, and the mobilization of nations were faltering at the starting line. The symbolic arrival of a new millennium created a historic opportunity to reset the counter to zero.

Soaring Hope in 2000 with the Adoption of the Millennium Development Goals

The 189 member states of the UN seized upon this positive mood to reaffirm their faith that lasting peace and international security can be possible only by guaranteeing the economic and social well-being of all people. The leaders of the member states hoped to define and implement a new strategy of cooperation, adjusted to the realities and changing needs of the 21st century.

The leaders met on September 5, 2000, in New York, in what was the largest meeting of heads of state and government the world had ever seen, the Millennium Summit. Guided by the idea that every program should focus on humanity to construct a global community that leaves no one behind, this Millennium Summit concluded with the unanimous adoption of a solemn declaration, the Millennium Declaration: eight objectives for fair and lasting development, created and promoted in large part by Kofi Annan, the secretary-general of the UN at the time, to be achieved within the next 15 years.

The Millennium Declaration was a turning point. For the first time in history, humankind gave itself unified and measurable goals in a form different in substance from the usual declarations or the previous "consensuses." The resolution brought together in a single text all the objectives that had been set at various international conferences in the previous decade. "It is a vastly useful initiative," noted our working group in 2004, focused on water. "The odds are most [heads of state] have forgotten these goals. It covers the whole of the tasks set out for the nations of the world—North and South combined—for the human community. They should be taught in every school and posted at every town hall."[1]

The Millennium Development Goals (MDGs) set eight grand principles and concrete objectives that constituted a global plan of action broken down into 20 quantifiable tasks, each measured by 60 statistical indicators. The plan offered precise, quantifiable measures in the fight against extreme poverty in all its dimensions. In theory each country's budget would reflect these priorities, because they flowed from a "respect for the fundamental goals of the entire human family" (see the box on the next page).

The Millennium Development Goals were still focused on public action, public influence, and public methods. That would change at the UN conference in Monterrey, Mexico, in 2002, but cooperation wasn't yet thought of as truly multidimensional, spanning businesses, financial institutions, and civil society. It remained confined to the relationships among individual nations—but the idea of partnership was gradually gaining traction. Development funding focused on financial transfers from northern countries to southern countries, according to the principle of solidarity reaffirmed by the UN, in which there are bilateral transfers of public funds balanced out by the cancellation of a share of the debt of the countries receiving aid.

This public mobilization to serve the common good appeared to be unquestioned, at least while the global economy remained strong. We were still in the era of "Great Moderation," as later economists called it, and global growth was supported by an international financial system that seemed incredibly efficient in terms of the wealth it was able to create and redistribute. The challenge of achieving the MDGs was foremost a challenge to increase state and international institutions' contributions to official development assistance (ODA).[2] Could humanity get there? It was up to the public sector to answer that question.

Fifteen Years Later—Did We Do It?

Although we clearly could have done better, the extraordinary momentum with which the world united in 2000 pushed us to achieve an unprecedented number of goals in the 15 years. In less than one generation, developed nations increased their ODA by two-thirds, from $81 billion to over $130 billion.[3]

Debt–service ratios dropped to one-fourth of their 2000 levels, thus reducing the financial burden on developing nations, even if not always to a sustainable point.[4]

THE MILLENNIUM DEVELOPMENT GOALS

1. Eradicate Extreme Hunger and Poverty

a. Halve, between 1990 and 2015, the proportion of people whose income is less than $1 a day.

b. Halve, between 1990 and 2015, the proportion of people who suffer from hunger.

2. Achieve Universal Primary Education

a. Ensure that, by 2015, children everywhere, boys and girls alike, will be able to complete a full course of primary schooling.

3. Promote Gender Equality and Empower Women

a. Eliminate gender disparity in primary and secondary education, preferably by 2005, and in all levels of education no later than 2015.

4. Reduce Child Mortality

a. Reduce by two-thirds, between 1990 and 2015, the under-five mortality rate.

5. Improve Maternal Health

a. Reduce by three-quarters, between 1990 and 2015, the maternal mortality rate.

6. Combat HIV/AIDS, Malaria, and Other Diseases

a. Have halted by 2015 and begun to reverse the spread of HIV/AIDS.

b. Have halted by 2015 and begun to reverse the incidence of malaria and other major diseases.

7. Ensure Environmental Sustainability

a. Integrate the principles of sustainable development into country policies and programs and reverse the loss of environmental resources.

b. Halve, by 2015, the proportion of people without sustainable access to safe drinking water and basic sanitation.

c. Have achieved by 2020 a significant improvement in the lives of at least 100 million slum dwellers.

8. Develop a Global Partnership for Development

a. Develop further an open, rule-based, predictable, nondiscriminatory trading and financial system.

b. Address the special needs of the Least Developed Countries (LDCs).

c. Address the special needs of landlocked developing countries and small island developing states.

d. Deal comprehensively with the debt problems of developing countries through national and international measures in order to make debt sustainable in the long term.

e. In cooperation with developing countries, develop and implement strategies for decent and productive work for youth.

f. In cooperation with pharmaceutical companies, provide access to affordable essential drugs in developing countries.

g. In cooperation with the private sector, make the benefits of new technologies, especially information and communications technology, available to all.

This historic progress can be attributed to a long list of factors, led by economic growth, most spectacularly that in China. Because of this, many development problems are now on track for resolution. For instance, by 2013 the number of individuals living below the international poverty line had fallen by 500 million.[5] By 2008 real advances had occurred in the wider availability of AIDS treatments, increased agricultural productivity, higher education rates, and greater access to clean water and sanitation.[6] By 2010 the rate of people without access to improved drinking water had been reduced by half. In 2012 the UN confirmed that it would be able to reach its goal of reducing poverty worldwide by 2015. Some 200 million people living in slums had already seen an improvement in their living conditions—exceeding the goal. In 2012 equality in primary education between boys and girls was also achieved.[7] This is the glass half full.

Of course, major challenges remain, beginning with the great disparities we still see between countries and among the various populations within individual countries. China achieved rapid economic growth, but progress was uneven in Africa, less developed countries, landlocked countries, and small isolated developing states. Some MDGs have not yet been achieved: those in maternal, neonatal, and infant health, and in the eradication of hunger. In 2013 one out of eight people still went to bed hungry.[8] Despite concerted efforts, ODA has not yet reached the target level, 0.7 percent of the gross national product (GNP) of every developed nation, identified more than 40 years ago. This is the glass half empty.

Humans Planning and Realities Intervening

The first 15 years of the new millennium did not unfold according to plan. The world become much more complex, and events took some dramatic turns. We are still not sure where those transformations will take us. The changes that touched us are multiple and profound, and their effects are still being felt.

A New Economic Cartography: The Rise of the Emerging World

The first major change completely redrew the global economic map. While packing for my move from Paris to Washington in early 2013, I came across a box of papers that contained notes from classes I had taken in preparation to attend business school. In 1985 and 1986, we were still talking about Soviet planning and the reforms of Stalin and Brezhnev. These subjects seem outlandish today! At that time, only the four Asian Tigers (South Korea, Hong Kong, Singapore, and Taiwan) and Japan were thought of as economic powers by the West: China was in the background, India was considered a lost cause, and the running joke about Brazil was that it was a country "with potential" but no energy. The G7 (Group of Seven) nations dominated the world, and the European Union was ascendant. For the years leading up to 2000, we walked a well-trodden path—at the time, we didn't even have the acronym BRIC (Brazil, Russia, India, and China; coined in 2001, it became BRICS in 2011 with the addition of South Africa). Today we take for granted the emergence of powerful economic competitors to the traditional economic powers—but who would have believed, even in 2000, that China could in the foreseeable future surpass the United States as the top world economy?[9] Who would have believed that France would have to bitterly settle for a ninth-place ranking behind the two economic giants, followed by India, Japan, Russia, Germany, Brazil, and even Indonesia?[10] And who would have believed that in 2012 India would attain a GNP so large that, added to China's, the two would be expected to quickly surpass the total for the combined G7 economies?[11] This transformation of the world economic map, created by the growing power of emerging economies, could have large and severe repercussions on development funding.

Demography Prevailing

The second major structural change, closely linked to the first despite how often we underestimate the connection, was the toppling of the balance of world demographics. Today, there are 1 billion more of us than in 2000, a total of 7 billion inhabitants on earth; another 1 billion inhabitants are forecast for 2030. This demographic explosion, however, has not been evenly distributed: some countries are aging while others are getting younger; some populations are dwindling while others are exploding. These changes in demographics are redefining the relationships between the global economic powers. Aging populations mean lower average incomes with higher health expenses, which put a strain on GNP, reducing innovation and resulting in slower growth for the nation—not to mention a smaller army, which weakens the sphere of influence militarily.

Older industrial nations like Japan and nations in Europe, and perhaps soon the United States should it choose to build barriers to immigration, are seeing demographic decline and risk being overtaken by countries with younger populations, such as Indonesia, Brazil, Mexico, or Turkey; thinking more long term, they could also be overtaken by countries in sub-Saharan Africa, which are in the middle of a population boom (by 2100, the continent will make up over one-fourth of the world's population). The intermediate case, China, is interesting: this emerging power could age out before it becomes wealthy, given the reduction of its active population in the past two years resulting from 35 years of having a single-child policy (now officially ended).[12] Immigration restrictions are also having an impact in China, as they have to a lesser extent in the United States and Europe. Will emerging markets be able to reverse this trend? The outcome is less than certain. The Chinese will have to transform their demographic "weight" into demographic "dividends"—meaning they will have to succeed in attracting more working-age adults than children under the care of adults—in order to support their economic growth. One thing is certain: in the space of a single generation, these demographic trends have already begun to reshape the global hierarchy.

Galloping Urbanization

Another consequence of the demographic explosion, in itself a fundamental change from the past 15 years, is the rampant urbanization and emergence of metropolises that is redefining the sovereignty of space in the United States and beyond. "Who knows of this city?" asked the three directors of McKinsey Global Institute,[13] evoking the case of Kumasi, a city in Ghana most people had never heard of, with a population in the millions. Like Kumasi, cities with more than 1 million inhabitants are cropping up like mushrooms in the emerging areas of the world with such speed that we no longer have the time to even learn their names. China alone has more than 40 cities, such as Luoyang, with more than 2 million inhabitants.[14] Africa now boasts more than 50 large cities. And while more than half of humankind has lived in cities for a long time, a growing proportion is concentrating in these unknown metropolises, which are starting to compete for power with national governments. The McKinsey authors postulate that by 2025, a single regional city in China, Tianjin, will have a GNP equal to that of Sweden, and that in the decades that follow, half of the world's economic growth will come from 440 cities, like Kumasi or Santa Catarina, Brazil. This boom of "subsovereigns," to use the international jargon, has a major significance with respect to the architecture of regional and global power, in economic, political, and even cultural terms. My wife discovered this after driving two hours from Shanghai to deliver a speech at a brand new, gigantic university that partners with Duke University (Duke Kunshan University); the world no longer revolves around just the Sorbonne, Oxford, and Harvard.

Another major issue in urbanization is the sustainable development of cities and their ability to accommodate population booms with adequate infrastructure and measures to combat inequality. The concentration of humanity requires modernization and rationalization, in other words, which require considerable investments that not all cities are able to make, even if they know where to begin. For example, I had an interesting and emotional conversation on this topic with M.Y. Nawandish, the mayor of Kabul, whose population today numbers a shocking 7 million and 1 million cars (compared to 600,000 inhabitants and a few dozen cars in 2002, when America entered Afghanistan). How can a city absorb such an influx when it has practically no paved roads and unstable access to water and electricity, and people are not safe on its streets? Which fix should be the first priority?

I was equally touched by a trip I took to Jakarta that offered a window into an Indonesia with mind-boggling economic growth but still massive inequality: the contrast between the worst slums, which I visited in the morning, and the huge Maserati retailer displaying his goods in the city center a few hours later next to a Bell & Ross boutique was striking. It shook up my take on the MDGs: although we had technically achieved goal 7.c ("Have achieved by 2020 a significant improvement in the lives of at least 100 million slum dwellers"), urbanization has progressed so fast that we have not improved conditions for many other people.[15]

A First Hint of the Global Financial Crisis

Another change that has made the situation more complex in recent years is the 2007–2008 financial and economic crisis, the magnitude of which no one in 2000 could have imagined. We will get into this in greater detail in Chapter 2. For now, let's just remember that the crisis has been shown to be possibly more significant than the one in 1929, which led us into one of our darkest times. Truly, in 2007–2008 we feared we were just a step away from the collapse of the global financial system. Once we saw that the system would hold, the cards were reshuffled: from a debt-based system dominated by banks, the world has turned to a system more and more dominated by institutional investors and asset owners like pension funds. This is a major change in terms of its implications for the funding of economies and development, monetary policy, investment techniques, and more. The crisis also created a system that appears to defy reason, where up to one-third of global public debt has at one time been contracted at negative interest rates, and "central banks" have lived up to their names better than ever. In short, the financial phase of the crisis set in motion a long cycle of global recession and threatened many of the development goals set in 2000. For example, the jobs deficit, affecting youth in particular, grew by 67 million around the world between 2007–2008 and 2013.[16] ODA growth slowed over the long term, a reduction that primarily threatens those countries that are already the most fragile.

Private Initiatives Everywhere

The developments in the first decade of the 21st century brought about another decisive change, this one much more positive in my eyes: recognition not of the "end of history" but of the role of the private sector and the market economy in development. This is likely one of the most significant and least visible changes since 2000. Although the MDG strategy leaned heavily on ODA growth, in 15 years, this has actually declined relative to other sources of funding, such as foreign direct investment, funds transfers (remittances), and, more broadly, the influx of private North–South and South–South investment. We are seeing a real seesaw movement: compare the $135 billion that ODA had reached, year in and year out, by 2015 to the $435 billion of funds transfers initiated in 2014 by migrants. This impressive total, which grows every year, is fragile in nature: migrants from Georgia, Kazakhstan, and Central Asia who worked in the petroleum industry in Russia lost their jobs with the drop in oil prices, and many find themselves unable to send money back to their home countries. We should watch this issue closely, since some countries have become dependent upon this source of funding: funds transfers by migrants represent 42 percent of GNP for Tajikistan, 32 percent of GNP for Kyrgyzstan, 29 percent for Nepal, and 25 percent for Moldova.[17] This kind of reversal requires that the situation be reconsidered: What role could ODA play here? How can these precious dollars best be used? How can we transform these public transfers into catalysts?

Finding answers to these questions is even more important because we now understand that the private sector (large companies and small-and medium-size businesses alike), far from being the devil, is actually the engine for growth. The World Bank estimates that 600 million jobs must be created in the next 15 years, or more than 3 million each month, to keep up with population growth. Civil service jobs certainly won't fill all this need! My trips to Africa support this statement: The primary problem for heads of sub-Saharan states, whose employment markets grow more abundant each year by the hundreds of thousands, and even by millions of youths, is how to create enough jobs for them. The question is even more crucial in countries like Côte d'Ivoire, which is coming out of a decade of civil war and needs to rehabilitate and reintroduce thousands of child soldiers into society. When the World Bank sets up training programs for masonry, carpentry, hairdressing, and similar occupations, the graduates must be able to use their training to find a job and to integrate into a real economy, or else we condemn these youths to picking up arms again. Interestingly enough, one of the keys to promoting this environment is an emphasis on a favorable climate for investment, good governance, and business.[18]

The Digital Revolution: On Its Way

Finally, let us not forget the pervasiveness of the digital revolution, among the great global transformations that have occurred since 2000, with all the opportunities and pitfalls it brings. When we entered the third millennium, obsessed as we were by the fear of a worldwide year 2000 (Y2K) bug, we still wondered what the Internet might become besides just another shiny gadget. Fifteen years later, many companies bear witness to its effects: like Kodak, many went under, unable to adapt to the new world in which any smartphone has a hundred times the horsepower of the 1969 NASA supercomputer that got us to the moon. So many things have changed in the span of a single generation, so much of a "new kind of human" has developed, vividly referred to as "Thumbelina" by Michel Serres: our children and grandchildren are now *digital natives,* who "no longer have the same bodies, life expectancies, or means of communication, they no longer perceive the world the same, no longer live in the same environment, no longer occupy the same space."[19] For this generation, "the language has changed, labor has mutated."[20] The number of cell phones sold has risen from fewer than 1 billion to more than 6 billion in just a few years![21]

This revolution has fed many hopes that we would never have dared dream of 15 years ago. Today's information technology and communications, by supporting access to knowledge and global interdependence of business, has the potential to accelerate human progress, reduce inequality, and give birth to communities of learning. It greatly stimulates scientific and technological innovation in fields as varied as medicine, energy, automobile manufacturing, and agriculture. In this digital age, we might have the capability to resolve the issue of world hunger, because every day we know with greater precision how to improve our soil, where we should irrigate, and when is the best moment to harvest; but more importantly, we know how to store, distribute, and trade what is produced. Humankind has never been able to interact so easily or rapidly, and we have never had so much choice in how we do so.

At the same time, we have entered into an era in which companies are panicked by the thought of being "Uberized" by the likes of Google, Facebook, Amazon, Airbnb, and of course by Uber itself. Such "exponential organizations" (ExOs), to borrow Salim Ismail's term,[22] were able to create a competitive advantage from available data and the network effect to build a disruptive model with 10 times the impact of organizations founded on the old linear model. These organizations were able to use the global economic displacement better than anyone to implement a paradigm shift from politics-based change to one based on consumer freedom—yet another consequence of the digital revolution that must be accounted for in matters of finance as well as government, as intertwined as the two are. Incumbent financial actors are also threatened by digital changes best felt with the emergence of "fintech" (financial technology) and the changes led by the blockchain. It is too early to say, but business models are likely to be transformed profoundly and at an unprecedented scale.

The Emergence of New Global Concerns

The emergence of new global preoccupations, as well as new questions that go beyond the traditional global public goods, also forces us to consider the world with new eyes. Take, for instance, the concerns with climate change and with refugees. In 2000 climate change was still debatable, but now it's widely accepted as fact, and we know that people living in poverty are the first to be affected, and most lastingly affected, by global warming. There is no more room for debate—we have to treat this at the global level, in coordination with the local, regional, and national levels, even if the decision by President Trump to withdraw the United States from the Paris climate change agreement has reignited some discussion. Similarly, the issue of refugees affects the entire international community and cannot be resolved by building walls (except where those stand as indicators of the most barefaced of demagogues). These issues affect the financial model that has persisted to this day.

Women Moving Up the Ladder: The Right Thing as Well as the Smart Thing

In 2000 I never would have had the unforgettable experience I had as a leader of the World Bank, on assignment in Dakar, Senegal, for International Women's Day. After attending a dinner with a group of 50 women from a variety of professions (including journalists, lawyers, and civil servants), we were shown a film in which Senegalese people, including two young women miming levels on a ladder, expressed their hope to someday reach the same level as men. My reaction was, *How horrible that we are still there! I dream of a world in which it is women, holding firm to the ladder, who reach down to bring men up to their level. Diversity—and I mean that in both senses—is an inestimable wealth. I can't imagine a world that is composed of only men, or only women.* This was rarely a matter for discussion at the beginning of the 21st century, despite an important international agenda. Now, as I discuss in Chapter 14, we are seeing the slow spread of an approach to finance through the prism of gender.

Proper Governance: The New Name of the Game

Before I end this admittedly nonexhaustive summary of the first decade and a half of our century, I want to mention something else new: the increase in expectations more often based on issues of *governance.* In 2000 this word, in its current meaning, barely existed; we spoke more often of *government.* The emergence of this idea of *governance* reflects a radical new approach to the management of globalization. As our water group said in 2004,

> Governance is a management method and not a system of government.... Governance is a triangle defined by public powers, private interests (industrial, agricultural, commercial), and the civil community formed by consumers and users. The triangle's size varies according to whether it is measured at the municipal, national, or international level.... It indicates that ... public powers have been stripped of their role as sole representative of the general interest. They ... no longer represent solely the interests of the State, its budget, and its sovereign powers.[23]

In other words, in the space of one generation, we have moved away from living in only a Westphalian world, one that is dominated by state power, to living in a much more complicated world in which the private sector and civil society both participate in decision making. We are now part of a world in which we were able to come to an agreement between nations on common goals, a world much harder to control, in which we have to completely reframe our discussions to find efficiency without harm to legitimacy. All this is anything but obvious, and in Chapters 9 and 10, we will see how the government/governance interplay is often painful and leads to disagreements.

Now What?

In 2015, the global community reached the deadline for achieving our Millennium Development Goals. Despite remarkable progress, we are far from eradicating the ills of the world. New problems have also arisen. We have never been less certain about the future of globalization.

Even though our world has been radically transformed since 2000, we do not need to give up on improving our global community. Our perspectives may have shifted and reshifted, but that does not mean we have to abandon our ideas. When world leaders met in Rio de Janeiro in 2012 for the United Nations Conference on Sustainable Development, they set new common goals for 2030 to define the big picture of international cooperation. If nothing else, this has given us a compass, with one priority left unchanged: eradicating extreme poverty across our planet. Natural trends and evolution are not enough, but the means, and the willingness, are there. Like Kennedy choosing to go to the moon in 1960, I have a dream: that we choose to do the things necessary to eradicate extreme poverty, not because they are easy but because they are hard.

That said, we cannot ignore the world's recent upheavals and emerging expectations. It seems inconceivable to begin again as we did in 2000 to plan for a worldwide commitment to support development. The UN knowledge group emphasized this point:

> To fulfill our vision of promoting sustainable development, we must go beyond the MDGs. They did not focus enough on reaching the very poorest and most excluded people. They were silent on the devastating effects of conflict and violence on development. The importance to development of good governance and institutions that guarantee the rule of law, free speech and open and accountable government was not included, nor the need for inclusive growth to provide jobs. Most seriously, the MDGs fell short by not integrating the economic, social, and environmental aspects of sustainable development as envisaged in the Millennium Declaration, and by not addressing the need to promote sustainable patterns of consumption and production. The result was that environment and development were never properly brought together. People were working hard—but often separately—on interlinked problems.[24]

How can we get the world reengaged in a viable action plan? How can we provide the means to reach our goals, and how can we fund them in the first place when we still depend upon a system of international cooperation that so heavily draws on what we inherited from the 20th century, with all its obvious limitations and how close it came to collapse? And can we avoid having to completely reinvent the system? Can we transition seamlessly? Obviously, as we will see in more detail in Chapter 3, finance as it was organized not only did not save the world but contributed to almost bringing it down. Future development of finance will have to take into consideration the changes discussed in this chapter: the role of emerging powers, the digital changes, as well as the new needs and the new actors.

To avoid a repeat, we need to be able to look to the financial system. This will help us answer the question we face today, which echoes a line from William Butler Yeats's "The Second Coming": will the center hold? And beyond that: can the center reinvent itself?

CHAPTER 2

The 2007–2008 Financial Crisis

Modern economic history is clearly divided into a pre-subprime and a post-subprime era. In 2007–2008 the world experienced the worst financial crisis since World War II, or maybe even since the 1930s. We are still not completely over it. And we are still uncertain as to whether the center—understood as our ability to make the system work—will hold, at least in its current shape. How can a financial system that seemed so solid reach the brink of collapse? We need to understand the sequence that occurred before bringing the common good into our reasoning. The Tower of Babel was so beautiful, why not build it higher? We can draw many lessons from this major crisis, and those lessons deserve serious consideration if we want to put our world and economy on a path that makes sense.

The Miracle of 1944: The Bretton Woods System

Everything started in the summer of 1944 with the signing of the Bretton Woods Agreement in the United States. The urgency then was to try to rebuild the Western world after the terrible war had torn it apart while ensuring the financial stability that strengthens international commerce. The lessons of the 1930s had been learned: the major advanced economies agreed on a system of fixed exchange rates, organized around the gold standard and the US dollar, which was the only currency convertible into gold. The mission of the central banks was to maintain a fixed parity between the national currencies and the reference currency. However, the exchange rate could be adjusted as needed, under the vigilant eye of the international community. Against a backdrop of strong economic growth, and because it was regulated (with a limitation on flows of capital between countries as well as restrictions on domestic credit, to avoid international speculation and domestic debt), the system worked relatively well during the 1950s and 1960s.

The depletion of the American current account balance, due primarily to the Vietnam War that the government was financing, sounded the death knell for this well-regulated mechanism. Since American gold reserves were entrusted with securing the whole system, their depletion undermined partners' confidence. You may remember that at the time, Charles de Gaulle expressed his desire to exchange France's francs for gold, and prepared to do so. In 1971 faced with watching the entire US gold reserve fly off to major exporting countries, President Nixon decided to suspend the convertibility of the US dollar into gold. This decision marked a turning point in international financial relationships: from a fixed exchange system, we moved to a flexible exchange system, "officially" adopted in 1976 by the Jamaica Accords that acknowledged the generalized floating of currencies. The obligation we had to central banks to stabilize exchange rates, and thus to have sufficient exchange reserves, was then cancelled.

The Deconstruction of the System and the Hidden Vices of a Well-Lubricated System

The election of Margaret Thatcher in 1979 in the United Kingdom, and then Ronald Reagan in 1980 in the United States, buried the Bretton Woods Agreement even deeper by starting a widespread revolution of financial liberalism. Controls on cross-border capital flows were lifted in advanced economies as well as in an increasing number of emerging countries, conferring a larger role on international commercial banks. At the same time, a large majority of countries lifted their restrictions on domestic credit, opening up an unbridled increase in real estate financing. Debt soared, and nominal financial flows increased, with greater and greater multiples of "real" underlying flows (e.g., trade and investments).

This liberalization of financial markets in the 1980s and 1990s ushered the world into an era of deregulation and massive debt. In the context of free competition, financial markets interconnected a bit more each day and became, in Adair Turner's words, "markets like any other," and credit became "a product like any other," to be provided "at lowest cost and in optimal quantities."[1] Household debt no longer financed new capital investment but rather purchases of already existing assets, especially property.

The mechanism had its virtues. During the 30 years of financial liberalism and this international financial revolution, global poverty was reduced more than at any time in human history: in 1980 some 50 percent of the human population lived in poverty, compared to 10 percent today.[2] This is the same dynamic that allowed the UN to affirm, in all seriousness, that eliminating this scourge from the face of the earth by 2030 was within our grasp. Finance is one of the critical ingredients that have enabled us to spread well-being, allocate resources in an optimal manner, and create growth without inflation, thanks to the positive trade-offs being made.

But also during this time, Western economies became deeply indebted. Humanity has been living on credit—governments, banks, companies, and households all play their own roles in this dangerous game, on a big or small scale according to the country. Everywhere, finance gained a greater weight compared to the "real economy." Adair Turner notes that finance's share in the American and British economies tripled between 1950 and 2000. In advanced economies, private sector debt increased from an average of 50 percent to 170 percent of national income between 1950 and 2006; likewise, capital flows between countries grew much faster than actual long-term investment.[3] The extent of financial activities as a percentage of GDP has hit two peaks: in 1929 and 2007. It's hard to believe that this is a simple coincidence. The cash machine was in overdrive to the point of creating well-known aberrations like the empty buildings in Spain and China or factories running at half strength.

When Icarus Flew Too Close to the Sun: Excessive Confidence, Despite the Warnings

The alarm had well and truly sounded several times, but no one wanted to pay attention to those who seemed to be crying wolf. The Asian financial crisis of 1997–1998 was the fifth time the world had seen a serious monetary and financial crisis in the space of 20 years. Most economists, as well as financial regulators and central banks, wanted to believe in the virtuous cycle of free debt creation and the multiplication of financial innovations such as securitization in the service of economic growth.[4] So long as the system seemed rational, profitable, and socially useful, so long as central banks were there to ensure control, led by the best people, why worry?[5]

The system's growing complexity, with increasingly sophisticated control and risk distribution mechanisms, in some ways represented a measure of stability: the more we distributed risks and dispersed debt, the more the system seemed to be self-correcting. Adair

Turner notes that on the eve of the subprime crisis, the complexity of the secure credit system and shadow banking was "staggering":[6]

> The Federal Reserve Bank of New York attempted to map all the possible circuits and interconnections on a single map. It printed the results on a 0.90x120cm (35x47 in) sheet of paper and recommended that anyone who wanted to understand the system do the same. It was impossible to represent it on a sheet of paper so small, and yet, it was already difficult to read the instructions.[7]

But the sophistication was reassuring, and it maintained the illusion of a "Great Moderation."

I did not truly understand the excesses in the system until I witnessed the swelling and then bursting of the dot-com bubble as an investment banker at Lazard in London and then New York. I had scarcely left the Ministry of Finance, with my beliefs in the rationality of French technocracy intact, when I found myself in a senseless world where you had to put ".com" on all pitches made to clients. I personally produced "W HSmith.com" and "Sainsbury.com." Theworst part is that it worked!

As an illustration, a major player in certification[8] saw its stock price soar in 2000 simply because it had signed a contract with a company that presented itself as the business web portal for China's external trade, by betting on the "first mover advantage" and "winner takes all": at that time, people could, quite seriously and without laughing, calculate that a minimum fee per transaction experiencing exponential growth would fall into the pocket of the certifier that entered the market first, thus making it shoot up in value. Vivendi, for instance, led at that time by Jean-Marie Messier, acquired the vizzavi.fr portal from an unknown person who had already filed the name (vis@vis) for the "modest sum" of 24 million French francs, or more than $4 million today! The values no longer made any sense. The speculative bubble grew steadily until it was ready to implode, with asset depreciations, bankruptcies, and the economic recession we all remember. There was an excess of finance to be purged.

Despite Alerts, Unquestionable Finance

The abuses continued, as well as the illusion of an untouchable financial system. It is interesting to consider September 11, 2001, from this viewpoint. On that day, the very heart of global finance was dealt a serious blow. I witnessed this human tragedy firsthand from the windows of my office at Lazard, on the 61st floor of a building at Rockefeller Center, where I had an unobstructed view of the World Trade Center. None of us who were there will ever forget it: it was a beautiful fall day ... and then a plane crashed into the Twin Towers right before our eyes. They evacuated our building, the phone network overloaded, rumors started, and panic grew. We found ourselves in the lobby, across the street from NBC headquarters, which was scrolling the morning's news in a loop like it was any other day—stock prices going up, Michael Jordan making a comeback to the NBA, and two planes hitting the Twin Towers. The atmosphere was surreal. Then we were allowed to return to our homes. When I went to the site a week later, I was immediately struck by a strong odor of asbestos and the countless bits of letterhead heaped on the ground. I was overwhelmed by a sense of loss. But things quickly went back to normal. The day after the disaster, I got a phone call from one of my Japanese clients who worked in one of the Twin Towers. He told me that he had lost all the data on a transaction we had worked on the previous week. He asked me to intercede with Tokyo so we could move forward and reconstruct the file. September 11 was staggering in its implications, and at the same time it was reassuring to see that life went on. Wall Street also went back to business quickly, even if stock markets saw a decline (naturally). The financial system had demonstrated amazing resiliency, as if all of the actors wanted to show that they would not let it fall. The fact that Wall Street had been hit and could resume working days after the attack seemed to stress the extraordinary resilience of the system. Like many at that time, I was puzzled. The US war against Afghanistan and Iraq paradoxically helped, by improving the health of the overall economy. That said, the September 11 attacks contributed to the idea that finance was a Tower of Babel looming over us all, which we could blindly trust.

2007–2011: The Fall of the Tower of Babel

What had to happen finally did. All it took was a grain of sand to clog up the mechanism and make the system implode. We had left finance without a master. The subprime crisis in the summer of 2007 was a harsh reminder that this was a profoundly irrational blind force, and that it was the toy of players with motivations that were often different from those who signed the Millennium Declaration and agreed on the Millennium Development Goals.

The subprimes, poor-quality mortgages in an amount based on the value of the property, were recklessly granted to less and less creditworthy US households, starting in the early 2000s. The whole concept was based on a rapid, continuous increase in property prices, without anyone thinking about prices going down.[9] By transforming, securitizing, and marketing these mortgages, the financial mills were offering products with higher yields because of more and more sophisticated bundling methods and ever-increasing complexity in financial modeling. It would have been enough that the American real estate market reversed itself at the beginning of 2007 to put nearly 3 million households in default, sending the nation's banks into a tailspin, and triggering an international financial crisis, but, in fact, the foundation of the entire financial products system was constructed out of high-risk components. The subprime assets were dispersed to virtually every corner of the earth, exposing the system to a risk that we thought was diluted and distributed to those with greater "appetites." Henri de Castries, then CEO of AXA, used a particularly strong image to summarize the situation at the time—the subprimes are essentially like the anchovies in a salade Niçoise. They don't amount to much on their own, but if they're rotten, it's enough to ruin the whole salad.[10]

That is how, after a string of implosions in 2007, the entire system started to gradually disintegrate. The chain reaction that followed made participants feel as though they were sliding downhill in a toboggan with no way to stop. For my part, I had just joined Crédit Agricole in Paris a week before it all started, in charge of finance at one of the largest banks in the world with a balance sheet of over $2 trillion. Suddenly, I was in the eye of a hurricane.

In August 2007 the announcement by the bank BNP Paribas of a temporary freeze on three funds exposed to subprime risk hinted that this would be more than just an American crisis. The European central banks, first among them the European Central Bank (ECB), were already forced to fly to the market's rescue. The Kerviel affair, in which a rogue trader cost the investment bank Société Générale €5 billion, was exposed in January 2008 and nearly signed Société Générale's death warrant. The affair highlighted an even greater loss of control and the scale of the threat that weighed on the global financial system. In March, Wall Street went in the red and the markets panicked before moving up again at the news of JPMorgan Chase's takeover of the investment bank Bear Stearns at fire sale prices, with the decisive support of the Federal Reserve.

On September 15 an event took place that was emblematic of the crisis: 150-year-old Lehman Brothers, the fourth-largest investment bank in the United States, filed for bankruptcy, the largest in American financial history. Alan Greenspan famously said, "I've never seen anything like this!" The shock for global finance became even worse because at the same time, the prestigious investment bank Merrill Lynch was bought by Bank of America. Then insurance giant American International Group (AIG) announced the emergency sale of $20 billion in assets. A few days later, Goldman Sachs and Morgan Stanley gave up their status as investment banks to transform themselves into commercial banks, that is, normal banks that accept deposits and have access to the Federal Reserve's refinancing capacities. On October 3, the federal government adopted Treasury Secretary Henry Paulson's plan to save the American economy. The historic government intervention totaled $700 billion. France followed suit by adopting a "plan to support financing of the national economy" on October 13 (in fact, it was a plan to support banking institutions). Several days later, the European banks had to recapitalize again.

Throughout that long, terrible fall, pervaded with the craziest rumors and the utmost uncertainty, a loss of confidence could be seen among the financial players. Entering the crisis meetings each morning at Crédit Agricole, we would ask each other what new bank we were going to have to stop trading with, sending to every trader on the planet the horrible instruction "Do not deal." It was hard for us to be the first to pull away the ladder, but clearly it was impossible to be the last! In the end, the central banks found themselves set up as traders of last resort. That black year ended with the arrest, in December, of financier Bernie Madoff, perpetrator of a massive $50 billion fraud through his investment fund. The glass is full! Enough was enough! As Warren Buffett noted, with dark irony, only when the tide goes out do you discover who's been swimming naked.

The following year, 2009, was a triumph of internationalism and regulation. Two G20 summits—in London in April and in Pittsburgh in September—were followed by a meeting in St. Andrews, Scotland, in November of the finance ministers and governors of central banks for those same countries. The participants defined a framework for the financial system that included creation of a Financial Stability Board, consideration of banks' off–balance sheet accounts in calculating prudential ratios, reform of accounting standards, and a compilation by the Organisation for Economic Co-operation and Development (OECD) of a list of countries that refused to exchange tax information with other governments. They also agreed on measures to restart the global economy, in particular with an agreement to bolster the resources of the International Monetary Fund (IMF). In the meantime, announcements about a return to profitability for American and European banks abounded.

The lull in troubling developments (if we can call it that, as growth was at a low ebb during this time) did not last long. In October 2009, the first tensions appeared that would lead to the euro crisis. The newly elected Greek Socialist government revealed the truth behind the country's public finances—a deficit of 12.7 percent of GDP, compared to the 6 percent that had been claimed. In January 2010, Brussels jumped in, and the 27 member countries of the EU, led by Germany, held a summit in February to try to solve the problem. An agreement on a Greek bailout plan was finally reached in May: aid of €110 billion—on a scale unheard of anywhere in the world—shared between the EU and the IMF to be granted in exchange for a painful austerity cure. Several days later, it was the Eurozone's turn as €750 billion was mobilized over three years to support the single currency, which was being attacked from all sides, and strengthen the budgetary discipline of member states. At the same time, the ECB acquired €74 billion in sovereign debt securities (Greek and Portuguese securities in particular) in order to reassure investors. In November the EU granted financial aid to Ireland.

During this time, the G20 continued to play a role in coordinating financial and economic policies. Summits in Toronto and Seoul struggled to pave the way to sustainable and balanced growth. But summer 2011 reignited the panic with the shock of leaders losing power: Papandreou in Greece and Berlusconi in Italy lost power in November, under pressure from their peers, a first in history. The year 2011 ended with a marathon meeting in Brussels, where the seventh summit in two years was held with the goal of saving Europe. When the Brits rejected the reforms proposed by France and Germany, the feeling was, as the December 10 issue of *Le Monde* put it, "L'Europe à 28, c'est fini" (The EU-28 is no more). It was a pronouncement that was six years too early. France's loss of its own triple-A rating in January 2012, previously flaunted as a national treasure by France's president, injected another shock wave, and a sense that the country had lost its bearings. And to increase the confusion in France, as previously in the United States, the end result in 2011 of this "catastrophic" downgrading was ... lower lending costs. You lose your prime status, and despite that you pay less than before thanks to the general fall of rates. Many people were legitimately wondering how this could make sense.

The financial crisis led the world to an uncomfortable place. No real precedents existed to help this navigation into uncharted waters. And little trust was left for the helmsmen. And the loss of trust was not just among members of Occupy Wall Street and the equivalent movements that emerged in different countries. Now that the world had narrowly escaped a complete implosion, finance had become a kind of public enemy number one. It was far from being connected to any form of common good.

CHAPTER 3

One Main Lesson: Trust Is Gone

The Revelations of an Unprecedented Financial Catastrophe

The economic decline of 2007–2011 resulted from a triple crisis, which compounded the effects of a more "traditional" excess debt crisis, and helps explain the unexpected force and extent of its damage.

A Crisis of Innovation Out of Control

Above all, this was a crisis of financial innovation. Rapid development of securitization, off–balance sheet refinancing vehicles, and the infinite pooling of the subprime mortgages all contributed to the uncontrolled chain reaction that almost killed the system. Carried away by the idea of the great economic progress that the system was supposed to enable, financiers had adapted a number of products without trying very hard to measure the consequences. The connection between cause and effect was lost. They created debt, and with that debt they redeemed assets, the yields of which encouraged them to create more and more debt, thanks to financial innovations that grew more and more inventive, until all control was gone. Left to its own devices, the instrument manufactured artificial wealth until the bubble burst. The biggest lesson we can take from the 2007–2008 crisis is that, to paraphrase Rebelais, "Finance without conscience is but the ruin of the world."[1] Domesticated, finance is a good servant, but left to itself, it becomes a poor master. Uncontrolled and allowed to run wild, it can lead the world to disaster. Paul Volcker, former chair of the Federal Reserve who advised Barack Obama on financial reform, bitterly said that there have been few true financial innovations and that the last real one was the ATM.

We must not forget that, contrary to traditional teaching, financial markets can be, and often are, dominated by the irrational. One example is the October 1987 crash, when the Dow Jones Industrial Average lost 22.7 percent of its value in a single day, even though there was no new information to explain the sell-off. The economy was certainly in a phase with sharply rising long-term interest rates, but why this black day? Sociologists talk about a "tipping point" or a "tolerance threshold," meaning the critical moment when a singular phenomenon becomes commonplace. In the case of the stock market, this means that during a certain period, the players overlook a trend until it is so noticeable that the collective confidence shifts. Movements on the stock market are never permanent or regular but instead are marked by seesaws and adjustments. There is mimicry as well as mania. This was the case for tulips in Holland in the 17th century.[2] In two weeks, tulips rose in price from 50 to 1,000 florins without any discernible reason. A buying mania took hold, the masses followed suit, and then suddenly there was a panic and a crash. In both cases, a force that was both irrational and irresistible had taken over the markets, pushing prices higher until they suddenly broke and started their decline, ending with another crash. Every time, people say "this time it's different,"[3] but the phenomenon occurs over and over again, always taking us by surprise.

In the case of the 2007–2008 crisis, the problem was that, despite the inherent irrationality of the system, we wanted to believe, more urgently than ever, in the absolute rationality and effectiveness of our financial instruments. The alliance of finance with digital technology undoubtedly contributes to the persistence of this illusion. An algorithmic tool pushed the players to systematize use of value models, which gradually became standards. This is the danger of any model, which by definition simplifies reality. Human beings have always tended to want to substitute the representation for the real, even when it is just so that we can make a decision. With financial models, built around averages from which they too regularly deviate,[4] the temptation to depart from them is often too great, at the risk of forgetting that this even is a departure. The models give false reassurance that extreme events are off limits and tempt us to test these limits. At heart the financial language and digital language are two of a kind. They are both universal languages, which, left unchecked, act as irresistible forces. Thus, their convergence can be explosive. The convergence led to a major crisis in 2007–2008. Driven by a unique and irresistible language, the temptation of Babel is ancient and universal.

A Crisis of Incomplete Globalization

At the same time, 2007–2008 was a crisis of financial globalization itself. Starting in 1971, reinforced and pursued throughout the 1970s, 1980s, and 1990s with the liberalization of capital flows beyond national borders, and then with ever more sophisticated distribution of credit risks, the financial system did not stop growing, spreading, interconnecting, and creating interdependencies, to the point that, if any part whatsoever should fail, the whole would be weakened immediately.

Does this mean this crisis was truly "global"? I can still hear the Indian finance minister, P. Chidambaram, ironically noting that we call crises that affect the United States and Europe "global" while those that happen in India are deemed to be "local." In fact, today the international financial economy is largely dominated by advanced economies (in the narrowest sense, the G7 countries; more broadly, members of the OECD). The world's largest banks are still European, American, Japanese, and Australian, as are the major institutional investors, despite the emergence of Chinese players. Emerging countries feel like hostages to a system in which they would like to have more of a say. This is the purpose of the discussions that took place at the G20 summits starting in 2008. Remember that in the worst hours of the crisis, when we were repeatedly at the brink of a global bankruptcy, it was China that contributed to the rescue of the global economy, even if the debt it created then appeared as a sign of fragility a few years later. As the Chinese famously said, it was time to save capitalism. With its 2009–2010 stimulus policy, China made itself into one of the world's economic locomotives. A number of financial flows were redirected then to emerging countries that had resisted the crash better, even if some of them are now seeing a painful economic turnaround.

A Crisis of Inappropriate and Poorly Supervised Regulation

It was a crisis of deregulation. Remember that deregulation was a key component of the neoliberal approach. We have not been able to regulate our global financial system; its complexity and distribution have largely escaped legislators' grasp. A similar situation arose in the Middle Ages with regard to the Church not knowing how to rule on the regulation of weapons. The Church ruled yes to those whose effects you could see, such as axes and maces, and no to those you couldn't see, such as ballistae and catapults. Not only have regulations barely been adequate to track the development of global finance, but the international community, blinded by its faith in the alleged benefits of the system, allowed existing regulations to be reduced. It granted an ever-increasing share of the assessment to financial actors—de facto self-assessment—who became bigger and bigger. Some banks attained balance sheets equal to the size of the GDP of major countries—close to $2 trillion for JPMorgan Chase and Bank of America, for example, which was comparable to France's GDP. These actors were themselves left to blunt their own regulations, relying only on measurement and compensation mechanisms and incentives that had lost any idea of the collective. They took the system in an insane direction.

In short, we did not know how to control the forces the deregulation had unleashed. In the prophetic words of Adair Turner, "This catastrophe was entirely self-inflicted and avoidable."[5]

Finally, a Devastating Crisis of Confidence

Finally, the economic damage caused by the 2007–2008 financial crisis revealed itself dramatically. After the Great Moderation, global community fell into a Great Recession that we have not yet completely recovered from. The cost of bailing out the financial system per se did not, however, weigh that much in the balance. In all the advanced economies, the governments support of the banks cost, in total, over 3 percent of GDP.[6] But, at the same time, millions of people had lost their homes, their jobs, or seen their incomes and standards of living fall. Public debt increased in a spectacular fashion (in advanced countries, by an average of 34 percent of GDP between 2007 and 2014[7]) at the same time that public development aid, the first target of austerity cures, shrank. This was a modern confirmation of the old adage that "when the fat grow thin, the thin die," as I explained in a book published around that time.[8] Paul Tucker, then number two at the Bank of England, predicted 25 lost years. We are still counting ... But the financial crisis had a still more damaging consequence in the long-term: the profound loss of confidence in banks, governments, elites, and "the system" in general. The public was appalled to learn that many bankers granted risky mortgages to Americans, as well as Irish, Spanish, and British real estate developers; that some had acted dishonestly by manipulating the LIBOR (London Interbank Offered Rate) or selling securities of questionable value to less scrupulous investors.[9] François Hollande's speech at Le Bourget, France, at the beginning of his presidential campaign on January 22, 2012, perfectly summarized the state of mind of many at the time:

> My true adversary ... does not have a name, a face, or a party. It will never present itself as a candidate, will never be elected, and yet, it governs. This adversary is the world of finance. Right in front of our eyes, over twenty years, finance has taken control of the economy, society,

> and our lives.... This control has become an empire. And the crisis that has raged since September 15, 2008, has strengthened, rather than weakening it.

I was overwhelmed by the negative image of bankers perpetrated by the media throughout the crisis, and by the popular resentment for them, because of the disparities between bankers and themselves. During the four years I spent at Crédit Agricole, I went to the bank's meetings of members, shareholders, and customers in various regions of France. I remember in particular my first such town hall in Blois, France, in March 2009, when Crédit Agricole shares were worth less than €6, compared to €30 before the crisis.[10] The first question I was asked came from an older gentleman, leaning on his cane: "How much do you make, monsieur, and how much do all of these people, who have ruined me, make, who have put my grandson out of a job, and said nothing to us?" This man, along with many others, had been hurt by the crisis and the economic recession that followed. They had to pay and will pay more in the future, along with their children for this debacle for which they bore no responsibility. I so deeply felt for him for what he had revealed that night. They did not get the explanations they deserved to justify the emergency measures adopted to save the system. We should not be surprised that confidence vanished. As Deputy Prime Minister Tharman Shanmugaratnam of Singapore said in a speech in Aix en Provence, France, in July

2017, the three biggest issues we are facing today are all consequences of the crisis: the stagnation of the middle class in most advanced economies, the renewed lack of convergence between advanced economies and the rest of the world, and, more importantly, the loss of trust in most, if not all, domestic institutions as well as international ones. Of course, these issues are interrelated.

King Finance Suddenly Naked

For France one of the symbolic turning points occurred in the summer of 2008. The theme that dominated the national debate in France at that time was the *Revenu de solidarité active* (minimum social income) proposed by Minister Martin Hirsch. The experts struggled with whether this was necessary and if we should dedicate a budget of €500 million, €600 million, or €800 million to it. In September Lehman Brothers filed for bankruptcy. In no time, Nicolas Sarkozy mobilized €420 billion to fly to the rescue of the banks, while the United States found $700 billion for Wall Street. In short, we fought for two months to decide how many millions of euros to give to the poor, and one month later we had pulled billions out of a hat for finance! The irony cut deeper because in France these two subjects were being voted on in the same bill. The rupture with the people was inevitable. We will never be able to explain to the French people, no more than to the American people or any other citizens of the world, that this €400 billion or $700 billion were ultimately a good deal for governments, which made money out of the bailouts, that they were, above all, to avoid a disaster for every country by heading off the collapse of the banking system.

The second rupture came on September 24, 2008, in Toulon, France, when President Sarkozy declared that he would not accept "a single depositor losing a single euro," that he would mobilize the state to protect citizens' deposits. Suddenly, 65 million French people asked, "Why were my deposits at risk?" Until then only a very few had realized that a bank was not a safe where their money patiently waited but that the banks reinjected the deposits into the financial system to use these resources, transform them, and reallocate them to the four corners of the world. Luckily, the Toulon speech did not trigger a panic and prompt the population to form lines in front of the banks to withdraw their savings. But all the financial players were quaking in their wingtips! This statement made in France echoed all over the world. People suddenly discovered what was behind the counters and ATMs of their banks. A famous cartoon spread around the world that said, "The 2008 Nobel Prize in Economics goes to Mrs. Jones for keeping her savings at home." I keep a framed copy of that cartoon in my office.

People realized that finance was not what they thought it was and that, when unleashed, it was more complex and dangerous than initially envisaged. This amazing force we thought we had created to serve us had run out of control. Most people had admired finance without questioning it. Suddenly the veil was cut into pieces and finance appeared naked. And this was a scary vision.

Governments, like bankers, are still paying for their errors and flawed teachings. People are angry today because they have the feeling they have been "had." They have gotten the impression that governments saved the powerful—these "cosmocrats," to use John Micklethwait's term,[11] people who are based in London or Paris and know New York and Singapore better than Detroit, Birmingham, or Marseilles—and abandoned the rest to deal with their own problems. The current global wave of populism is an expression of this vast disenchantment.

Even more disturbing is that the markets, as well as the governments themselves, question banks and central banks. All you have to do is watch the current debates in Germany over the "dictatorship" of the ECB, or the recurring temptation of the US Congress to increase its control over the Federal Reserve or have its decisions constrained by rules. In the eurozone, as in the G20 circle, everyone suspects everyone else of wanting to depreciate its currency, creating tension on the exchange market. As for investors, they have become ultrasensitive to reputation risks. An asset manager I met in 2010 in San Francisco as part of a Crédit Agricole quarterly road show told me: "I am no longer buying bank stocks for three reasons: (1) because people don't like you anymore, if they ever liked you; (2) because with the new rules in effect, your profitability will decrease; (3) because even if you turn out to be profitable, you're risky because people don't really like you [see number 1] and you will easily be taxed or fined in the future, so you don't interest me."

Don't even try to talk about a bank to a Scottish investor. In Edinburgh, where I had a chance to do a road show in 2009, the people I met were ashamed that two of the largest bank disasters in the United Kingdom were caused by the Royal Bank of Scotland and the Bank of Scotland.

Without Trust: No Capitalism, No Market Economy, and No Democracy

This loss of trust capital is the biggest loss caused by the financial crisis. This was Nicolas Sarkozy's message during his speech in Lyon on January 19, 2012: "This is not an economic crisis, it is a financial crisis that created a crisis of confidence, which created an economic crisis." The entire capitalist system, our entire modern Western civilization, relies on trust. Without it we can no longer make loans, make plans, or cooperate. Alain Peyrefitte analyzed this mechanism well in his book *La société de confiance* (The trust society): if development in Europe was possible, it was thanks to an "ethos of trust," which upended the traditional taboos and favored innovation, mobility, competition, and rational and responsible initiatives. Without trust the entire society built by our ancestors is undermined. Yet this is precisely the poison that the financial crisis injected. Our system does not work as well today as it did 10 years ago because we have lost faith in it. And this issue goes well beyond finance. For example, think about the shock wave created by Volkswagen and its fraud concerning the automobile pollution measures or the Panama Papers or various accounting scandals. The level of trust in the system has decreased, putting the system in danger. Rebuilding this trust is an urgent task, one without which our world cannot thrive.[12]

A System Awaiting Rebuilding, but also Reform: Regaining Control over Money

The financial system was almost wiped out, but it finally managed to recover. By relying on the G20, the international community managed to bail out the financial institutions, set an agenda among the players, and establish new rules, including those for compensation. People, at least those who had and always will have access, can continue to place their money in the bank, deposit salaries electronically, and pay with credit cards. Currencies did not disappear, and a deflationary spiral was avoided. The financial system managed to organize itself. For now, we have avoided the catastrophic scenario of a repetition of the 1930s.

Make no mistake, however, about the nature of this restoration. The system has done nothing more than shore up the breaches and patch up the cracks. It has not in any way been rebuilt; it has not been given new foundations, and it certainly has not been given an overhaul. If it was necessary to ensure that dishonest or incompetent banks are sanctioned, that no bank becomes "too big to fail," that financiers are compensated based on the overall performance and the duration of the undertaking and not just their individual performance, or that taxpayers will never again be asked to rescue the bankers like they did in 2008, the regulatory reforms are not focused on the crisis's true problem, namely, that the financial mechanism is left to its own devices. Today, it is urgent to get this mechanism back under control.

To serve the common good, we need to regain control over money. To do this, we must give the players in the international financial system a new compass. The system has such a compass, but it does not know how or why to read it, or even the direction the market should be facing. Without figuring this out, we could see another major crisis that we cannot afford.

Institutional Investors: The New Depository of Trust in the Reshuffled System

If we need to rebuild the international financial system, we first need to know which players to call on to rebuild it, and we need to agree on who does what. Yet another major consequence of the crisis is the transformation of an economy dominated by the banks, now constrained by regulation, into a world where institutional investors reign: pension funds, insurers, sovereign funds, and other asset managers now have a predominant weight in the international financial system (soon they should be managing close to $100 trillion) and are the repository of our trust; they are managing our money! This reshuffling of the cards poses a number of questions that urgently need to be answered if we want to maintain control over how our money is used.

What regulations should we adopt when some banking business is being sent outside the banks into shadow banking, where regulations are different? Since 2008 the financial system has put in place more solid regulations to control the banks and limit the risk of a new financial crisis. The problem is that some of the risks now lie outside these traditional institutions. How can we make sure that the new version of global finance is effectively controlled?

How can the resources held by the various players be mobilized to benefit the real economy, without depriving the investors, contributors, and retirees in the world? How can development, and specifically infrastructure, be financed? In fact, because of the regulatory changes and market expectations, today it is more costly and less attractive for a bank to grant long-term loans for complex, risky, and exotic projects. How can we make sure that institutional investors are ready to take the reins? They hold a more central place than ever in the financing of the economy and do not operate like banks (see Chapter 14). How can we guide them to a place where they are financing a shared prosperity for all?

The Meaning of Managing $5,000,000,000,000

We must collectively learn to maintain the stability of the international financial system in which these new institutional investors have more weight than the banks do, are more concentrated, and correlate more with one another. Today, the world has around 20 major asset management companies, such as Blackrock (the largest with close to $5 trillion in assets), Vanguard, and Amundi (which each manage more than $1 trillion), the latter based in France. At the risk of exaggerating, I suggest that humanity may end up depending on a close circle of chief investors and chief economists to allocate savings. These investors will say that their management is highly decentralized and fragmented and therefore has little chance of going in the same direction, but who will guarantee for us that all these people are not going to think in the same way at the same time, leading to a widespread financial panic—with the catastrophic consequences that we have all seen? We still don't have the answer, and we will likely have to go through another financial crisis to test these scenarios. It is then fair to say that the shadow banking system is a real concern for institutions like the IMF, as well as for central bankers.

Technological Disruption Added to the Equation

The current financial system, as reshaped by the 2007–2008 crisis, is even more fragile than before because of the profound disruptions caused by technology. These disruptions include the development of online banking—combined with a vast movement to close physical branches—high-frequency trading, and even asset management by robots. Faced with these innovations, how can we make sure that they benefit everyone and do not create new gaps in society? The growing number of banking apps that are trusted by the younger generation also shows a loss of faith in traditional banking.

There are so many questions that we need to face head on, which remain the major challenges that the last crisis confronted us with: the challenges of regulation, globalization, and financial innovation. The question at the heart of all of our problems today is how can a poor master become a good servant? Can we reform a system that has laudable ambitions but that has taken a wrong turn? How can we restore a trust that must be earned, not demanded? Where do we start? The clock is ticking. How can we make sure that ultimately we all win? Can we regain control over finance and money?

CHAPTER 4

Great Hope II. All Together Now!

The global financial and economic crisis that was triggered in 2007 threw us far off the cohesive and collaborative course the global community had set for ourselves in 2000. Would we have achieved all the MDGs, or performed better, if this calamity hadn't occurred? It's hard to say, given how much the economic maps have also changed, along with the transformations of demographic balance, funding methods, and the major players in development. As we will see in this chapter, 2015 was an exceptional year, as hopefully the history books will show, and it provided humanity a unique opportunity to bring back to the table essential issues we had lost sight of during years of discord and shock.

Three World Summits to Bring Back the Millennium Spirit

For whatever reason, some years are more symbolically charged than others. The year 2015 was one such year. It may be too soon to categorically declare it a historic year, but 2015 was, at the very least, an opportunity to lay out a new roadmap for international cooperation through 2030, with the aim of establishing lasting, universal development.

When in 2015 we considered all the upheavals that had taken place since 2000, we came to understand that the global community must organize our efforts in a different way. We realized that we must adapt our technologies and redouble our ambitions if we were to re-create the terms and conditions for a credible hope for our near and distant future. Working on the senior management team of the World Bank, I found myself at the forefront of this effort.

Addis Ababa: Financing Development

The first summit meeting to open up the path to the anticipated adoption of the Sustainable Development Goals (SDGs) by the United Nations in September was the Third International Conference on Financing for Development, held in Addis Ababa from July 13 to July 16, 2015. Hosting such a high-level global event on its turf was in itself a coup for Ethiopia, one of the developing nations of East Africa: this role as a host was even more symbolic because the mobilization of domestic resources for development (e.g., taxation), prioritized over receipt of external aid, was a major theme of the conference. Besides evaluating the progress reached in the implementation of the Monterrey Consensus (2002) and the Doha Declaration (2008), this summit addressed new or developing issues posed by the United Nations' development support programs after 2015. The funds that were needed to realize the SDGs totaled in the trillions of dollars annually, so discussions focused on practical means to mobilize such resources within a difficult economic context. The Addis Ababa Action Agenda, adopted at the close of the conference, sent a clear message about the importance of climate issues and the need to integrate them into political development conversations. In a sense, this conference set the tone for the two other key summits in 2015, as well as for the annual meetings of the World Bank Group and the IMF organized in Lima, Peru, in October.

New York: Achieving the Sustainable Development Goals

The second meeting of 2015 was the United Nations General Assembly, held in New York from September 25 to 27, which officially established the global community's commitment to goals that were even more ambitious than the MDGs, despite the post-2000 problems. In 15 years, the international community increased the 8 objectives to 17 and expanded the 21 targets to 169, relying on a holistic, universal, and transformative vision of sustainable development. Where the MDGs centered primarily on social themes, the SDGs attempted to cover all dimensions of sustainable development: economic growth, social inclusion, and environmental protection—all in the hopes of accounting for existing synergies between the goals set for these three areas. Furthermore, whereas the MDGs mainly targeted developing nations, the SDGs have attempted to make sure no one is left behind: they apply to both rich countries and poor, which is a first in the world's approach to development. They come with a more or less audacious promise, that despite our current economic situation and the threat of climate change, poverty will be eliminated by 2030, through the mobilization of every possible effort. The unanimous adoption by the 193 member states of the United Nations of the 2030 Agenda for Sustainable Development (see the box on next page) received a standing ovation by the delegations!

Paris: Addressing the Challenge of Climate Change

The 21st Conference of the Parties (COP21) to the United Nations Framework Convention on Climate Change (UNFCCC), held from November 30 to December 11 in Paris, ended the year with a major leap forward for the planet in terms of sustainable prosperity. World leaders recognized that the elimination of poverty must be accompanied by strategies to reinforce economic growth and respond to a range of social needs without harming the environment or affecting the climate. They needed to adopt a binding agreement about the lasting reduction of greenhouse gas emissions. And they did it! On December 12, 2015, the 197 parties to the agreement committed to taking measures to cap global temperature change to no more than 2°C above preindustrial levels, and to attempt to reduce this increase to less than 1.5°C. This agreement represents a major advance for the world, particularly because it is the first time in history that we have recognized that respect for human rights—specifically the rights to health and the rights of indigenous peoples, migrants, children, and disabled people—is an integral part of the fight against climate change.

SUSTAINABLE DEVELOPMENT GOALS

1. End poverty in all its forms everywhere.

2. End hunger, achieve food security and improved nutrition, and promote sustainable agriculture.

3. Ensure healthy lives and promote well-being for all at all ages.

4. Ensure inclusive and equitable quality education and promote lifelong learning opportunities for all.

5. Achieve gender equality and empower all women and girls.

6. Ensure availability and sustainable management of water and sanitation for all.

7. Ensure access to affordable, reliable, sustainable, and modern energy for all.

8. Promote sustained, inclusive, and sustainable economic growth, full and productive employment, and decent work for all.

9. Build resilient infrastructure, promote inclusive and sustainable industrialization, and foster innovation.

10. Reduce inequality within and among countries.

11. Make cities and human settlements inclusive, safe, resilient, and sustainable.

12. Ensure sustainable consumption and production patterns.

13. Take urgent action to combat climate change and its impacts.

14. Conserve and sustainably use the oceans, seas, and marine resources for sustainable development.

15. Protect, restore, and promote sustainable use of terrestrial ecosystems, sustainably manage forests, combat desertification and halt and reverse land degradation, and halt biodiversity loss.

16. Promote peaceful and inclusive societies for sustainable development, provide access to justice for all, and build effective, accountable, and inclusive institutions at all levels.

17. Strengthen the means of implementation and revitalize the global partnership for sustainable development.

The Emergence of a New Spirit of Cooperation

In addition to defining statements of principle, these three summits that punctuated 2015 created a promising trend for our future. At the same time that they were governed by the traditional diplomatic dynamic between nations that meetings, roundtables, workshops, forums, conferences, and the like end with the creation of an agreement and signature of heads of state, these summits also benefited from a smooth mobilization of representatives of all members of society: businesses; foundations; NGOs; government agencies; investors; regional, national, and international intergovernmental institutions; elected officials; and citizens. Unexpected coalitions came together to spark debate, create momentum, and, in short, to foster agreement. This catalytic phenomenon is quite new, and it made the summits more productive and even, considering the circus-like aspect, fascinating.

From Billions to Trillions: A Paradigm Shift

The Addis Ababa conference was momentous for me because I had gone to promote an unprecedented document for which I was the lead author: *From Billions to Trillions.* [1] As surprising at it may sound, this was the first time that all the international development finance actors involved had signed a statement together. It was a small but real revolution for the world of multilateral organizations! The idea was to affirm our conviction that the challenges facing sustainable development funding were not insurmountable, because the total savings and public and private investments in the world were, in theory, sufficient to meet the need. I made sure that the report would be written in the most accessible English possible and that its title would boldly and clearly embody our ambitions.

The billions to trillions approach is a fundamental tenet for how we address the huge needs facing us. We are faced with a reality that the investments that need to be met run into the trillions of dollars while the public funds available run only into the billions. This so-called financing gap is daunting when viewed in its aggregate.

Bridging this gap is at the heart of a new financial system, a way of using finance that is needed to finance sustainable development. This way will require the recomposition of a number of different and important elements. Much-improved domestic resource mobilization is one factor. This can be done through more-efficient tax systems and better tax collection, as well as by taking a closer look at how to increase (move money from under the mattress) and to better use domestic savings (for example, reviewing the regulations around how the funds can be used without compromising the ability of players to meet their own liability requirements). Another critical factor is generating a higher return per dollar of public finance. Adopting a more thoughtful and rigorous way of using public finance can mobilize multiples of private investments, be that through first/second loss mechanisms or more usable forms of guarantees or other risk mitigation instruments, that is, mobilizing public resources where they can most make a difference in terms of risk assessment, perception, and actual use.[2] Approaches such as these were articulated in the *Billions to Trillions* report. By bringing together the various actors in the field, we were able to set out a framework, one which we must now begin to implement with a greater sense of urgency.

This new form of mobilization could be seen in Paris. Certainly, the success of COP21 was a success for French diplomacy, which reversed the protocol of the Copenhagen conference of 2009, in which heads of state did not arrive until the end to approve the results of negotiations (when it was already too late). In Paris world leaders were asked to attend from the start of the conference to signify their commitment and show negotiators following their lead that they could not fail. This success is also clearly the result of an international consensus that has been growing for years with respect to the estimated cost of climate change and its repercussions,[3] which billions of people are already beginning to see, particularly our most vulnerable populations. The mutual agreements made before the conference between the two largest producers of greenhouse gases, China and the United States, are the best example of this success, even if adverse views remain powerful in the United States and led to the decision by President Trump to exit from the Paris climate accord. There is no doubt that the enormous public health issues linked to air pollution in Beijing and other cities in China also came into play to get agreement on this historic accord.

Interestingly, the decision made by the United States to withdraw from the Paris climate accord highlighted in an unexpected manner the changes that the negotiation and its conclusion have brought to world diplomacy. It was not the first time that the United States has left an agreement that it had signed. The United States withdrew from the Kyoto Protocol, for instance, creating a negative momentum around that agreement. This time it is different. The reaction from around the world, and from many in the United States, shows that this agreement goes beyond traditional diplomacy organized between sovereign states. The withdrawal of the United States is unlikely to break the momentum. All other signatories immediately jumped in to confirm their commitments. And within the United States, a number of states, cities, corporations, and NGOs voiced their continuing support. In a way, with or without US support, the agreement is opening the way to new global understandings. Of course, climate is a specific issue and to a large extent, one of a kind. But we should acknowledge that it is about to create a fascinating precedent.

COP21 would never have enjoyed such success, nor would the conferences in Addis Ababa and New York, without the efforts beforehand of all the participating groups in the fight against global climate change; the unprecedented media coverage to raise public awareness; proposals by large businesses for audacious and sustainable solutions to speed up the process; a clear and stable framework to orient the strategic investments of private actors; initiatives such as the Breakthrough Energy Coalitions launched by Mark Zuckerberg and Bill Gates to finance the search for solutions to the clean energy problem; the demonstrations of the world's NGOs at numerous kiosks at the Génération Climat space in Bourget or the Grand Palais in Paris; and the involvement of the World Bank, which invited a thousand businesses to support a declaration on carbon price signals.[4]

COP21 is one of the first examples of open diplomacy in history, thanks to a big push from the global community, catalyzed by the mobilization of new information technologies, communications technologies, and social networks in particular. Under this pressure, nations found it more difficult to stifle the excitement, more costly for the negotiations to fail. They had to participate. Throughout this final stage of the extraordinary drama that was 2015, the global community was able to implement an efficient method for cooperation between every voice that had something to say, without silencing anyone and without producing a meaningless statement. Difficulties persist, but this simple fact sustains hope.

Finding Another Way to Finance Development: An Experimental Blip

The Addis Ababa conference also contributed to the emergence of a new age of cooperation by fostering an unprecedented approach to development funding based on global partnership.

This approach was not entirely novel, but it certainly had never garnered this much interest. The water group noted as much in our 2004 book: "Partnership is a major conceptual contribution, unfortunately welcomed by skepticism and indifference at the United Nations conference on 'development funding' in Monterrey."[5] By partnership we meant an "equal dialogue" requiring that "no one may offload their responsibility to another" and "acceptance of a common path along new trails in globalization, with the requisite care for the footsteps of others." It was to be a multidimensional relationship extended by states to businesses, institutions, and civil society.

Within the framework of the MDGs, our global group's work on "funding for water infrastructures" was a revelation in this respect. The question we posed was clear: how can we finance access to drinking water and sanitation for the billions of people who do not have it? The question in itself was revolutionary: "We had been asking ourselves about our priorities and objectives for thirty years, and we had been debating technical solutions for twenty. But the questions of means, of money, had never been posed in such clear terms before February 2002. It was no longer a philosophical question. It was prosaic, as practical as could be."[6]

This is how we gathered 20 men and women from diverse backgrounds around the same table, "industrialists, representatives of non-governmental organizations, private and public bankers, development specialists, and politicians. Their legitimacy resides solely in their skills and their good will."[7] In the first meetings, we confronted the most divergent positions and interests,[8] and raised doubts: "The odds are stacked against the ability of these twenty well-wishers, as inspired as they may be, to reach a dynamic consensus rather than the usual lukewarm results."[9] Yet "the unexpected happened. The members of this group, none of them gentle dreamers or idealists, all men and women of experience ... gradually shed their working façades and began to act as free people."[10] After 15 months of discussion, the so-called wise men managed to put more than 80 measures on the table, several of them completely novel but totally in reach. At the heart of this technically and financially realistic project was a simple idea: "Before the question of financial resources comes into play, the problem of water is a question of good governance, coordination, and mobilization of all the actors featured in a complex chain of intervention."[11]

From this prophetic experience, strengthened by the Landau report that followed (see Chapter 15), I gained one of my deepest convictions: when people agree to sit around the table in good faith, when they are capable of acknowledging and making sense of their differences, it is possible, even if sometimes difficult, to overcome them together to solve the most complex questions about topics that are vital to humanity.

The year 2015 offered an opportunity to restore this partnership logic in an attempt to find pragmatic solutions to funding the SDGs, all in the spirit of the *Billions to Trillions* report. Knowing that all the institutional investors in the world manage $70 trillion, more or less the same as global GDP and expected to reach $100 trillion by 2020, you can't help but think there must be a solution to the problem of how to finance sustainable development, and it can't be boiled down to official development assistance (ODA) alone. Naturally, this means that we have to travel off the beaten path and mobilize all our available strength to connect even the most distant actors and encourage them to collaborate on the same projects and use the same financial system (its tools and institutions) as a catalyst. We must move from a state-focused, bilateral mind-set to a system based on partnership and learn a way to better connect public and private money, and national and international resources. Regaining control means building shared control and shared objectives truly in line with the common good.

Turning Words into Action: Baby Steps to Cultural Transition

A few signs of this revolutionary mind-set still remain. Although in 2015 we were able to find the words to express our interest in working together, to write our reports, and better still, to create international agreements, it is still premature to think that we are ready to act in accordance with this new modus operandi.

The transition between the old ways and the new ways will be long. I have experienced firsthand the tensions that arise in preparation for these summit meetings between the strength of evidence and the snail's pace at which international processes advance. In fact, civilian and partnership mobilization can be destabilizing for traditional diplomacy, accustomed as it is to protocols regulated down to the minutest levels. How can we manage the discussions taking so many different directions, and how can we understand them when they are happening not just in multiple official diplomatic languages but in dozens of civilian languages? How can we work together without being tied to the same expectations on the times and places for actions? How can we talk about private money to a public that may understand the use of formulas but not the practical realities behind them? And, of course, although legislators may instruct their administrations about how they should use public funds, no one has the power to dictate to the private sector. The public and private sectors have a tenacious and mutual suspicion toward each other that will take time to ease. Can we wait that long?

Such is the challenge we face today: after having the feeling of a job well done in 2015, how do we avoid a painful letdown going forward? How can we turn our words into actions? How can we make sure that the commitments we made in an exceptional year take solid form, rather than remaining vague hopes?

We made great strides in sustaining the hope of 2000 and making our dreams reality—in fact, our ambitions have gotten bigger. But the 2030 Agenda for Sustainable Development, which set forth the SDGs, remains a significant tome, with its 17 objectives and 169 targets. Chancellor Angela Merkel once dared the participants in a meeting to recite them all from memory. Such is the nature of bureaucratic compromise: we had to please everyone. The main skill needed to give these commitments substance is, above all, the ability to explain them. Before these documents can change the daily life of global citizens, particularly the poorest, we must get agreement on the significant efforts needed.

The SDGs are not legally binding. We hope that governments will take it upon themselves to set up national frameworks to achieve these goals, follow up on them, and measure their nation's progress.

However, the adoption of the Paris climate accord, which brought an end to 20 laborious years of negotiations, did not mean that the parties involved would automatically follow the precepts of the agreement; the 55 countries that represent 55 percent of worldwide greenhouse gas emissions had to ratify it before it entered into force. This ratification was reached within a year at a record speed. After the symbolic political gesture of adopting the accord, and the legal process of ratification, we have to move to implement the necessary measures—if sufficient funds are there to do so.

The year 2015 could turn out to be a historic one, but, today, a few years later, it is not yet certain. Popular support is fleeting and fades quickly, sometimes much faster than its upswing. How much is left of the wave of emotion that swept Europe after the publication of the photo of little Aylan, washed up on a beach in Turkey? The pendulum always swings back and forth between the poles of unifying, symbolic, and emotional moments on one side, and fear and retreat on the other side. The outcomes of elections held within months in 2016 and 2017 in the United Kingdom, the United States, and France all reflected these emotions and tensions, even if they unfolded in different ways. Thinking back on the warmth and support that rolled in to the people of France after the terrorist attack in Nice, those feelings of national unity seem so far away. Let us hope, after the difficult events many countries faced in 2016–2017 that the coming years will see humanity swing in a positive direction.

Struck by the strength of the crisis and the cost of having let finance swing out of control, the global community has started to discuss new ways of operating in order to regain control of finance and money. That new way means, first and foremost, collective thinking and action. It also means putting the common good first and discussing what we mean by that. The commitments reached in 2015 are a good and reasonable framework. We have the boat. We have a compass. It is time to sail. But the seas are still treacherous.

CHAPTER 5

Renewed Centrifugal Forces

Ten years after the financial crisis, we are still facing headwinds. Our enthusiasm for 2015 turned to dismay for 2016 and 2017. After the great hope sparked by people coming together around shared and ambitious objectives, centrifugal forces are reasserting themselves. Tensions of all sorts, more or less contained until now, have come to the surface. Nothing seems to be spared. Economic, geopolitical, social, and cultural uncertainties abound, including anemic economic growth, ongoing wars, the European crisis; terrorism, populism, climate change, digital hacking, and the refugee crisis bring fears of the unknown and uncertainty. Our goal of regaining control of money to serve the common good is indeed facing some headwinds. But these headwinds can be seen as a call for action and can present cases where finances properly controlled can make a difference.

The Economic Hangover: End of a Cycle with No Precedent

The years since 2000 began with a positive development. China integrated into international commerce with its entry in 2001 into the World Trade Organization (WTO) and developed a model based on low-price production and exports, public expenses, and an artificially low exchange rate for the yuan.[1] It was a win-win for everyone: European and American consumers have access to cheaper products, while suppliers of commodities and value-added goods and services can sell their products at high prices on the Chinese market. During this time, China has made a major economic leap, becoming the second most powerful global power and forming one of the largest foreign currency reserves on the planet.[2] We forget that it was China that played a crucial role in saving the world from bankruptcy in 2008–2009 by restarting the global economy. As the Chinese said behind closed doors at that time, "Saving private capitalism is a priority!"

We knew that China's dynamic, based on a model that originated during a period of profound imbalances, could not last forever. We are actually coming out of a historic convergence of three movements without real precedent: China catching up with the world economically, the "commodities super cycle," and an unconventional monetary policy in the United States. All three movements will obviously continue to play a role going forward, but they are unlikely to be as highly charged and have the same high level of convergence.

China Slowdown

The first trend, China's slowdown from double-digit to single-digit growth, is nothing more than a return to normality. While it is welcome, this normalization was nonetheless frightening for those who had bet on the potential of emerging markets. These markets, led by China, managed all the same to contribute 60 percent of worldwide economic growth over the past 10 years and avoided the recession in 2009! The collapse of the Shanghai and Shenzhen stock markets in the summer of 2015, which until then had been powered mostly by flows out of individual Chinese savings accounts, was a confirmation of this return to normality. Above all, the slowdown in Chinese growth revealed the new impact of this economy globally. The poorly communicated decision to depreciate the yuan in the summer of 2015 contributed to market turbulence by focusing attention on that for several months and kindling doubts about the quality of China's statistical apparatus. It also illustrated financial players' doubts: one could simplistically say that everything that the Chinese leadership did previously was considered with benevolence and admiration, and suddenly everything they did was questionable and mistrusted, especially because China's ongoing transformation to an economy based on a more value-added production model, and more focused on domestic consumption and services, looked to be off to a slow and uncertain start. As Mohamed El-Erian, chief economic adviser at Allianz and chairman of former president Barack Obama's Global Development Council, stated, "The regular upheavals this transition will cause will give the rest of the planet cold sweats."[3] By its growth normalizing, China had a full impact on a globalization, which remains imperfectly modeled. When the Asian financial crisis flared up in 1997, it had little impact on growth in Europe and the United States. In 2015 we had to adjust the model: the Asian economy was no longer 10 percent of global GDP but 25 percent, and the tremors could be felt around the world.

The End of the Commodities Super Cycle

The second trend is the end of the "commodities super cycle." With uninterrupted growth of more than 10 percent annually over 30 years, China became the leading consumer and principal importer of most commodities (agricultural, mineral, and petrochemical): in 2015 it accounted for over 50 percent of global aluminum consumption, 50 percent of carbon and nickel consumption, 30 percent of cotton and rice consumption, and 12 percent of oil consumption.[4] The slowing of Chinese economic activity, confirmed by the collapse of the stock market and paired with the devaluation of the yuan, against a background of slow economic growth elsewhere, led in recent years to a fall in commodities prices, which accelerated in 2015. Commodities lost 40 to 60 percent of their value in one year, despite the beginnings of a rebound in 2016 that is expected to continue for few years, although not to come back to the previous excessive levels. These losses were a shock for the global economy—a positive shock for importers like the

European Union or India but a negative shock for exporters, particularly those in emerging countries.

Unconventional Monetary Policies: About to End?

The third trend in 2015–2017 may be the end of the monetary policy implemented by the US Federal Reserve, imitated by other major central banks, of low interest rates and easy credit (this point will be discussed later in more detail).[5] We suspected that this extraordinary policy could not last long. But we were still not prepared to have to renounce it, and certainly not to see all of these phenomena interrupted at the same time! In one blow, the markets had lost all of their bearings. The drug had been good, and stopping it was dizzying.

The Uncharted Waters of Finance: A Transfusion and the Need to Stop It, but How and When?

The markets were all the more disoriented because global finance is still in recovery mode and for several years has been in "uncharted waters," an expression often heard in international meetings, much to my surprise. One of the most insidious consequences of the 2007–2008 crisis is that in order to revive anemic worldwide growth, the financial system has been put completely into the hands of the central banks, which have never lived up well to their names than during the past decade. What will the Fed say? The ECB? The Bank of Japan? The Bank of England? The whole world now waits on these financial institutions commissioned by governments—but legally independent on a daily basis—that have flooded the planet with liquidity to put out the massive fires represented by the crisis. We are now a bit closer to extinguishing the fires, but we have not yet repaired the water damage. The house is standing, but the foundation is shaky and there are cracks in the walls. Rather than implement structural reform, the governments, often underplaying their own structural and fiscal tools, have left unconventional monetary policies, designed as temporary measures, to prosper, placing central banks at the center of "the only game in town," as Mohamed El-Erian has called it.[6]

As a result, we have low, or even negative, interest rates: over $10 trillion in government bonds are or have been issued this way. This is a new phenomenon in the world of finance. Apart from a brief time in Hong Kong in the 1980s, we have never lowered rates to the point of asking commercial banks to pay central banks to deposit their reserves there instead of being paid for the deposits. This short-term refinancing process is combined with a long-term practice called "quantitative easing," initiated by the US Federal Reserve, which has since been imitated by central banks in the United Kingdom, Japan, and Europe. It involves buying bonds in bulk (sovereign, government, or even corporate bonds) to influence the market, lower interest rates over time, and thereby exert pressure across the whole rate curve, to stimulate demand via cheaper credit and a wealth effect.

From this point of view, the world is still getting a transfusion, and this remedy could turn out to be toxic if administered for too long. This is the core of the thesis developed by El-Erian: anemic global growth could soon transform into an economic recession, and the accompanying social troubles that result, if politicians in charge do not act quickly. For other financial experts, as long as global growth is kept around 3 percent with monetary injections, the system will hold. Adam Posen considers that the world has, for the first time in a long time, found a sustainable pace of growth that encourages a slow but sure economic recovery.[7]

In fact, the experts do not all agree about what direction we should take. After the phenomenal increase of wealth in the world during the past two centuries as a result of the Industrial Revolution, have we entered into a "new mediocre" phase (to use the concept advanced by Christine Lagarde, IMF managing director, a spin on El-Erian's "new normal"), or even a "secular stagnation" phase (according to Larry Summers)? In a talk given in May 2016 at the Peterson Institute,[8] David Lipton, number two at the IMF, provided a good summary of the two major theories we are grappling with today. On one side, some experts consider that the current slowdown is an effect of a crisis that we have not cleansed from the system, with symptoms such as late debt adjustments, persistent production surpluses, disagreements over monetary policy, perverse effects from austerity cures, and impediments to investment and consumption. On the other side, other experts feel that the low growth is itself a symptom of a scarcity of profitable investments, a condition that started well before the 2008 crisis and is indicated by 15 years of low interest rates while savings grew. This is economist Larry Summers's theory, which predicts long-term secular stagnation.

In any event, how can we find the optimal balance between investment and savings under such conditions? How can we compensate for the underlying weaknesses of the labor market in advanced economies, which have lower rates of growth in their active populations and lower rates of productivity? How can we redirect monetary policy when we know that the world is weighed down by debt? How do we get agreement from emerging countries that had a large potential for growth and were on pace to catch up, according to the IMF's mid-range forecasts, but were reduced to two-thirds of the expected pace for 10 years?

As David Lipton noted, the economic development model that experts and decision makers advocated during the 1970s—a globalization promising a bright future, synonymous with an opening of commerce, integration of foreign direct investment, convergence of advanced and emerging economies thanks to capital accumulation, education initiatives, and improved productivity enabled by technology—no longer works. The current political tensions in Brazil, Russia, Mexico, and even South Africa reflect popular disappointment in the barely realized convergence. Lipton is talking about a "counterintuitive phenomenon." The fact is that globalization, faced with multiple transformations in recent years, is currently going through a complicated phase where both models and underlying analyses are being readjusted and reworked. It is not insignificant that the annual forecasts from the IMF, the World Bank, and the OECD are regularly reexamined and revised, most often downward.

For many people, the future of globalization has dimmed. The fear of market volatility outweighs the potential gains to be won from financial interconnection. In 2016 and 2017, the global economy was characterized by exacerbated anxiety and tensions on the one hand, and recovery prospects on the other. The rebound in the stock market that followed the US election, while strong, has again raised questions about its causes and its sustainability. Tensions on trade policies are on the rise again as demonstrated in a number of international forums.

Geopolitical Clashes

Furthermore, the geopolitical context is tense. The world is currently experiencing its highest level of instability in several decades, likely the highest since the Cuban Missile Crisis in 1962. According to the Uppsala Conflict Data Program, armed conflicts have returned to record levels since the end of the Cold War, and from this point of view 2014 turns out to be the second most deadly year on the global scale since World War II.[9]

Fortunately, the current geopolitical instability is not global, but its effects are felt in many areas as tensions spread to five continents. The Middle East has been torn apart by conflicts, both civil and multinational, against a backdrop of the failure of some of these states. Ukraine and Russia confronted each other right up to the Eurovision stage.[10] The United States and China oppose each other over territorial disputes in the South China Sea, where bordering countries more or less peacefully challenge all who use it. Emerging economies are starting to openly contest advanced economies' stranglehold on international finance. North Korea threatens to use nuclear weapons. The existence of a series of powder kegs in the Sahel in sub-Saharan Africa raises fears of the emergence of a new Afghanistan, without any solutions for stabilizing the area either politically or economically. Other perils exist in the ongoing conflicts in the Horn of Africa and the escalation of the security situation in western Africa, or even in the destabilization of Venezuela as well as a number of countries that are dependent on its petroleum exports.

The tensions are exacerbated by the challenges that petroleum-exporting countries are currently facing. While the fall in oil prices remains relatively good news for importing countries,[11] it, combined with lower prices for other commodities, has had an increased impact in areas where geopolitical stability is closely tied to economic health. The Middle East is a textbook case, where the lower prices weaken Iraq and Syria even further, sandwiched as they are between major players in the region such as Egypt, Iran, Saudi Arabia, and Turkey. Decisions made on social and economic changes by the Saudi royal family over the past two years show the gravity of the upheaval, as well as the magnitude of the adjustments needed. Although many still doubt the capability of Saudi Arabia to implement the objectives it set out, the changes were recognition that the status quo was untenable. The oil crisis introduced additional weakness in influential countries like Russia, which is also burdened by international sanctions related to the crisis in Ukraine, and Brazil, which has been torn apart by a major political crisis. Other countries affected are those that are highly dependent on "black gold," such as Nigeria, Angola, Algeria, and Venezuela.

Terrorism represents another aggravating factor. Kabul, Baghdad, Sana'a, Toulouse, Jakarta, Ankara, Brussels, Paris, Copenhagen, Tunis, Beirut, San Bernardino, Sousse, Bamako, Ouagadougou, Grand-Bassam, Lahore, Orlando, Istanbul, Nice, Manchester, London.[12] The list of terrorist attacks keeps getting longer, the mindless violence increasing in indescribable degrees of horror. There is no longer any region of the world that seems safe. Not only does this wave of attacks feed defiance and fear within the global community, it weighs heavily on border controls and international financial flows—which are subjects of debates and tensions between the countries of the world.

The current instability in Europe is the sad result of this convergence of economic and geopolitical tensions. With the questioning of the Schengen Area,[13] the Brexit shock, and the inability to mount a coordinated response to the refugee crisis, the stability of the European Union has never been more severely compromised. Nationalist movements are on the rise, and they have placed extreme right parties at the gates of power. The euro crisis marked the beginning of this break with reality: after a first alert during the failure of the 2005 referendums in France and Holland (on ratifying the constitution for the EU), the financial and then economic storms in 2008–2011 caused lasting harm to European populations in a system seen to be opaque, unjust, and undemocratic.

Even worse, the financial crisis has reopened old wounds between members of the EU. To me, as an Alsatian growing up on the German border, I always heard my grandfather explain that the Rhine was not a border but a passage, I grew up full of dreams of a "closer union between the peoples of Europe," and I was disturbed to hear Germans strike out at the Greeks, telling them they just needed to sell their islands to soak up their debts, and the Greeks responding that they did not need to take lessons from those who raised the Nazi flag over the Acropolis. I was also saddened to hear people refer to dealing with "PIIGS" (Portugal, Ireland, Italy, Greece, and

Spain), meaning countries on the edges of Europe. It was a slur so common that I had to use it myself as a reference in some presentations.

After the North–South tensions around the euro crisis, the refugee crisis revealed disturbing tensions between the east and west of the EU. The refugee crisis worried me even more than the euro crisis. The euro crisis was perceived as a "technical crisis" for which a solution could be found with a few spare billions—while the refugee crisis raised questions about our common values. What do we share? This more existential question, which gets to the heart of things, will be much more difficult to answer.

The World at New Risk

To these numerous sources of concern are added new threats: climate change, the digital revolution, and pandemics.

Climate Change: Feeling the Heat

The visible impacts of human activity on the climate and extreme climate conditions are starting to exacerbate instability in regions already stressed by low economic growth and, in many cases, geopolitical tensions: look at Nigeria, Syria, and Yemen to start. We know without a doubt that for the poorest regions, starting with sub-Saharan Africa, the additional impact of global warming will be stronger and more disastrous in coming years. The report published by the World

Bank at the end of 2014, *Turn Down the Heat: Confronting the New Climate Normal,* [14] is unequivocal in this regard: from now until the middle of the century, Earth's atmosphere is locked in to warming of nearly 1.5°C (3.6°F) compared to the preindustrial period, but even a mildly ambitious carbon reduction program could change this. The UN warned in April 2016 that over the course of the preceding 12 months, the world had seen the number of droughts double (triggered in part by the warm El Niño equatorial current), threatening food security for 100 million people.[15] This climate phenomenon also caused a coral die-off, with severe consequences for the marine ecosystem. The floods that have deluged coastal regions in France and other countries in recent years remind us that the whole world is affected by these catastrophes. For example, rising sea levels will have a severe impact on Morocco, where over 60 percent of the population and over 90 percent of businesses are located in major cities along the Atlantic. We will likely face even larger population migrations in coming decades than those caused by the comparatively simple yet still unsolved Syrian refugee crisis.

These forecasts look even more threatening when you consider that the Paris climate accord, as ambitious and necessary as it is, is only a first step, still insufficient to effectively limit these effects. As the UN noted on the eve of the signing of this agreement, "there is a real danger of being overwhelmed by the rapid increase of the pace of climate change, unless the signatories significantly increase their commitments to reduce greenhouse gas emissions." In practical terms, this means that "the world needs to make a stand now for a rapid transition from fossil fuels to renewable energy sources."[16] The world otherwise risks repeated humanitarian crises and enormous economic losses, with geopolitical consequences that we still have a hard time imagining today. Former president Barack Obama's foreign policy focused much less on the crisis in Syria than it did on climate change with respect to its potential impact on American security. The new administration, although it is a work in progress, has on both of these issues, a significantly different view, as confirmed in particular by President Trump's decision to withdraw from the Paris climate accord.

Digital Anxiety on the Rise

The digital revolution raises as many questions as it does hopes. Will the Uberization and robotization of the planet take our data, our privacy, our jobs, and our national sovereignties away from us? In their ambition to replace governments in all their domains, are Google, Apple, Facebook, Amazon (GAFA) and other web giants going to standardize the world while at the same time destabilizing the most fragile institutions, aggravating individualism, and deepening the wealth divide? If Silicon Valley becomes the heart of a new empire, where will we find the ways and means to an equitably connected world? Like finance, digital technology is a mindless force that, unless domesticated, can lead humanity to its ruin. As with financial language, binary language can lead to hubris: such is the pride of the people who build a Tower of Babel to the sky! The "exponential organizations" that are shaping globalization today may well promise us a peaceful, liberating revolution and pursuit of the good of all, but their disproportionate weight in the global economy raises many questions. These organizations are even more frightening in countries like France, and Europe in general, which don't know how to create their own digital rivals (aside from a few Scandinavian unicorns), despite a swarm of initiatives.

In a Connected World, Higher Pandemic Risks

In our ever more connected world, the risk of a pandemic is high. Since 2000 this threat has materialized more and more often: *E. coli,* mad cow disease, bird flu, H1N1 virus, Ebola virus, Zika virus, MERS virus. Every three years or so, an epidemic launches from a more or less remote part of the planet. The scientific community and public authorities are convinced that this phenomenon will continue and accelerate. Today the earth has nearly 7.5 billion inhabitants, more than half of these humans are crowded together in giant cities, and the predominance of meat in our diet leads to increasing concentrations of animals—these are some of many factors that lead to the development of pathogenic viruses that, combined with the constant increase in air and sea interconnectivity, make the risk of a major global epidemic more likely. The World Bank estimates that a Spanish-flu–type epidemic, spread by airborne transmission, would kill over 33 million people in 250 days and cost the world over $3.6 trillion (or 4.8 percent of its GDP). Bill Gates said in Munich in February 2017: "Whether it occurs by a quirk of nature or at the hand of a terrorist, epidemiologists say a fast-moving airborne pathogen could kill more than 30 million people in less than a year. And they say there is a reasonable probability the world will experience such an outbreak in the next 10 to 15 years."

Winds are blowing from everywhere and it is difficult for anybody to make sense of what is going on. What is coming seems gigantic and off the scale. Finance, which contributed with the crisis to unleash these hurricanes, seems an ideal culprit and at this stage not yet a contributor to a solution. With that in mind finance is high on the list of enemies of the common good and a great contributor to the social frustration felt in so many places.

CHAPTER 6

Frustration and Political Unrest

Unprecedented Social Frustration

In this complicated and unstable world in which threats are materializing at regular intervals, people feel that the current system is unsustainable. To countries like the United States or France that engineered or shaped previous global financial systems, the current path of globalization seems to be uncertain, and their populations now shudder at the prospect of the decline of their countries.

However, in the midst of this uncertainty, the global community has never been so rich, it has never produced so much, it has never consumed so much, and it has never invested so much.[1] But this global community of extraordinary abundance is not one of shared abundance: inequality has been reduced between countries, even while within some countries, it has clearly widened. This is particularly true for developed countries and certain emerging countries with strong rates of growth. Lifespan and standard of living of the middle class are no longer going up, and the wealth of the elites has increased while real salaries have decreased. Yet income inequality, combined with inequalities of wealth and opportunity (those that hinder people from expressing and revealing all of their potential through lack of access to education or care—as Saint-Exupéry says, "What torments me is not the humps nor the hollows nor the ugliness. It is the sight, a little bit in all these men, of Mozart murdered"[2]) has made growth unstable and generated immense frustration in societies.

An Unprecedented Level of Wealth Creation

Popular protest movements, such as Occupy Wall Street in the United States and the Indignés/Indignados antiausterity demonstrations in Europe, are proliferating. They demonstrate how some people have lost confidence in capitalism or in their institutions (government, media, and companies) to serve them and help them build a future. Electoral successes or progress for populists such as Donald Trump, Nigel Farage, or Marine Le Pen will show that the concerns go further than the visible manifestations of a few and have become more mainstream. That is the high price of the global financial crisis that is still being paid. Ordinary citizens feel they have been "had." They harbor a deep resentment at finding out that the market economy, the financial system, and the system in general, do not work for them but function solely for the benefit of a few—starting with bankers and the elites.

Prosperity Not a Benefit to All: Seemingly Something Hidden

This crisis of confidence is further aggravated by the release of secret information by whistleblowers. WikiLeaks, founded by Julian Assange, has leaked sensitive documents; Edward Snowden, former consultant for the National Security Agency, has released classified information; and the Panama Papers, made public by an anonymous source, detail the tax evasion practices of many world figures. The increasing transparency of our modern world allows us to learn about thorny issues, but it also fuels the everything-is-rotten camp and their conspiracy theories. These revelations reinforce the public's feeling that things are being hidden from them, that the deck is stacked, and that the elites of this world keep the largest slice of the pie for themselves. (It is embarrassing that it is not only the "usual suspects" from countries known for corruption but also the leaders of supposedly clean countries, such as the prime ministers of Iceland and the United Kingdom, who were named during the Panama Papers financial scandal.) We cannot pretend to ignore, while at the same time deploring, the anger, disenchantment, and even disgust of citizens in the face of such events.

The Temptation to Simplify and Withdraw

In the face of this generalized suspicion, exacerbated by the empowerment of individuals and the increasing belief in the equal value of all opinions, the legitimacy of traditional authority and forms of government is being questioned and challenged.

In France, Europe, and elsewhere, defiance of authority and fear of the unknown are prevalent, in part because leadership has never been so weak, or even entirely absent. The United States can no longer be the sheriff of the world as in the past, nor can any other nations, at a time when no one can act in isolation anymore. The success of positions against free trade in the US election campaign opened up a cycle of withdrawal from trade agreements, which was confirmed after President Trump took office. Europe no longer works collectively to respond to the world's emergencies, cooperation that was sidelined by a visionary and unified Franco-German partnership before possibly being revived by the election of Emmanuel Macron. The British government failed to avoid the referendum on Brexit demanded by the nationalists and risked a crisis—and it lost. Spain remained without a government for months. Belgium revealed the fragility of its sovereign functions through its uncertain management of recent attacks. Turkey saw its internal divisions grow after the failed coup against President Erdogan, and executive powers were increased by referendum. The Russo-Ukrainian conflict is still going on. Somalia is still a failed state. Iraq, Syria, and now Libya are facing Islamic State (IS) challenges. China hesitates to assume its role in world leadership. I could continue this list: the planet has never been faced with so many crises of authority.

The world is more complicated to govern than it was 15 years ago. The time of the G7, when Western powers influenced or even dictated the international agenda, has passed; now the G20, which extended membership to emerging countries, gathers members who share neither the same values nor the same priorities. The world is not far from being that of "G-Zero," as Ian Bremmer wrote in December 2015.[3] However, these international summits, as imperfect as they are, are indispensable. We cannot take the risk of letting the engine run untended and get the upper hand over the people who are in charge. We must make *leaders summits* into actual *leadership summits:* find ways to let this leadership express itself! We must prefer decision and action to carefully crafted but empty communiqués.

The current situation represents a real danger for democracies and the world. The failure of world leadership, while authority is being challenged, combined with social unrest and fear of the unknown in this topsy-turvy world, creates an explosive cocktail that feeds the success of demagogues over pragmatic problem solvers. Throughout the world, we are witnessing a breakthrough, if not a slow but sure climb, of populism and extremism that gives voters simple "common sense answers," that tell them what they want to hear. Whether it is Donald Trump in the United States, Marine Le Pen in France, Rodrigo

Duterte in the Philippines, Viktor Orbán in Hungary, Boris Johnson (the former mayor of London who campaigned for Brexit) in the United Kingdom, the Law and Justice (PiS) party in Poland, the FPÖ in Austria, the Alternative für Deutschland in Germany, or even the Golden Dawn in Greece, the radical and xenophobic followers concerned with "de-demonizing" their autocratic style are mounting serious electoral challenges around the world. When times are hard, when confidence is low, it is so much easier to lay the blame on some group (the elites, the refugees, Muslims) and suggest leaving Europe, closing borders, building a wall, and withdrawing, than it is to explain the tough truth that we need to roll up our sleeves and try to work together because we simply can't do anything on our own.

We need to find answers to the central question of borders so we can rein in finance to serve a common good and put globalization on the right path. We need to demonstrate that if we all work together, we can solve the world's problems—the economy, finance, education, health, climate, migration—and to do that, we need to go beyond borders while respecting these same comforting boundaries. Everyone needs to feel at home somewhere. Yet the world has a need to work together like never before. The Old World in particular, the same one that is trying to retreat within itself today, has never been in such need of people from elsewhere to renew itself. How do we cope at a time when Europe, which offers humanity a transnational model of cooperation, is threatening to implode? And when the United States, which shaped the present global order, questions it so deeply?

Another, equally fundamental question is the state of the middle class in Western democracies, which shaped the current international financial system. In France the *Trente Glorieuses* ("thirty glorious years" from 1945 to 1975) led to the emergence of a middle class, which became the backbone of democracy. When the middle class is weakened, when it can no longer keep pace to represent its members' social progress, when it no longer seems to be represented, the heart of democracy itself is under attack. Faced with the continued slowdown of global economic growth and growing inequality, faced with risks that threaten the universal dream of peace and prosperity, should we conclude that the emergence of this middle class was nothing but an accident of history? Is this population segment doomed to shrink? Has the weakening of the middle class endangered democratic systems?

We cannot ignore these crucial questions if we want to restore meaning to our models, and not just our economic models but our political, social, and cultural models as well. In the absence of quick answers, the centrifugal forces unleashed around the world today could overwhelm the system that we have built.

Above all, we must not surrender to siren call of pessimism. I have not made my suggestions to add to Cassandra's lamentations of the world but to emphasize how the current environment, with the many threats it is facing, including its ultra-low or negative interest rates, maintains this cognitive bias that leads us to concentrate on *what can go wrong* rather than *what can go right.* This irresistible temptation thrills us to the point of letting fear lead us—even though we will see that we have the means to overcome it. As General Douglas MacArthur said on the purpose of youth, "When your heart is covered with the snows of pessimism and the ice of cynicism, then, and then only, are you grown old. And then, indeed, as the ballad says, you just fade away."

Finance, unbridled, led us to where we are: in a state of questioning and disarray. We are on the verge of pessimism and cynicism. There is not much each of us can do, right? However, this is precisely the moment when we must engage and discuss what comes next. What if finance could change the course of the endeavor? What if finance could save the world?

CHAPTER 7

Humanity at a Crossroads

In the 2005 Woody Allen film *Match Point,* a tennis ball hits the top of the net—and hesitates between the two sides. Depending on which side it falls, one of the players will lose, and the other will win. Will humanity reach such a point? "Against a global background with no historical precedent, the near future is particularly indecipherable," Michel Cicurel, then CEO of the private bank Compagnie Financière Edmond de Rothschild, observed in 2007.[1] Now, more than ever, "our planet wobbles between various perspectives." Tempted by fear, courage, and hope, we should not let chance or fate decide for us. On which side of the net will the ball fall?

Not Letting the Wrong Story Enter the History Books

Today, the future of globalization is at a crossroads. Our actions can still lead to the worst or to the best time in history. It is up to us to make it good and avoid the easy route out—down the slippery slope with the force of gravity. It is not the first time in our history when we have faced such a choice, but perhaps it is the first time we have encountered one when we are so much more interconnected on a global basis. Being surefooted in our way forward is critical.

If we leave the active forces at play, if in our weakness we simply leave it up to future generations to clean up after our mess, we could leave an inheritance that could be made up of debts rather than assets, and these will act as disruptive forces that inevitably prevail over the forces of unity. Do we really want to replay the scenario of the 1930s by letting things spin out of control?

Resistance to O-H-I-O

By letting nationalists, imperialists, protectionists, regionalists, and individualists thrive—by letting each country close its borders, fill the gaps, establish currency reserves, and wait for things to get better, according to the lonely O-H-I-O (own house in order) strategy referred to by David Lipton,[2] we will let the mediocre run the show. By letting the English—more likely than the Scots or the Irish—go their own way outside Europe and dissolve the Schengen Area, by letting China and Russia maneuver within their zones of influence, by letting the Islamic State grow, by letting the planet heat up, by letting GAFA appropriate our data, by letting Greece starve, by letting the refugees drown, by letting the poorest countries flounder—in short, by renouncing political, economic, and international financial cooperation, by cutting the connections we so carefully tied, one after another—we will do nothing more than fall into a new version of the 1930s.

Remember Churchill's famous warning: "A people who forget their past are condemned to repeat it."[3] Europe should not manage the refugee crisis the same way the Roman Empire did 16 centuries ago, faced with an influx of what were then called "barbarians," meaning the populations pushed toward the west by the Huns whom we could compare to the Islamic State today. The sated, decadent empire collapsed under its own weight because it could not find a way to absorb these populations intelligently and reconstruct the social contract.

The Alternative of Evil

The American political scientist Ian Bremmer, president of the Eurasia Group, sees three possible trajectories for globalization, two of which are nothing to celebrate. The first is a top-down trajectory (an oligarchic model), whereby the elites suppress the base, and globalization slows or even stops for a "global subclass" (those citizens deemed unproductive or destitute), under the effect of real or virtual borders erected by governments and societies to exclude these citizens. This is a path that I compare to that of the Roman Empire: *līmes* (defenses) at the borders to keep out the barbarians and *panem et circenses* (bread and circuses) on the inside to contain the population; this worked for several centuries, but of course, neither Twitter nor Facebook existed at the time. The second is a bottom-up trajectory (a revolutionary model), whereby the base takes the power from the elites: globalization slows or even stops for the rich, social instability spreads, and cyberattacks along with forced transparency (among other asymmetrical responses) hinder institutions blocked from operating effectively. This scenario would somewhat echo a French Revolution–type path and would mean an abrupt elimination of privilege.

Although the future will doubtless take a less clear-cut trajectory, we should not believe that these types of extreme risks can never happen. That was the error of the financial players in 2007, who were persuaded that a financial catastrophe would occur only every hundred years, that a crisis of this type would not happen (the last having been in 1929). This is an example of Nassim Nicholas Taleb's black swan theory. People were convinced that swans had to be white until someone discovered a black specimen in Australia. Taleb, a leading expert in the epistemology of probabilities, shows how random and highly improbable events punctuate our lives.[4] Who would have said, even five years ago, that the conflict in Syria was going to produce millions of refugees to the point of endangering Europe, including Germany, where it is a central issue? Who would have predicted that David Cameron would announce holding a referendum on Brexit in the middle of a terrorism crisis on European soil—and who would have bet even on the eve of election night that the out vote would end up winning the next morning?[5]

We should also not believe that catastrophes happen only to other people. We are all living on the same planet. We cannot, at least not yet, break free from this blue sphere immortalized in 1972 by NASA. Our destinies are all linked: if some threats caused by centrifugal forces come to pass—geopolitical, economic, financial, climatic, pandemic, or digital—we will all be affected. We cannot escape globalization; regardless of the trajectory it takes, we will not be able to wriggle out of it.

An Ambitious Third Way: The Redesign of Our Condominium

The third trajectory, which Bremmer called "condominium," would work like co-owned residences: under pressure, despite antimarket forces, governments (and companies) remodel the social contract to reduce inequality and enable the middle class to regain its position and prospects; globalization continues in its current form, seeking to benefit everyone while adapting to localization of supply chains. It would be neither the collapse of an empire nor a revolution but rather the owners carrying out building maintenance: repairing the elevator, clearing up the stairwells, and getting the neighbors to talk to one another.

This is one of the alternative versions of history that humanity still has the chance of writing today: one for which the outline was defined in 2015, the history of a tamed globalization that grants all humans, without exception, access to a better life. Clearly, we will never fully achieve this objective, which remains an ideal. But the objective can create positive energy. It sets out an asymptotic path toward a happier world, toward humanity entering a new Enlightened Age, a new Renaissance.

This version of history will require even more effort. As self-fulfilling as the worst options are, the third option will require even more courage, engagement, responsibility, and leadership to write. Choosing the path of hope will be difficult.

A Lesson from History: The Worst Is Never Certain

But choosing hope will be worth it! In May 2010 Jacques de Chalendar,[6] inspector general of finances, was the oldest of us attending a lunch I had organized at Crédit Agricole. Around the table sat a broad sampling of the French administrative and economic elites discussing the Greek crisis, which was then reaching its peak for the first time. Jacques de Chalendar spoke toward the end of the meal, saying, "I joined the administration during World War II, at a time when things were truly going badly, when the future could not have looked bleaker. At that time, no one would have thought that France would see its best years afterward, with the *Trente Glorieuses.* You, who are in charge today, instead of lamenting, roll up your sleeves. Work to rebuild your country!" This plea overwhelmed me. It put things in perspective: those of us who are managers are often so immersed in the immediate future that we have a tendency to overvalue bad news and pass over good news. What if Europe and the world, instead of shrugging their collective shoulders, said that this is the dawn of their best days? Wouldn't that be more courageous?

"Run Toward Our Own Risk": Times of Opportunity

This is a historic moment. The financial and economic crisis left behind a world where growth stagnated and where we may never find the stability of the *Trente Glorieuses* or the Great Moderation. Yet it is a world where there are still reservoirs of growth,[7] which we have the means to integrate into the international system. Demographics, in particular, remains a major force. The population of the planet will increase by 3 billion in the coming decades! Still, in this postcrisis world, interest rates are so low that yields are almost nonexistent. Banks have ceded their dominance to institutional investors, which will soon be managing $100 trillion: these players will unquestionably have a role within the macroeconomic equilibrium. The world also has a unique cooperative institution in the G20, which in 2009 was able to respond in historic fashion to the global financial crisis. While not all voices are represented at that table directly, the role international organizations must play is critical in enabling global cooperation.

At the same time, the UN has set out a sustainable development plan for the next 15 years. These common objectives are ambitious and vulnerable, but they are there, ratified by three international agreements. Debates and new approaches proliferate around the idea of ethical, socially responsible financing that is capable of leaving the dictatorship of quarterly reports behind and thinking in the long term, to direct investments toward viable projects, full of meaning and offering a future for humanity.[8]

Climate change in particular concerns an increasing number of financial players who have the power to make a difference—starting with international insurers. Mark Carney, governor of the Bank of England and chair of the Financial Stability Board (FSB), delivered a historic speech in this regard in September 2015, in which he insisted on the need to take climate risk into account in global finance:

> The need to manage emerging, mega risks is as important as ever.... While there is always room for scientific disagreement about climate change (as there is with any scientific issue) I have found that insurers are among the most determined advocates for tackling it sooner rather than later. And little wonder. While others have been debating the theory, you have been dealing with the reality: Since the 1980s the number of registered

> weather-related loss events has tripled; and inflation-adjusted insurance losses from these events have increased from an annual average of around $10 billion in the 1980s to around $50 billion over the past decade.[9]

Global financial stability, and in the long-term the wealth of the global community, will be threatened by these upheavals. Mark Carney identified three great risks:

- ***Physical:*** "current consequences of climate—and meteorological—events on insurance liability and on the value of financial assets, such as floods and storms that cause property damage or disrupt trade."
- ***Liability-related:*** "potential risks to come, if parties who suffer losses or damages due to the effects of climate change seek compensation from those they hold responsible. Such procedures could occur in a few decades and they could hit carbon extractors and emitters the hardest and, when they have liability insurance coverage, their insurers."
- ***Transition-related:*** "financial risks resulting from the process of adjustment towards a lower-carbon economy. Changes in policy, technology, and physical risks could prompt a reassessment of the value of a large range of assets as costs and opportunities become apparent."[10]

At these three levels, finance and climate are closely linked. We cannot address one of them without the other.

Has the time come to reinvent the financial system, redefine the role of the players in the global investment ecosystem, and rebuild the foundations of cooperation? Many decision makers agree that we need to act. What are we waiting for? We are running out of time. The fast pace of technological change, combined with geopolitical instability and the consequences of a warming climate, form a short-term threat to the world economy. As Mark Carney emphasized in September 2015, "The window of opportunity is finite and shrinking." We need to act today; we should always run toward our risks, to paraphrase René Char's poem.[11] Let's not wait until it is too late! It is time to regain control.

"Them" Means Us!

"Us" means each and every one of us. "Them" means the politicians, directors, executives, and managers whom we sometimes judge, a bit too quickly but sometimes quite reasonably, as being irresponsible.

Of course, "they" have a duty to set a good example. They have responsibilities: as citizens, shareholders, or employees, we have tied ourselves to them by contract and delegated responsibilities to them. They have the duty to represent us well. They need to have the courage to get their hands dirty instead of seeking to keep them clean at all costs, which is the best way to do nothing in a world that is by definition imperfect.[12] They need to stay on the bridge facing the storm, fending off emergencies, and scanning the horizon. During the financial crisis, I put it this way: "It is for holding the outposts that directors receive their benefits and compensation—not for being 'pencil-pushers'!"[13] They have the duty to withhold signs of cynicism when signing partnerships, treaties, and national or international commitments, to have the political courage to implement them, and the dignity to respect their promises.

Despite everything that happened in the financial crisis and everything I witnessed, I still believe in the international agreements, the power of symbols, and the virtue of declarations of principle. It is a way to tackle reality, even if it is not enough. The world would be better off if we took treaties more seriously. For example, in the case of the Helsinki Accords in 1975, when the Soviet Union at the end of the Brezhnev era agreed to sign the Declaration on Principles Guiding Relations between Participating States (including human rights and fundamental liberties), who could have imagined that this would open up a breach that would contribute to the breakdown of the Soviet system? When a government signs a paper, it is committed, sometimes for much longer than it expects.

But for this reason, we must remember that our representatives' signatures also commit us: whether as citizens or users of public services, we must comply with them. When a head of state signs an agreement like COP21 or the United Nations agreement on sustainable development initiatives, when they commit to sustainable development in the name of the country they lead, this signature commits us all: public authorities, companies, NGOs, and citizens. We all have the responsibility to take ownership of the subject ourselves. We all have the responsibility to stay alert and play our role by monitoring the actions taken to ensure that these agreements are fully implemented. We must remember that we have all the power, through our ballots, but also through the choices we make when we invest and consume, and when we use our own voices, in this era of social networks, to sanction the key figures in our society. We cannot waive this essential right, which is also a responsibility.

"We" Are All in Charge

We are all riding the wave of the globalization movement that swept our planet—none of us can escape it. But globalization in itself is not good or bad: like finance, it does not have a soul; it simply is what it does. In other words, don't submit to it. We all have the power to control globalization, too. If we must assume that we are committed collectively, by the democratic political system as well as by circumstances, then we must also assume we can commit ourselves individually to recognize our capacity for action in the world, each at our own level, as a power and a responsibility inherent to each and every one of us.

"Them" means us! That was the other great lesson that Michel Camdessus taught me: we are all responsible—some more than others, certainly—for the dawn of a better humanity. Every person on earth, no matter where they live, has a share of responsibility: This is true whether they are the leader of a country, city, company, institution, or NGO, a citizen with a vote and an ability to invest in public spaces or pay their taxes, an individual exercising their freedom of speech on the Internet, a member of an association paying their membership fees, a consumer making purchases, an employee making charitable contributions through their paycheck, or a shareholder, saver, or pensioner putting their money in shares or savings accounts. Inhabitants of poor and undemocratic countries will have much less freedom to act, but my time at the World Bank convinced me that every man and every woman, even those in remote areas, can change many things where they are. But obviously the more you have, the bigger the responsibility.

If we want to collectively create a good history together, all of us must exercise our individual power.

The Time to Reboot the Global Financial System So That It Can Serve the Common Good

What we need to do, then, is to recognize that we cannot act alone in this interconnected world where the problems keep getting bigger and more global.

The immense yet necessary ambitions the global community drafted for itself in 2015 will become reality only if we can unite all the intelligence and energy of countries to one another, and within. We need cooperation between the public, private, and community players collectively. We must succeed in moving away from the O-H-I-O strategy to the "C-A-lifornia strategy: Collective Action (or we could opt for Ian Bremmer's "condominium" idea).

However, we must recognize that nothing is harder in an individualistic world: the reciprocal mistrust is so anchored, so tenacious (particularly in countries like the United States or France, where the divide between public and private culture and mentalities is still deep—but this is really the case in most of the "united" nations). It is so much easier to oppose on principle, to stand firm on your interests and positions! But I believe that such movement is possible; I have seen it in all summits, projects, meetings, and working groups in which I have participated in the past 15 years, and particularly in the Paris climate change conference.

Finance still harbors the potential for integration—despite the disillusionment of the past decade. This poor master can also be a good servant: although it was once part of the problem, now it can be part of the solution. And this is not only because finance, like technology, is a universal language, an inventive tool that when used well allows wealth to circulate, unify, and create value, to help people and their various institutions work together. It is also because, as mentioned earlier, in our roles as citizens, taxpayers, consumers, investors, shareholders, savers, pensioners, association members, and so forth, we can all work on humanity's investment portfolio. Thanks to the largely free circulation of capital, the actions of each of us can have a positive impact on the planet. The same financial globalization that, starting in 2007, led to stagnation could well be a globalization that puts the world back on the right path.

But to get back on the right path, we need to take the opportunity we are offered today to reinvent the international financial system. That is, to build a controlled system, with not too much and not too little regulation, where the lines of solidarity between countries are reconsidered. A system where Wall Street or the City of London does not decide for the rest of the planet, giving no one else a say, whether advanced or developing countries, investors or regulators, central banks or savers. A system where innovation competes to find the best answers for financing the world's needs. A system that relies on existing institutions, properly reformed, and that knows how to use them best and reengages with the spirit of 2009 displayed by the international community at the height of the financial crisis, when they created the G20 and before everyone went back to their own domestic agendas and made it no more than a powerless talk shop.

We have yet to repair the system undermined by the 2007–2008 crisis, other than to plug up the breaches. We have not followed through on the reforms needed. As Jacques de Chalendar rightly said: Let's roll up our sleeves and rebuild *now:* all the tools are here, within our grasp! The ball can and will fall on the side of the net we choose. But like improving our game in tennis, improving the financial system means that we need to go back to the basics.

PART TWO

Resetting Finance for the Benefit of All

Part 2 examines a finance reset, focusing on products, markets, innovation, and behaviors. It delves into how we should view finance as a tool for everyone.

The new way of thinking discussed here is to see finance for what it really is, a tool. As we know, the hand is in control of the tool and not the tool in control of the hand. This basic principle should never be forgotten. The genie has been let out of the bottle, so now our collective efforts must be on regaining control over it. That control is well within our grasp, and only by gaining control can we achieve our aims. This endeavor does require us to revisit our understanding of how we can control finance and the ways in which we can channel its power. Understanding the key tenets underpinning finance is critical to us being able to implement the changes we need.

Chapter 8 looks at the key principles that anchor finance as I reboot it and take it back to basics. I look at how we can control this powerful tool and the road we need to take to get there, including regulation and reform. Chapter 9 discusses the overarching issues and principles that must be safeguarded as we go through the process of change. In particular, these include maintaining a culture of responsibility and ethics, ensuring appropriate governance, and renewing the focus on the long term. Chapter 10 looks at what is already underway, the silent and still nascent revolution in finance that needs to be encouraged and nurtured, which has already begun giving hope for the future.

CHAPTER 8

Back to Basics

The financial crisis of 2007–2008 and the deep global economic recession that followed have made finance seem like the enemy to many citizens in the world. What should have brought people riches led them into poverty and darkened their prospects, with a seemingly small minority benefiting from everyone else's malaise. But to condemn finance outright is to deprive humanity of an essential tool: although it is assuredly a poor master, finance can also be a great servant. Finance, rebooted, can help save the world. It has a colossal amount of stored energy waiting to be released and a prodigious potential to serve the common good once again. The trick is to reeducate, to lead by example, to learn to control the chain reaction, to direct its strength, and to use it well. "If you give me good politics, I will give you good finance," said Baron Louis, minister of finance for the July Monarchy in France in the first half of the 19th century. As long as we work toward goals that make sense, the money will follow.

Back to Basics

I worked on the executive team of a universal bank during the global financial crisis. When in 2012 I left

Crédit Agricole to join Société Générale, I had doubts about the basic good of my field and the utility of the tool to which I had devoted the majority of my life. I arrived to find teams dispirited, under pressure, and knocked off balance by Jérôme Kerviel's conviction as a rogue trader and four uninterrupted, intense years of crisis, culminating in the second half of 2011 with speculative attacks on the share price that were started by baseless rumors.[1]

Concerned about collective mobilization and preoccupied by the deteriorating environment, I asked Michel Camdessus to speak to them. I had worked with him for more than a decade, and he was always a source of inspiration. The question I posed for his talk was "Is it possible to reenchant finance?"[2] Camdessus delivered a memorable answer, which was comforting and motivated everyone at Société Générale to carry on. In short, we were to get back to the basics. Rather than renounce finance, we were to distill it back to its essence and reconnect it to the real world, to remember why humankind invented it. Some of the most brilliant minds are drawn to the finance industry—it was time to mobilize them!

Finance: First and Foremost Just a Tool

As I've said before, finance is truly no more than a tool at the service of humankind. Through savings, investment, risk distribution, and analytics-based predictions, financiers are able to make time and space our allies and build our own futures. Finance is also a powerful means of liberation. Consider this insight from Jean Boissonat, one of the best-known French business journalists and my mentor, who recently passed away: "In the 1930s, vouchers were handed out for the purchase of bread and other staples. How humiliating! Imposing a specific end use for expenditures is disrespectful and denies a person's free will—it denies their individualism."[3]

I am always shocked to hear condescending remarks about the place of the poor—"If I give them money, they'll only drink it away." So what! Drinking isn't the problem in this scenario; it's the lack of dignity. I have always been convinced that financial autonomy, access to credit, and savings contribute to an individual's freedom, allowing them to dream big and make their ideas come to life. It is precisely this core tenet that we should all reembrace when we think about the best way to use money for the greater good. It is not to adopt what can sometimes be the rather patronizing views of the elite but to ensure that the power resides with everyone.

Finance: An Extremely Powerful Tool Like No Other

Financial inclusion programs play a major role in helping to empower people. Queen Máxima of the Netherlands, having herself worked on Wall Street, is an active champion of financial inclusion, and I have had several opportunities to collaborate with her. Despite some economists' doubts about their effectiveness, microcredit programs offer the chance for participants to take charge of their own lives and rejoin the global market. I get emotional remembering a woman I spoke with while I was in Bihar, one of the poorest and most heavily populated Indian states located at the base of the Himalayas. I entered the village, dripping with sweat in the 105° heat, to meet with a group of women to hear about the progress of a village project deployed by the World Bank in their community, one of hundreds of such projects. The idea was to create a village minibank funded by the institution to support local initiatives. I sat for an hour on the ground talking with one woman, roughly my age in years but who looked 20 years older, evidence of our different life trajectories. Her gaze fascinated me (I still keep her photograph in my office), and so did her story:

> Five years ago, I was nobody; I lost my husband after he fell from a tree [and this created a precarious situation for me in India, as widows are considered nonexistent]. I found myself with eight children, all unmarried [another real problem, since we count on dowries here]. But thanks to microcredit, I bought my first goat, then a second, then a third, until now I have a herd of 15 goats. I also created a small notions store. Everything has changed for me. Now, I do exist, I have a name, and my children are married.

The simplest financial mechanism in the world can change the lives of women, and they can be free; such is the empowering force of the market. From helping one woman to oiling the wheels of international systems, it is the same money, even if it takes different forms.

The Universal Appeal of Finance

Finance is a precious instrument for use in the service of the economy. It is also a catalyst for cohesion: as a universal language, it is a pliable tool to get women and men cooperating with one another across borders. It allows us to share our wealth and coordinate our efforts. For example, through a limited liability company, we can combine smaller contributions into a larger amount of initial capital to increase the number of lives we can touch. On the flip side, finance requires trust and cooperation: you can't be a financier all on your own, and finance is not possible if you just shove your dollars under the mattress.

For all these reasons, finance can be a decisive source of leverage and, today more than ever, development. Whenever human society has a need for physical or social infrastructure, in particular for access to healthcare or education, it also has a need for financial infrastructure, whether it be a banking system or financial markets. Securitization, discredited through the use made of it to package subprimes, nonetheless allows issuers and investors to distribute and diversify their risks. It remains a useful instrument to efficiently channel financial resources to the real economy.

The mobilization of domestic savings is another powerful source of leverage: after all, our Western economies used this tool to grow during the 19th century, launching the steel industry and railways in the United States, England, France, and Germany. Chinese savings—mandatory,to a large extent—like Japanese savings years before, also contributed to equipping and developing these two countries.

The large public institutions created in 1944 by the Bretton Woods Agreement, the IMF and the World Bank, were specifically mandated to support such development in the medium and long term. This required careful and clear leadership, delivered then by the United States as well as the United Kingdom. More than ever, while the major SDGs of 2015 await implementation, these institutions play a critical role in the preservation of financial stability and in the search for the money needed to fund the transition to clean energy, build infrastructure, and provide access for all to healthcare, education, energy, and technology. Visiting the yurt of a shepherd on the remote Mongolian steppe, I was stunned to see his traditional tent home decked out with the latest modern technologies. I was there in the context of a World Bank program on universal access to electricity provided by individual off-grid solar panels.[4] Invited into his home, I found the man, dressed in a style two centuries old, who offered me yak butter tea (a specialty) in a timeless room containing the traditional Buddhist bed and altar—plus a flat-screen TV and a Wi-Fi–enabled mobile phone. Even more surprising, thanks to his cell phone connection, this sheep and goat herder had access to agricultural insurance to manage the risks associated with his livestock, which faced threats such as extreme temperatures from one season to another. All this was possible through just a few solar panels!

"Devil's Dung but a Very Good Manure"

At its root, finance is like money as Saint Teresa of Ávila described it: "the devil's dung, but it makes very good manure." This financial instrument was horribly corrupted in the years leading up to the financial crisis by actors who if not ill intentioned were at least indifferent. Uncontrolled, finance has become a blind and uncontrollable force. But it would be such a shame to renounce it—the world would lose so much! Instead, we should take back the reins of this tool, which has long attracted the brightest minds, and remobilize our efforts for the common good. Let's continue to encourage innovation, as long as the end result has lasting benefits for humankind. We must remember, this finance, this money, is ours not theirs; reasserting control and driving its use by clear signaling is our collective responsibility.

Finance Development, Not Just Growth

To reassert control, we must learn how to better distinguish growth from development. I often cite the 1987 declaration of the Ecumenical Council of Churches: "Growth as an end in itself is the strategy of cancer cells. It is the uncontrolled proliferation without limit or regard for the system supporting it that leads to its degeneration and its death. Development, on the other hand, is the strategy of embryos: putting things it needs in its proper place at the proper time, with care to respect the relationships between them."

What a strong image! At its most basic, growth leads to the creation of GDP. It is not very complicated: all you have to do is rev it up and let it go. We could manage to create an extraordinary level of GDP! Growth is this mechanical augmentation of wealth produced, whatever the wealth may be, and some harm that is its means of proliferation. On the other hand, development (meaning harmonious, thoughtful, controlled growth) is much higher maintenance and sophisticated, and it is the only viable trajectory for globalization. We cannot allow globalization to be overtaken by this cancerous logic of a finance that can be anything and allow anything. The same is true for digital technology. We urgently need to put humanity back at the center of it, to ensure that the tools we invent are used solely for the benefit of humankind. We must get back on the path of development rather than growth, and not only for the poorest countries. All countries face the challenge, wealthy ones included. This is the ambition of the 2015 SDGs.

Rekindling a love for finance, then, is nothing else but giving it back some meaning: a meaning it had lost, or maybe had neglected for some generations. We have to give it meaning and heart; this is core to rebuilding the trust. This is the message I was asked to instill at my last Société Générale speech presenting the bank's 2012 annual accounts. I developed the image in three stages: (1) "The Core–T1 Ratio is Good," (2) "Group Logo as a Red and Black Heart, and (3) "The Care–T1 Ratio is Better!"[5] Finance is not just a matter of ratios, it's also a matter of care—a matter of the heart (*coeur* in French).

Avoiding the Temptation of Cynicism

To address this matter of the heart, we have to rid ourselves of any cynicism we may have once had toward finance's clients, their peers, and the profession. Without a doubt, we cannot reenchant finance if the actors who had used and abused this instrument, even in small part, continue to play the system and shirk responsibility, waiting for the crisis to pass. It would be too easy to pretend, given the pipe dreams of reform, that global finance is a force too big to do anything about and that the system will simply have to adapt. We have seen where this kind of logic leads us.

Yet some habits persist! Cynicism's roots go deep. For instance, consider the manipulations of the LIBOR interest rates, or those on the foreign exchange market in the United Kingdom, which continued long after the start of the financial crisis. The thoughts expressed directly from the mouths of the bosses at the large American banks in 2010, when worldwide regulations were being established, also bear witness to this. In the spring when Congress was beginning to review the Dodd-Frank Act, one of them told me, "What instructions did we give our lobbyists in Washington? It was simple: legislation is necessary, it's the price we have to pay for what we've done, but make it so it's not too painful." The underlying message being, they would wash their hands clean and get back to the same dirty business.

I heard a similarly striking message in September 2010 in Brussels, at the Eurofi meeting (known as "the bankers salon"). I was grabbing a quick bite for lunch with some of international finance's biggest names, and I asked one of them, "Will the Dodd-Frank law mean you have to review your banking model?"

"Oh, you know this framework law, it's a bit like the Bible, over 2,000 pages that you just need to learn to interpret," he answered. "The only difference is, of course, the authors of the Bible are dead!"

"But you will still have to give up *some* of your practices!" one of my French colleagues retorted.

"You know what the market's like," he said. "It's not a fire station where you wait for the alarm call to pull on your boots and helmet to go put out the fire, then head back to the station. The market is like a moving walkway at the airport: It moves 24/7. I wake up at 5:00a.m. and step onto the walkway. When my client arrives at 5:05, I help him up; then when he leaves, I stay on to follow the market in order to be able to help him. You see what I mean?"

I was shocked and I still am. And I tried to express my views at the time and have since then.

This story truly reflects the spirit of the era, in which we clung to the idea of an uncontrolled market with the conviction that no law could ever change it. It is this mind-set that so many find abhorrent and that caused significant swaths of the public to lose trust in the whole system and raise existential questions.

The Temptation of Total Regulation

The opposite extreme, to base the reform of the financial system on regulation alone, would not be helpful. Certainly, getting finance back in the hands of regulators and legislators is necessary, even indispensable to regaining control of the blind force we had allowed to run free. To control means to define rules and sanctions, to set up radar, guards, and arbitrators, to set goals more sustainable than the obsession with earning ever-increasing wealth. Before long, the financial system had encouraged collective greed—remember the famous "Greed is good" slogan popularized in 1987 by Michael Douglas's character in Oliver Stone's film *Wall Street*—among underwriters, bankers, insurers, and savers and the morally reprehensible behaviors of a select number of heads of large businesses. It was time to get the lines moving.

The responsibility for regulation was largely incumbent upon national governments, central banks, and the international cooperation of the G20. In the United States, for example, the Dodd-Frank Act, now threatened, was adopted by Congress in July 2010. Dodd-Frank created a Financial Stability Oversight Council (FSOC) and tasked the Federal Reserve with the surveillance of global risk. These mechanisms gave the United States the ability not only to influence but to lead a race to adopt the highest and most efficient forms of regulations consistent with each country's aims. Beyond the regulation of derivative product markets to reduce the accumulation of risks, or the obligation of lenders' solvency for real estate loans, one important aspect of the law focused on commercial banks, which can no longer hold more than 3 percent of their own funds in shares in hedge funds or capital investment funds. Another significant change, in principle, was that taxpayers could no longer be asked to bail out financial enterprises in trouble. These, at any rate, were Dodd-Frank's stated goals.

In this new environment, the creation of the Financial Stability Board (FSB) at the G20 meeting in London in April 2009 represented an important event. This council, drawing from the G20 heads of central banks and chairmen of the treasuries of member states, as well as certain international organizations such as the IMF, World Bank, and the OECD, today constitutes the steering body for worldwide financial stability. It is tasked with identifying the system vulnerabilities and defining standards (or the coordination of their development around the world) to manage them, in collaboration with international standard setters. For example, the FSB defined a list of systemically important international banks, those considered "too big to fail," the collapse of which would cause a complete breakdown in global finance. Such banks, compared to other banks, have additional capital requirements. The FSB also looked into the organization of derivatives markets, systematically encouraging the use of official clearinghouses.[6] It also promoted principles regarding remuneration of market operators and the identification of the institutions that act as counterparts to a financial transaction.

In order to protect us from a new systemic threat, the Basel Committee of the Bank for International Settlements adopted new ratios for bank solvency in September 2010 (called "Basel III"), that raised the minimum capital required of banks.[7] The establishment at the end of 2015 of loss absorption mechanisms (total loss-absorbing capacity [TLAC] at the global level[8]) has rounded out this prevention system. The final regulatory effort to date was the adoption in May 2016 by the G7 finance ministers and central bankers of an action plan to strengthen the global fight against financial terrorism. The work continues.

Gaps remain in these international regulations. The exposure of banks to sovereign debt (up to now considered to be risk-free and thus exempt from the limits imposed on bank assets made up of corporate and household debt) is still not regulated and has created disagreements among the ministries of finance of the EU. Discussions about what could be called "Basel IV," and in particular the use of in-house models validated by regulators as opposed to standard approaches identical for all, are ongoing.

The Rise of Market-Based Finance, aka Shadow Banking

Shadow banking is a so-called parallel banking system, known more now as market-based finance, which encompasses those actors and activities that contribute to the economy through nonbank funding. This system is not in itself bad, but it has not been subjected to the same attention as the banking system. That said, we should not think of it as a Wild West situation in which anything goes: pension funds, hedge funds, life insurers, stock managers, and the like are all regulated, sometimes strictly. But it would be worthwhile for us to integrate the supervision and regulation of this system into a global approach to the funding of our economies.

The global approach that has been developed has facilitated a significant improvement in global standards. The participation of all the largest economies in particular is critical. Such a multilateral approach is at risk amid the rising nationalism around the world. It is easy to turn one's back on such forums because they can be cumbersome. However, to do so would be to risk that some other forms would fill the vacuum, which could lead to unintended consequences that may be much harder to change in the future. Matters of finance have become predominantly global issues; taking a nationalistic approach will inevitably lead to a breakdown and result in stark imbalances. Even if this nationalist approach seems tempting and easier rhetorically, there will be no control regained solely at the domestic level.

We must consider several changes that have occurred in the shadow banking system: the change in scale of a sector that represents just under $100 trillion of assets under management; rapid growth outside of the United States and Europe, in China, for example; the proliferation of connections between all actors in the financing of the economy, both bank and nonbank based. Beyond the piecemeal regulatory contribution of this system, there is also the question of the manner of financing our economies: How much debt should there be? How much capital? How much for banks? How much for the market? What level of profitability? What level of transformation?[9] These questions do not appear to garner the same response from every country. But they cannot be ignored or addressed separately over too long a period. We must use a holistic approach that will spark debate at a sufficient level about the conditions for financing economies: at the level of nations, of regional unions or alliances, and in some cases of the world. The question of financing infrastructure is a classic: the whole world recognizes the enormous need for roads, ports, airports, power plants, and the like, and has called for a greater involvement of the private sector, but at the same time, no one has mobilized to address the regulatory checks or behaviors that hinder a greater involvement of pension funds or insurers and push the banking sector away. The regulatory approach should combine the negative (don't do that!) with the positive (do that!), prescriptive (you must!), and incentive (do this to your benefit!).

Beware of Unintended Consequences

Some regulations, however, have clearly resulted in unexpected effects, or so-called unintended consequences. The case of correspondent banking was a revelation to me, as I acknowledged in a 2015 article cowritten with Mark Carney.[10] Until the 2007–2008 crisis, several large international banks (such as Deutsche Bank, JPMorgan Chase, and BNP Paribas) acted as ports of entry to the international financial system by offering up the use of their infrastructures to financial institutions from many countries. These so-called correspondent banks allowed local banks to give their clients access to the services of a more distant institution such as for currency exchange or transfer of funds to a foreign account. Capital flows traveled via these intermediaries, and each domestic market was connected to the world. With the crisis and regulation of the system, fines, from the Americans in particular, proliferated against banks that did not respect embargos or anti–money-laundering rules.[11] Faced with significant sums of losses sustained, a number of establishments decided to pause their correspondent banking activities in Libya, Mexico, Saudi Arabia, or Somalia, having calculated that the risk of doing business with them was too high—or at least that they were not compensated for such risk. As a result, we have isolated or are likely to isolate some emerging or developing economies from the international financial system.[12]

Regulators cannot ignore such consequences. To do so would be neglectful of the purpose of the financial reforms undertaken by the G20, specifically the support of an open and flexible global financial sector that truly serves the economies of the world. It would also encourage the circulation of illicit funds through unofficial channels. We have to understand the magnitude of this problem and its causes, to ascertain facts, drawing once more on the experience of the World Bank Group and other development players.

We should then also standardize the application of international norms, create interpreting bodies for them (particularly interbank partnerships), and clarify the expectations and uses for technology to this end (specifically blockchains[13]).

In another field, the regulatory treatment of securitization, which is today subject to strict requirements, would also allow it to be reviewed because it could discourage investment. The EU has begun work on this issue.

If we wish to reset finance on a "purified" basis, we must find the right balance between a necessary arsenal of regulations and a necessary fluidity for circulation of capital. In short, we need to find the proper amount of breathing room for the financial system: the proper level of detail in the definition of roles, the proper degree of cooperation between regulator and regulated, and the proper level of sharing of responsibilities. Above all, we must think of the system as a whole, not as pieces. We have to start thinking about how to streamline everything. With this effort comes a real health warning. A move back to a relatively less regulated environment, if balanced correctly, may indeed make sense. We cannot view what happened with the global financial crisis as leading to finance simply being put in the penalty box, only for it now to be unleashed again in a postregulated world where we swing back too far the other way with respect to the level of oversight and checks and balances. If we go down that path, we will create a future certainty, a repeat of the same mistakes, and this time, perhaps, with even more far-reaching consequences. And, as one would expect, this reform will start by reestablishing at all levels a culture of accountability and responsibility.

CHAPTER 9

The New Names of the Game

During this reset of finance, the temptation to be prescriptive is natural. The hope to resolve everything through regulation is inevitable at times. But it would be regrettable if we were to discharge financial players of their responsibility. The perception that this was happening, particularly during the bank bailouts, was a significant contributing factor to the diminution of trust in the system. The challenge we face is how best to realign incentives and consequences.

Reestablishing a Culture of Responsibility

The issue of bankers' remuneration is a textbook question. I remember having had a debate on this topic in 2008 with reputable consultants. I felt that the problem of financiers was not so much their total compensation package as the manner in which the compensation was structured, particularly the habit of linking short-term measured performance to bonuses: it was an invitation to commit crimes! The consultants laughed in my face and told me I was naïve, that there was no way to change that. I replied, with some seriousness, that if we were unable to impose sound limits ourselves, then legislators would eventually get involved—and that's precisely what happened. Bankers have become probably the only professionals to have their compensation set by European directive! And Americans are so infuriated by the impunity that Wall Street decision makers seem to enjoy that the topic was brought up during the presidential campaign; first steps toward fixing this are quietly being put into place. It's a shame we had to get to this point and that financial professionals did not find it in themselves to self-regulate. It will be interesting to see how things develop now that the mood has changed.

This responsibility is a fundamental cultural concern. Although regulatory changes were undoubtedly necessary, they are in no way sufficient, because all they do is to codify procedures with only superficial changes to behaviors. Rekindling a love for finance requires that we reestablish a culture of accountability and responsibility among all the players in the game.

The Great Moderation that occurred in the years leading up to 2007, by establishing the idea that subdividing, redistributing, and insuring risks was a guarantee of the viability of the system, developed a culture of comfort in which decisions are detached from accountability because risk is distributed in an increasingly far-flung manner. No one is left responsible for participating in anything in this globalized machine spinning on its own. To get back to the fundamentals of finance will also mean renewing the spirit of capitalism as Henry Ford and others conceived it: capitalism that can exist and grow only with rigorous respect for ethics. This same thought occupied the ministers of finance and central banks of the G7 in May 2015 at their meeting in Dresden: how could they formulate a code for the banking profession, drafted as a collection of voluntary commitments for which the guiding ethical principles were rooted in the conscious understanding that finance is not an end unto itself but rather a means to serve the real economy and society, a means to promote investment, growth, and prosperity for all?

This call must also be heard throughout colleges and universities where ethics should be taught compulsorily and in the most practical manner. The way business cases became the norm decades ago, ethical cases should also become references in any curriculum.

No Longer Ignoring Ethical Fault Lines

On the question of financial ethics, we would benefit by listening to the wise voices of various religions. Through my involvement in the Semaines sociales de France, a hundred-year-old association dedicated to Christian social thought, I have long stood behind the Catholic social doctrine of a common good, grassroots participation in society, and a preferential option for the poor.[1] I have also attended several seminars at the Vatican, particularly an international seminar on the economy and the common good organized in July 2014 by the Pontifical Council for Justice and Peace, presided over by Cardinal Turkson, archbishop of Accra in Ghana. We debated the issue of sharing growth and making it inclusive, creating social and territorial cohesion, and maximizing the number of people served by finance. Religions have valuable messages for us on these topics. During one day of our seminar, Pope Francis joined us for lunch and warned us about the "anthropological reductionism" marking our era, denouncing an economic system dominated by the "culture of waste."[2] For all the leaders gathered together on that day, this call, along with the Pontifical exhortation in 2013 to fight against the "globalization of indifference" from the Italian island of Lampedusa, was a lifesaving wake-up call and a stimulus to act. In another meeting in 2017, Pope Francis said,

> Those who cause or allow others to be discarded—whether refugees, children who are abused or enslaved, or the poor who die on our streets in cold weather—become themselves like soulless machines. For they implicitly accept the principle that they too, sooner or later, will be discarded, when they no longer prove useful to a society that has made Mammon, the god of money, the center of its attention.... We need to learn compassion.... This compassion will enable those with responsibilities in the worlds of finance and politics to use their intelligence and their resources not merely to control and monitor the *effects* of globalization but ... also to correct its *orientation* whenever is necessary.[3]

Making Finance Intelligible for All

Into this culture of accountability that is to inform the reinvention of the system, we must integrate the needs of education. Finance has too often hidden behind the sophistication of its instruments, but its fundamental mechanisms are simple if you just take the time to explain them. Finance has tried for too long to make discussions unintelligible, sometimes through complacency, sometimes through bad faith or dishonesty. It may have seemed disdainful of the populations who nonetheless, through their money, fed into it. It is time for the players involved to commit to explaining systematically what they are doing. While access to finance is a determining factor of individual freedom, this freedom can be exercised only with a minimum level of knowledge. Every citizen of the world must be able to understand what it means to save, lend, and invest, and what these activities contribute to the economy. Without that, we will never be able to rebuild communities' trust in finance. The Dodd-Frank Act took a noteworthy step in this direction by creating a bureau of financial education and consumer protection, which is responsible for informing the public and analyzing the products provided to them. The European Union has put effort into its own online education tool, the Consumer Classroom,[4] to improve consumer awareness of financial matters and credit. These efforts naturally involve an attempt to answer more technical questions, including some of the least understood, such as those on accounting. They must, however, go beyond these first steps, and I would expect the education system to integrate more of these aspects in the curriculum.

We also have to start questioning the way financials are presented. The current accounting system, based on the so-called mark-to-market approach, in reality a liquidation value approach, is certainly consistent, but it has significant consequences in terms of economic reasoning: when you systematically reckon in market value or in replacement value, you affect the manner in which you think about the whole. To avoid this bias, you have to encourage integrated reporting efforts that aim to boil down a company's entire strategy into a few intelligible pages, rather than the 500-plus-page annual reports that get published. It is more important and necessary to be able to report in plain English on what a company is doing and with which objective than it is to just pile up pages in an opaque manner.

All financial professionals, all business and global institution leaders, must be able to contribute to such efforts and ensure that these efforts meet expectations without creating a new layer of complexity. A fundamental responsibility of our democracies is to remain accessible to the public, to allow citizens and employees to understand the larger goals of a government or a company, to provide these reform strategies, and to assist humankind in grasping the complexity of the world without oversimplifying.

Building a Balanced "Triangle of Governance"

We won't be able to reenchant finance with the flick of a magic wand. We have a lot of work to do. We will naturally need to start with regulatory changes, to the banking sector and beyond, integrating the entire financial sphere. And this necessary transformation is not enough on its own: we also have to reframe the behaviors of the actors involved, without relying too much on an ideal scenario in which they change on their own, suddenly "enlightened" with a sense of what is right.

The changes we make must include a realization that, despite growing doubts, better educated or more conscientious thought leaders can change practices or initiate the necessary changes—along the lines of the speeches that have been made recently supporting better accountability in finance by such renowned figures as Mark Carney, governor of the Bank of England and president of the FSB; Larry Fink, CEO of BlackRock; and Ronald Cohen, founder of the Big Society Capital project. In addition to these guiding voices, the most demanding investors and consumers will also exert pressure. Finance is equally influenced by changes to the fiscal parameters linked to compensation and attention given to externalities like the price of carbon. Although the rise in power of institutional investors (among them, a small number of influential actors), can be perceived as a risk, it can also represent an opportunity to reconstruct the financial world with more heart. International organizations, particularly development banks, will have an eminent responsibility in promoting, evaluating, and testing innovations and changes.

The combination of three forces—regulation; the role of financial actors, including the largest of them; and commitment of international organizations—could prove powerful and likely holds one of the keys of reform. Reform would also benefit from social pressures and the pioneering role of certain multinational companies like Unilever, Mars, and Danone, to name a few. In a sense, we are seeing this "triangle of governance" that the water group described in our book *Eau,* in which "public authorities, private interests (industrial, agricultural, commercial), and civil society comprising consumers and users rub shoulders."[5] There are three main distinctions to make among these three powers:

> Public authorities (which are neither suppressed nor replaced but included in the system of governance) send legislative and regulatory messages to civil society, which is meant to comply with them.... Governance creates balance within these regulations through the user's "best practices."...
>
> A second equilibrium is established between private, industrial, and commercial interests, and public powers. The latter admit the laws of the market: transparency of information, competition,

> a balance of price and quantity between supply and demand.... The rules of liberal economy are tempered by regulation (not rules) that public powers exert over private business....
>
> A third equilibrium, between civil society and private interests, between businesses and their clients, affects the quality of services offered (price included) and the nature of demands expressed by society. Clients can be users or members of the public; companies can be government bodies and public services; these semantics don't change the issue. There is always a producer side, and a consumer side.... This final equilibrium is a matter of submission of the economic side to the personal side.
>
> Each point of the triangle of governance attempts to control the proper functioning of the equilibriums in opposition.[6]

If we are to reenchant finance and regain control of this unparalleled but hard to tame tool we will have to continually seek to strike a balance between these points.

Conjuring the Tragedy of Horizons

Another imperative that should guide our reset of the financial system is putting an end to the tyranny of the short term in order to give better consideration to the long term in our collective actions and decisions.

Living "on the inside" during the 2007–2008 crisis and in the years that followed was a revelation for me in this respect. Being in charge of the finances of two of the largest banks in the world, I had to juggle two different depths of perception: thinking about the present moment so that the bank didn't hit an iceberg, and thinking 10 years into the future to determine how to rebuild in order to survive that long. In other words, "I had to be both an emergency responder and a scout to figure out the formula I should use at the right time."[7] The different time frames collided with one another.

The task for financial players, and more broadly politicians and technocrats, is to take into account all these different time frames. Mark Carney taught this lesson to the insurers at Lloyd's of London. In his speech "Breaking the Tragedy of the Horizon," a tragedy in which Carney includes climate change, he refers to the economic phenomenon of the tragedy of the commons. He shows how far removed is the climate problem (15 to 20 years out) from trading (one minute ahead), the issues of banking (the next quarter or year out), and the issues handled by the head of the central bank (three to five years out). In short, there is no single financial player in our current state of affairs who has an incentive to think about climate. As Mark Carney put it,

> We don't need an army of actuaries to tell us that the catastrophic impacts of climate change will be felt beyond the traditional horizons of most actors—imposing a cost on future generations that the current generation has no direct incentive to fix. That means beyond the business cycle, the political cycle, and the horizon of technocratic authorities, like central banks, who are bound by their mandates. The horizon for monetary policy extends out to 2–3 years. For financial stability it is a bit longer, but typically only to the outer boundaries of the credit cycle—about a decade. In other words, once climate change becomes a defining issue for financial stability, it may already be too late.[8]

It is the responsibility of financiers to work their magic on this tragedy of horizons, to make it understandable for all parties involved, in a simple and intelligible manner, that "the more we invest with foresight, the less we will regret in hindsight."

Moving Away from the Tyranny of Short-Termism

Larry Fink delivered another lesson to us in April 2016. In a letter addressed to the directors of the largest American and European businesses, this CEO of the global leader in asset management, BlackRock, urged businesses to get past the "culture of quarterly earnings hysteria," to detach from the immediate demands of investors to give new perspective to their strategies. Despite repeated calls for CEOs to embrace a long-term vision, "many companies continue to engage in practices that may undermine their ability to invest for the future." Systematizing the redistribution of profits to shareholders, warns Fink, is to act "at the expense of long-term value." This clearly threatens the survival of these companies, in a world in which "over the long-term, environmental, social and governance (ESG) issues—ranging from climate change to diversity to board effectiveness—have real and quantifiable financial impacts."[9]

The good news is that this letter appears to have received a warm welcome by its recipients. When you manage $5 trillion, you can have an undeniable influence on market practices!

These various calls for action are not seeking to eliminate finance, simply to reform it. We want to use it for what it can do: pushing out our horizon instead of simply accepting fate. Jean Favier, one of the most respected historians of our time, offers that lesson:

> Whatever man does is the future: the fate of peaks and swells, what we see and what we guess, the earthbound and our dreams. The horizon shows each of us the level and limits of our needs and abilities. There are horizons we accept and those that recede. One is sterile, the other exists. The other is only an idea, and it is fertile. One and the other have a relativity of spirit

> and instance. By encircling them, they define men and things, resources and partners. Intelligence knows how to expand the circle. It requires the will to create, which could be called audacity, or the spirit of enterprise. It also requires the immediate knowledge of realities that create the possibility, the distance of the desirable. Thus the horizon invents itself, within the confines of need and ambition.[10]

This was the miracle of the Age of Discovery: Europeans expanded their horizons in an extraordinary way when they stopped accepting the limits of the known world. It all began with Henry the Navigator, prince of Portugal, who decided one day to pay his sailors to attempt to navigate Cape Bojador, the southernmost point of the African coast known to Europe at the time, which until then had been considered impassable due to sea monsters. The first expedition was turned back, as was the second, but the third made it through and showed that there was nothing there to fear.[11] In a way, it was money that allowed these explorers to face their fears and move forward!

As I've said before, as long as finance is used well, it is our best tool to manage the long-term and unknown areas of our future. Imagine what would be possible if we could finally mobilize all our intelligence and energy with that perspective in mind! This requires a change in mind-set, a different way of thinking about finance and how we can all be smarter about changing behaviors. The good news is that this mobilization has already started and is taking the shape of a silent revolution.

CHAPTER 10

A Silent Revolution Is On

Rebooting finance means putting all the malleability and inventiveness of this tool back to work for the common good. It means using it wisely, reorienting the compass, getting it back onto the right course, giving it the right signals. We can't ignore or diminish the force of the market, the influence of investors, and the desire to be profitable. Instead, these forces need to be channeled for the better (rather than the worse). Further, we can't deny the immense energy of finance—we must harness this, too, borrowing its coding and using its protagonists (leading and incentivizing them in a different, new way) to manage investments in viable projects that give us a sense of the future. Numerous ideas, innovations, and initiatives have emerged with this goal in recent years that demonstrate just how useful finance can be, perhaps even more useful than we dared to imagine. We need to talk about these ideas a lot more and in terms easily understood by nonexperts. By showing in stark terms how finance is being developed to address some of the world's most pressing needs, we will aid in its rehabilitation. We also have to launch the various initiatives on a massive scale—as massive as we can manage as investors, savers, clients, and retirees.

Then we'll see that our 2015 goals are totally within reach. Perhaps one of the least understood factors is that our generation is at a point of inflection where we can make a step change by using finance as our servant to drive wholesale changes.

The Silent Revolution of the Markets

The social and solidarity economy is today in turmoil. Forums, test labs, and new approaches abound around the idea of intelligent, ethical finance that is socially responsible and capable of shedding the tyranny of quarterly results and thinking in the long term to build sustainable plans for humanity. Concepts like economics of mutuality (promoted by Bruno Roche and Jay Jakub[1]), a circular economy, impact investment, green bonds, and shared value no longer cause smirks and eye-rolling: the financial innovation logic they embody has sparked real interest not only from experts but also from public authorities and investors. Around the globe, many of these concepts are already working diligently to promote capitalism with feeling. A new financial system must be able to integrate this, without being naïve, into the new products and markets that follow.

HEC Paris's Finance 4 Good, Stanford Graduate School of Business's Impact Funding Lab and Responsible Business Lab, and Oxford University's Impact Investing Programme are just a few examples of the world's most prestigious schools positioning themselves at the head of the movement. In an example that reflects on the economy of mutuality, HEC Montréal created the International Research Centre on Cooperative Finance, for example. Rym Ayadi, its director, explained: "The race towards a homogeneous financial system ... proved to be at odds with the nature of the system which is, in essence, diverse in many aspects. Diversity results from the co-existence of more than one organizational form of finance, such as shareholder versus stakeholder-value financial institutions. Each one has its own incentive system and view about the way it contributes to the economy and society as a whole."[2]

Other fascinating initiatives are also under way to apply the concept of shared value proposed by Michael Porter, professor of management at Harvard and director of the Institute for Strategy and Competitiveness. This idea is far more engaging than corporate social responsibility, which has been adopted more or less voluntarily by organizations and which has led to accusations of opportunism in many cases. Instead, a company can take it one step further, Porter says, by "generating economic value in a way that also produces value for society."[3] More than simply protecting the environment from its impact and arming itself against the related negative externalities, a company can reshape the direction of its operation and integrate consideration for the needs and expectations of society into its strategies by refreshing its products and services to adapt to social needs, increasing productivity in its own value chain (through the commodities market, for example) and contributing to the creation of hubs, such as Silicon Valley in California or the many competitive clusters that already exist in France.

Today, shared-value initiatives are being used within many companies in a variety of sectors, from pharmaceuticals to banking to food production. The application of this concept to the banking industry, in particular, leads to imitation:[4] several large banks like Barclays, ING Group, JPMorgan Chase, Crédit Agricole, and Société Générale are understanding that their clients, ranging from the biggest institutional investors to businesses, jump at offers that respond to the new alternative energy market, from housing development to agricultural development. These social and environmental markets, increasingly seen as "profitable" with respect to the size of demand,[5] are major opportunities for banks to create shared value. They can increase profits while also reaffirming their *raison d'être* of serving the economy and society and financing solutions to local and global issues.

Dear Investors: On Social Impact

Another revolutionary approach has a bright future: social impact investment, also called, more simply, impact investment. It encompasses "all investments that deliberately aim at precise social goals as well as financial returns, and which measure the accomplishments made with respect to each."[6] It is clearly significant that the promoter of this idea, Sir

Ronald Cohen, the wealthy British businessman who founded Apax Partners (a private equity firm), is also considered one of the founding fathers of venture capital and private equity—in other words, a model of traditional finance became the figurehead of new finance. This is surely a sign. As we once discussed: "Basically, the 19th century was the age of *return* (the main question being, how much will my investment bring me?); the 20th century was the age of *risk-return* (will the return on my investment be enough to justify the risk I take?); and the 21st century appears to be the age of *risk-return-impact* (how much am I risking, how much can I earn, and what is my impact?)."

In short, we have moved from a two-dimensional to a three-dimensional vision of the financial market, in which investors are dedicated to concentrating on our ability to construct a better society, to everyone's benefit.

The latest novelty in this innovative approach to finance is the social impact bond: following green bonds, social impact bonds (first introduced in the United Kingdom, then launched into many other countries) are a "nontraditional form of debt issued by a state (or a public borrower) without a fixed interest rate but for a predetermined period in which it commits to paying for a significant social improvement [such as reducing the recidivism rate for prisoners] for a defined population."[7] This concept of social finance, initially developed to manage long-term social problems (like absenteeism, illiteracy, recidivism, and social exclusion), now tends to expand into domains such as education or public health, to benefit the most fragile populations (such as youth, the elderly, the disabled, or the homeless).

These new approaches to finance are in no way utopian. Impact investment is growing rapidly in the market. This type of investment has already allowed us to make advancements in reducing recidivism and improving healthcare for children and the elderly, and in financial inclusion, even if programs are not linear and some failures have been registered. Initiatives like the ones launched by Coca-Cola in Brazil and by Danone in Bangladesh have created local value and jobs.[8] In the wake of COP21, we saw a record volume of green bonds being issued worldwide in the first quarter of 2016 ($16.5 billion in just one quarter) by multilateral issuers (like the World Bank or European Investment Bank), large-scale enterprises (EDF Energy, Unilever, Air Liquide, Apple), and medium-size companies.

Without great fanfare, a revolution is taking place: as Cohen says, impact investment "brings the invisible heart of markets to guide their invisible hand."[9] Finance has the great advantage of being a flexible system that reacts mechanically to incentives. We just need to give it good incentives, such as the requirement that the impact of investments made on behalf of the client of a bank or a fund be positive, and that stocks bought be of social or environmental benefit, in order for the system to turn in the right direction. This linkage is sometimes misunderstood or creates mistrust in the public sphere. That is why it seems so urgent to me that we explain all the strategic roles of investors better. COP21 gave us a lesson by demonstrating that private and public players can work hand in hand. Now, we need to improve our application of this approach.

Finance and Climate: Toward a New Community of Shared Destiny

While the silent revolution stirring the markets has a special role to play in the fight against climate change, the discussion on climate has, to a certain degree, only emphasized the well-understood drag created by finance. Let's not kid ourselves: the $100 billion in public aid promised each year from North to South, an obligation of solidarity, will not by itself make a difference. The Copenhagen Summit of 2009 treated this amount as symbolic of our collective commitment. But $100 billion per year will not suffice to reduce the footprint of a global economy of $100 trillion. This transformation can happen only with market mobilization, and therefore with a change in the behaviors of the players involved.

Already, we are seeing an increasing number of companies and shareholders take the climate dimension into consideration when they choose investments and savings, market their products, and set up their accounting systems. More and more investors, in particular, are "greening up" their stock portfolios by withdrawing investments from carbon (as Amundi, a subsidiary of Crédit Agricole, did in 2015) and hydrocarbons (like the Rockefeller Foundation did in 2016, when it sold all of its shares in ExxonMobil) to redirect their money toward projects related to the energy transition. In 2014 Engie, a French electric utility, issued the largest volume of green bonds ever made by a private actor to date (€2.5 billion) to finance wind power, hydroelectricity, and energy efficiency. In October 2015, EDF Energy also distinguished itself by issuing a green bond for a record dollar amount of $1.25 billion. What's new is that these choices are not purely ethics based, but are also financially sound: "It makes little sense—financially or ethically—to continue holding investments in these companies ... [that] continue to explore for new sources of hydrocarbons," the Rockefeller Family Fund stated on March 23, 2016.[10]

Financial risk has effectively come of age. Economic actors can no longer ignore the "transition risk" described by Mark Carney, which threatens nothing less than global financial stability:

> Take, for example, the IPCC's [Intergovernmental Panel on Climate Change's] estimate of a carbon budget that would likely limit global temperature rises to 2 degrees above preindustrial levels. That budget amounts to between 1/□ th and □ rd [of the] world's proven reserves of oil, gas and coal. If that estimate is even approximately correct it

> would render the vast majority of reserves "stranded"—oil, gas and coal that will be literally unburnable without expensive carbon capture technology, which itself alters fossil fuel economics. The exposure of ... investors, including insurance companies, to these shifts is potentially huge.[11]

If these financial budgets, which today represent trillions of dollars in the global economy, were to devalue quickly, the world could experience a devastating crash. Given such conditions, Carney concludes, "financing the de-carbonization of our economy is a major opportunity for insurers as long-term investors." The fates of finance and the climate are, from here on out, connected—whatever comes to pass. Markets therefore have an interest in projecting as far into the future of this transition as possible. As Carney said, "The more we invest with foresight; the less we will regret in hindsight."[12]

In any case, Carney places the responsibility for providing a compass to the actors squarely upon policy makers, by making greenhouse gas emissions costly according to a fixed-price scale. This type of indicator would, by its nature, have a gradual influence on behavior. It would give the market the signal to do the necessary work by validating alternative energy in the long term. Companies, investors, and consumers would have all the items in hand to direct their choices to the benefit of greener solutions by incorporating a carbon tax into their economic models and project plans. "These carbon price mechanisms should not be considered a check on the global economy," explained Engie's president, Gérard Mestrallet, in 2015. "Quite the contrary—they will be a necessary accelerator of growth by creating confidence, stimulating investment and innovation, while setting up the conditions for fair competition."[13] This is one of the most powerful illustrations of the value that finance, properly applied, can be a creative force for the short-range, mid-range, and long-range future. By sending the right signals through an appropriate regulatory framework with the requisite degree of supervision and measurement, we can harness the energy of finance for the common good!

But Does It Scale?

The possibilities of using finance for the common good are just about limitless, in theory. I have personally been convinced of that since at least 2002, when I was a member of the World Panel on Financing Global Water Infrastructure working group led by Michel Camdessus, then again by his side in the office of the French president, and worked on many projects central to development finance.

Financing Access to Water

It was in the working group that I first experimented with financial innovation for the common good, beginning with universal access to clean water. Our working group quickly came to realize that nothing was as it seemed, because the common wisdom is that water is a gift from God, one of the most sacred resources. Too bad God didn't think to make the plumbing needed to distribute it! The needs in this field were massive: $180 billion per year to achieve the Millennium Development Goals, or twice as much funding as was then being made available (and nearly twice the total of contemporary official development assistance).[14] Of the 84 measures proposed in our study "Finance Water for All," the idea of a "sustainable tariff on drinking water" was the one we pushed: "To resolve the enormous financial problem, we must first turn to the most legitimate resource we have to use: self-funding, through a reasonable and efficient tariff policy," or in other words, a "realistic and socially applicable" policy. We were inspired by a successful experiment in South Africa, which drew on the principle that it made sense to pay higher rates for water used to fill a swimming pool or wash a car than for the water used to quench thirst. We suggested that the first few cubic meters of water should be free, and any above that would have a price. In this way, we defined a "tariff principle for the sustainable recovery of costs," using tariff formulas that attempted to "account for the abilities to contribute of different segments of the population" in order to grant the poorest "a much better service at an equal or lower price."[15]

A Small Levy on Plane Tickets

I was able to test out another intelligent use for finance as rapporteur-general alongside Jean-Pierre Landau, inspector general of finance, on the 2004 study *Les nouvelles contributions financières internationales* (New international financial contributions, also called the "Landau report") on financing global solidarity.[16] This is one of the innovations I am most proud of, because the creation in 2005 of the "Chirac tax" on airline tickets allowed us to solidify on a global level the idea of responsible globalization. Back in 2002, at the international conference in Monterrey on development funding, the president of France, Jacques Chirac, reminded us: "[It is] natural to envision the financing of humanization and the mastery of globalization through exactly that wealth which it engenders. We must therefore think more about the possibilities of international taxation for which the proceeds would be added to official development assistance."[17]

The idea was to invent an international fiscal policy that, by its leverage, would allow us to find the indispensable resources for development funding while minimizing the individual effort for consent. The importance of such an approach is also that it guarantees predictable and perennial resources that are not subject to the whims of parliamentary and democratic votes.

In 2003 the president of France assigned Jean-Pierre Landau and me to the task of putting together a working group embracing different points of view (from

ATTAC [Association for the Taxation of Financial Transactions and Aid to Citizens] to the IMF, the Ministry of Finance, the French Development Agency, Sir Tony Atkinson, and Oxfam). The highest-level experts, including economists, financiers, and tax specialists, were tasked with evaluating the feasibility of multiple options in finance innovation from a practical perspective, particularly the different possible forms of international taxes: microtaxes on financial transactions, taxes on foreign capital entering or leaving a tax haven, green taxes on ocean and air transportation, tiny pay-as-you-go taxes on airline tickets, and so on. It was this last option that we kept, for purely practical reasons, specifically because its implementation didn't create technical difficulties in collection, and also because of the connection between air transportation and globalization. With the effects of scale (at the time, 3 billion airline tickets were sold around the world each year), a universal and painless contribution of one dollar per ticket would have brought in, without compromising the economic balance of the industry, at least $3 billion.

This is one of the most extraordinary powers of finance: it allows, through the mechanism of a marginal charge on an economic activity, the widening of the solidarity base and the funding of a public good by mobilizing a fraction of the new wealth created by globalization, a large part of which had eluded state taxation systems. In this case, the Chirac tax on airline tickets allowed us to raise nearly €2 billion for the fight against AIDS and large-scale epidemics. France, along with about a dozen other countries, set up a partnership to allocate this money for the creation of an international center for medication purchases, dubbed Unitaid, which has become one of the pillars of financing access to healthcare worldwide. As a purchasing hub, Unitaid benefits from strength on the market to negotiate significantly lower prices with pharmaceutical companies. More than 80 percent of its budget goes to low-revenue countries.

Mobilize Today for Future Commitments

The Chirac tax is an even more interesting financial innovation when paired with another kind of innovation involving financial engineering. The idea, advanced by the United Kingdom, was to create a "simplified international finance" apparatus to pull together sustainable resources to fund vaccinations. The formula was that if a number of countries committed to donating 10 units per year for 10 years, we could recognize these multiyear commitments, mobilize the money immediately on the market (meaning, 100 units today), and reimburse the apparatus with future payments. Rather than giving a smaller amount each year, the funding efforts of states participating in the apparatus could be concentrated at the start by borrowing against the promised future amounts. That way, we create a much larger mass effect and quickly get noticeable results. That is how the International Finance Facility for Immunization (IFFIm) came about in 2006, with the mission of issuing equity bonds on financial markets regularly through the multiyear commitment of 10 states.[18] The funds raised were reinjected into the Global Alliance for Vaccines and Immunization, a public–private partnership delegated with the administrative functions and on-site implementation of the projects funded. To date IFFIm has collected $5.2 billion. Between just 2006 and 2008, this mechanism contributed to saving the lives of 3 million people living in developing countries! It is not just public reengineering of fiscal policy, which would not be new, but a genuine combination of efforts of all kinds.

Finance Controlled by a Firm Hand: The Sky Is the Limit

Finance can be used to set up an extraordinary and effective mechanism in a number of fields of application, allow bulk buying and advance purchases, and generate leverage. In the healthcare field, for instance, financial experiments have been conducted by modern philanthropic organizations like the Gates Foundation: by introducing guarantees into the market for vaccination, it allowed wide-scale use of vaccines and low-cost distribution in developing countries.

Along with Jean Todt (president of the International Automobile Federation, former CEO of Ferrari, and special envoy of the UN for road safety), I am leading discussions on ways to use financial mechanisms in the same vein. Road safety is an issue that affects more people than AIDS. On a global scale, 1.3 million deaths per year and 50 million injuries occur on the roads, the majority of which affect poor countries and pedestrians (many of whom are children: 500 kids die each day from traffic accidents). The difference with road safety, of course, is that we know the remedy: awareness campaigns that educate users of roads about the laws; enforcement of speed limits and laws against driving while under the influence of drugs or alcohol; improvement of radar, sidewalks, and speed bumps; and upgrades in public lighting. None of this is particularly expensive, but it could save hundreds of thousands of lives.[19] In order to consistently fund these solutions, we could come up with a microlevy or a microcontribution on automotive products—beginning with cars (80 million are sold each year), from which a "painless" contribution of just five dollars could sustainably generate hundreds of millions of dollars.

Similar ideas could be implemented in other fields like education. I am currently working on this topic with Gordon Brown, UN special envoy for global education, as well as the creation of the International Finance Facility for Education (IFFEd).

Financial players all need to do a much better job of communicating how each of these initiatives is working and the irreplaceable role of finance in their functioning. The appropriate combination of various facets of finance—collecting, mobilizing, and combining public and private resources and capacities—is required to address needs in an efficient manner. At the same time, we have to keep innovating, sourcing ideas from different stakeholders and then using the right mechanisms to test them quickly to see which ones warrant rolling out at scale. In Chapter 11, I look at one of our strongest forums for such tests, the multilateral institutions.

In Part 3, we will see how this controlled approach of finance can help restore trust in the multilateral system as well as foster a genuine cooperation between nations to serve the common good.

PART THREE

Finance at the Heart of Renewed International Cooperation

Part 3 discusses how finance is at the heart of a much-needed renewal of cooperation. Finance is a global matter and requires a concerted approach. However, finance is also more than that; it is also a tool for international cooperation. Controlled properly, finance can help the multilateral efforts to serve the common good in an effective manner.

If we are serious about addressing the challenges we all face in today's world, then we must resist the forces of unbridled nationalism. Finance is global and does not recognize international borders. We need to take control of the power of finance, not by inventing new, even more bureaucratic systems but by refining existing institutions and making them more efficient. We have to upgrade the operating system of globalization and make sure it does not leave to one side the citizens for the sake of the system. By doing this, we can increase the legitimacy of the institutions we have created and help channel finance and resources in the most appropriate ways. A key element is a sustained effort to improve the existing institutions; these are large, long-established organizations where the core value needs to be unleashed in a much more effective way. This improvement does not involve taking the path of least resistance.

Chapter 11 considers the system that has been built since World War II, its successes, and its limitations in today's world. Chapter 12 looks at how finance can help make the necessary adjustments to the system and truly create a tool to serve all of us.

CHAPTER 11

A Miracle to Be Preserved

We are faced with a hard truth, one we know and regularly tend to forget. No single world leader has ever had the capability to act alone to solve the world's great problems. That statement is more true today than ever. Whether the issue is climate change, migration, public health, digital technology, or most obviously capital flows, most issues now require cooperative and global action. Our leaders no longer have a choice. They must face the hard truth that the people they govern are frustrated and confused at being threatened, forgotten, and overwhelmed by giant superstructures that don't speak their language. They have been overtaken by a mechanism that seems disincarnate and as if it is operating on automatic pilot.

How do we rekindle international cooperation? How do we create or improve dialogue among the various advanced, emerging, and developing economies; the multilateral institutions; and even the weakened federations? How do we create unity to fight against the centrifugal forces that push us to reject the Other and withdraw within ourselves? How do we go from the O-H-I-O strategy to the C-A-lifornia strategy, that is, from the traditional concern of getting our own house in order to promoting collective action?

This is where finance has a historic role to play. Instead of being a simple item on the agenda in world governance, it can be a practical tool for mobilization—a tool so powerful that the international community will seize it and decide to define standards, adapt its regulatory and legislative framework, test and expand new modes of cooperation, and make sure that this tool is truly effective. We have the means to achieve our goals. The money is there, in the hands of private investors. The institutions are also there. They are only waiting to be better used! A new finance, rebuilt from the ground up, can be one of the best ways to give their actions a purpose.

The (Useful but Frustrating) Miracle of Current International Institutions

Kofi Annan, secretary-general of the UN, says about international institutions,

> At the beginning of the millennium, the UN reminded us the lessons it had learned from the interwar crisis. The architects of 1945 had learned just how destructive the stubborn refusal of any economic interdependence could be. During the 30s, the most unbridled economic nationalism and a policy of "everyone for themselves" and beggar thy neighbor was in vogue almost everywhere, degenerating into political retaliation,

> totalitarianism, and militarism in some countries, and isolationism in others. The League of Nations got off to a bad start trying to deal with these forces and never had a chance to fulfill its mission. This is why the post-war builders wisely chose the path of openness and cooperation. They created the United Nations, the Bretton Woods institutions, the GATT (which then became the World Trade Organization) and an entire series of organizations with the mission of making sure the system was functioning properly.... We are now harvesting the fruits of their labor.[1]

We must acknowledge that a small miracle occurred in 1944–1945 with the creation of a number of international institutions. It was visionary to focus on economic and financial cooperation to regulate the economies of the world. We have been lucky because it would be much more difficult, or even impossible in such a connected, complicated world, to invent tools with such ambition today. All of us alive today are custodians of this legacy. We could not do anything without it.

True, international organizations have created a giant, monstrously bureaucratic mechanism, which functions poorly in many respects—and sometimes functions so well that there is no need for a human at the wheel. True, this system, with its rituals, codes, programs, and agendas, generates inertia and frustrations. All that was probably inevitable.

An institution like the World Bank has 189 shareholder governments.[2] I saw the full impact of what such governance involved when I chaired its board meeting. Imagine 25 people meeting regularly to spend three hours talking: even if, as a whole, everyone says more or less the same thing, at times there are a few important nuances—some people think there is not enough equality between men and women, others that we are too focused on civil society, others that there is not enough civil service involvement. If each person talks for just five minutes, it would take over two hours to go around the table! During these meetings, my brain feels like it's split in half; one part says that this is an unbearable ritual, and the other whispers *maybe, but what is the alternative?* Is this not the price we pay so that the most powerful can sit around the same table with the least powerful so that they can be seen talking successively, representing the United States and the Seychelles (what beautiful symbolism!), and to prevent "the West" from deciding everything on its own in the name of the planet? Maybe everything can't be perfect, but this system, despite still being dominated by OECD countries, in particular the United States, strikes a balance, year in and year out, in mobilizing tens of billions of dollars for the benefit of the most vulnerable and setting a few rules for everyone to follow: on child labor, on respect for indigenous populations, and even on the preservation of biodiversity.

Hell Avoided

Dag Hammarskjöld, the UN's second secretary-general, who hailed from Sweden, has been quoted as saying, "The UN has not created a paradise, but it has avoided hell." Is awkwardness and dysfunction sufficient reason to give up such a benefit?

Wouldn't it be better to think about the reasoning behind all these rituals that at first glance seem so disconcerting? I am thinking about international summits, for example. In 2003 when I was working at the Élysée,[3] I found myself, still quite young, on the terrace of the Hotel Royal in Évian, in the midst of Vladimir Putin, Hu Jintao, George W. Bush, and Jacques Chirac. We were at the G8 summit, the weather was wonderful, and the most powerful world leaders were enjoying the sunlight, talking in small committees. I sidled over to Michel Camdessus, who had taken me under his wing and remarked, "This is horrible! So much wasted time! We manage to gather the world leaders and instead of sealing them up in a room to negotiate and make decisions, we give them a few hours to wander around without doing anything." Michel Camdessus replied, "Don't be so sure. This 'wasted time' is the most important time of the summit! All the rest is just choreography. We already knew generally what was going to happen. There were a few minor changes: everyone read the paper, the translators translated, and then, during the night, the sherpas molded the speeches into shape.... Now is the moment each person can learn to understand, to sympathize, and to ask things like, what are the key issues where you live? How are your wife and children doing? All at once, the next time they pick up the phone, they are going to start off by asking for personal news before politics. That is the strength, the added value of international summits. They create cohesion and human relationships."

I was able to verify the wisdom of these words myself in 2014, during the G20 summit in Australia. We had just finished—temporarily—withthe Ukraine crisis, and international relations between Russia and the United States were chilly. Vladimir Putin even went as far as to send a Russian fleet to Brisbane! Yet in a quiet moment, far from the reporters' microphones, I was surprised to see the Russian leader chatting with Barack Obama and Narendra Modi—proof that some parts of the summit's mechanism were still working, and proof also that it is crucial that such rituals exist, even with the fleeting worries they may produce.

Learning the Unspoken Languages of Cultures

These rituals are all the more useful as the international community diversifies and the need to understand intensifies. As the United Nations announced in 2000,

> We are now faced with a paradox. This is a multilateral system put in place after the war that makes the emergence and rise of a new globalization possible, but it is globalization which has gradually made this system obsolete. In other

> words, the institutions that arose after the war were designed for an international context, while we now live in a global context. And the main challenge that our current leaders now face is how to skillfully navigate a passage from one to the other.[4]

The passage we are navigating today means going from the G7 to the G20 format—without discarding the G7—and it involves learning the language and codes of dozens of new cultures and new countries.[5] While the Americans, French, English, Germans, Japanese, Canadians, and Italians know each other well—when the English open their mouths, the French, who have been confronting them since the Hundred Years' War, know when yes means no and when no means yes![6]—figuring out as much for an Indonesian or Argentinian, or for them to figure out the same for a French person or a Canadian by only their smiles and blinks, will take a few decades.

Personally, I have learned a lot these past few years, rubbing shoulders with representatives from emerging countries and learning about the various paths their lives have taken. I have in mind a dinner where my tablemate on the left was the South African minister of finance, and my tablemate on the right was a Chinese colleague from the World Bank and the head of the IFC. We were talking about education. The South African confided, "I got my education in prison. I spent 10 years there for being a member of the

ANC [African National Congress]." The Chinese man one-upped him: "I was born in 1958, into a Muslim family in Beijing, and I saw the ravages of the Cultural Revolution. Luckily for me, Deng Xiaoping opened the borders in 1980, and I had the chance to get one of the first visas to go study in the United States. Since then, I have worshiped this man: if he had not been there, if he had left the country in the hands of the Gang of Four who succeeded Mao Zedong, China today could have been a giant North Korea." This man led Goldman Sachs in China, then a major international institution, and today he is leading the project to leverage money in his country to invest in African development? What a difference in background, particularly from my classical route as a French technocrat, having passed an exam at 18—(and taken a second exam at 23 because I loved it!)—before starting my career. When you become aware of the life experiences of your peers from emerging countries, you see that they will not necessarily have the same vision of the world as you will, and that they will not necessarily want to be chummy. A Russian told me one day, "Really, if we scare you, it is because we know what it is to be hungry, to fight. Life does not have the same value for us as it does for you Americans and Europeans, who are so well fed; you are afraid to fight, to lose your comfort. You have lost the tragic meaning of history." How can you even respond to that?

A Steep Learning Curve but Worth Our Pain

We need to learn to better understand these populations who do not share our culture, values, political systems, and life paths, and who, in addition, do not have the same appetites as 15 years ago: their expectations have been multiplied and sophisticated. I was taken by surprise myself when, during a trip to Xiamen, China, I unexpectedly came across a group of workers at a construction site along a riverbank who were in the process of lifting a church and its vicarage so they could be moved elsewhere. I never would have thought that the Chinese would have reached this stage in their development where the preservation of historic monuments was a priority—yet that is indeed the case. Let's drop our prejudices about countries and cultures that often we have not taken the time to learn about and understand. We will learn about and cooperate with them by acting in good faith so we are all on a level playing field, in other words, by recognizing their legitimate right to take a larger role in decision making and international debates. This goes both ways: leaders in emerging countries should also be able to recognize the negative effects of, for example, their environmental or monetary policies on advanced economies. But this can be done only if all of us learn to respect our differences.

This business of respecting differences will not be easy. When we see how long it has taken Europe to learn this, when we see how fragile the respect is, even when the countries in the European Union share nearly the same history, the same civilization, we can see the difficulty in extending this to other continents. It is not because we speak the same language more and more often—the same Globish (a subset of English) or the same financial or digital language—that it will be less work to do. But we don't have a choice. We are living and working together and will be doing so more and more in the future for the good of humanity. We must promote the teaching of multilateralism, explain to the public that the self-sufficiency of countries is an illusion, and that the nostalgic dream of returning to an Elizabethan England, the France of Louis XIV, Imperial Russia, the Monroe Doctrine, or the Ottoman Empire will not come to anything.

For all that, denying the differences that distinguish us from one another would be just as counterproductive. Instead, we must learn to make these differences work for us, to create opportunities to work together. I am not imagining a uniform, Babelian world. If the whole planet spoke the same language, thought the same way, there would no longer be words or thoughts. (Bio)diversity is a priceless treasure for humanity. Instead of curling up, rejecting the other to preserve our own identity, we would do better to work together to help every country in the world develop its own cultural, economic, and social resources, to help create their own luxuries to be proud of, rather than trying to copy those of other countries.[7]

The World Bank, from this point of view of working together, is a precious organization that we should use more effectively. In a little more than 70 years, it has been able to create its own culture, which we can classify as universal: a mix of American political culture (with its universalist bias), economist and financial culture, development culture, and the contributions of the original cultures of its 189 member governments.[8] The profiles are much more diversified than in the past. As I said in 2015, "Nothing is fixed for eternity. The principles [of the World Bank] are subject to debate. We must keep them alive. Some people think that we impose the same vision everywhere. This is less and less the case. We are talking more and more about our 'partners.' The Chinese tell us, 'We have as much to offer you as you have to offer us.' They are right. Our institution, which could be extremely rigid—and still is, in many ways—has, bit by bit, managed to adapt and create a global model."[9]

Improve Legitimacy without Smashing Efficiency

In the mid-20th century, humanity, thanks to US vision and leadership, had succeeded in establishing visionary and useful institutions. We have already, over time, redirected these institutions' missions, combining them with complementary organizations. The UN, IMF, multilateral development banks, G7+, G20, G24, G77, FSB, European Parliament, and others are practical tools for international cooperation. Instead of deciding not to use them, let's make the most of them with a system that is not so bad. Rather than leaving them to fall apart and get bogged down in awkwardness and bureaucracy, rather than sweeping them aside, claiming that we have had enough with IMF and the World Bank, that it's better to see them disappear to escape the "tyranny of the financiers," let us focus our efforts on adapting these tools, modernizing them, and opening them up to the world and its new players: emerging countries, the private sector, and civil society.

We must move the international public domain out of the solely Westphalian system, centered on interstate relationships, where it has been stuck until now: the United Nations cannot be summarized as a union of nations, while ignoring the people; the European Union cannot be summarized as a union of states; the World Bank and IMF cannot be summarized as a meeting of shareholder governments represented by a board of directors. We must make this global governance system more accessible to people and diverse stakeholders engaged in our society and make it more transparent. It already has been made more digestible and intelligible in many ways, but often people are not aware of this. Simply putting thousands of pages of agreements, treaties, and reports online is not enough. We need to know how to promote them, to provide context and credit to these discussions and international commitments, which would make them more democratic as well. International organizations will make people dream and mobilize only when they have integrated participative democracy more into their action procedures and decision making.

In this new approach to global governance, one of our priorities must be to find an appropriate balance between effectiveness and legitimacy. Efficiency is the temptation of a directorate of the leaders of the most powerful countries (those of the G7 or the defunct G8) to instruct the rest of the world under the influence of their own interests—there is no question that decision making is faster with seven or eight. Legitimacy is the endeavor of everyone who feels they are a stakeholder in these decisions, whether they live in Trinidad and Tobago, the United States, or China, whether they are the president of the republic, a minister of finance, an entrepreneur, or simply a citizen. The G20 was created in 1998 to respond to the Asian economic crisis by gathering together the central bankers and ministers of finance of the 20 largest powers: the international community acknowledged that the seven or eight richest countries could no longer be the planet's sole decision makers.

But this framework, expanded to 20 megaphones, is reaching its limits today: in a world that is now interdependent and ultraconnected, how do you make sure you are listening to everyone who is not sitting around the table (and they are the majority)? How do you make sure that you take their interests into account? How do you handle problems specific to countries that are forgotten by the international financial system? How do you reintegrate those excluded by the regulations on correspondent banking, as discussed earlier? How do you impose the international standards defined by the FSB—a G20 organization, which covers 90 percent of global finance—on the 150-plus remaining states? We cannot ignore the claims of some African central bankers who feel forced to apply regulations that they were not involved in developing.

When we are faced with this problem of legitimacy, an institution like the World Bank should play a crucial role. In fact, the presence of this development bank is unique in the world: not only does it have a multinational network, but through its global access, it could be a "voice for the voiceless" within the international community. The World Bank Group is invited to G7 and G20 discussions and summits. It is a member of the FSB and is represented in a number of standard-setting organizations. This is not a symbolic status. This is access to the place where global consensus is shaped and where the rules that have an impact on the clients are discussed. In other words, the World Bank is in a position to express the opinions of people who are not present in the discussion and share their concerns, to ensure that the awareness of the interconnectedness of the planet is also heard. It can ask questions that no other organization would dream of asking: What is the impact of the new financial regulatory framework on emerging and developing economies? Are there unforeseen consequences, as in the case of correspondent banking? It can emphasize the importance of mitigating, measuring, and rolling up risk to the appropriate level. It needs to do even more: bring up the recurring question of the management of global public goods, insist on the cultural efforts required to agree on bringing high-level discussions closer to daily priorities in the field. The World Bank Group is the only one with the power to take on this mission with the intensity required. We are still not there. But we cannot give up. And it is in this spirit that I have acted each time I found myself in one or another of these forums. The need for a continued evolution of ongoing reform (time to adapt to a continually changing world rather than believing in a linear, rigid way of the status quo) is critical. Moving in that direction in a resolute manner could do a lot to improve the legitimacy of the institution. The pressure from civil society and the shareholders must drive the agenda and demand results. This is further strengthened by the current political climate around the world, in many parts of which there is no appetite to continue to write checks. Do more with what you have, be ruthlessly innovative and efficient—and repeat. It is these types of changes to the mind-set that are needed going forward.

CHAPTER 12

Time to Adjust, Though

Historically, international cooperation has been built on economic and financial cooperation. The institutions of 1944–1945 still stand as proof of this. More recently, the creation of the G20 showed that, in the event of an emergency, the global community still knows how to cooperate. The emergency, as it happens, was the financial catastrophe of 2007–2008, to which the world responded by strengthening the G20, made up of ministers of finance and central banks and itself created to respond to the 1997 Asian crisis, with a G20 made up of heads of state. The scale of the crisis called for a commitment from our top leaders. While this institutional innovation was later claimed by multiple leaders, in truth a first attempt was made back in 2003 in Évian, with an invitation by Jacques Chirac to leaders outside the G8 (such as Hu Jintao of China and King Abdullah of Saudi Arabia, as well as five African heads of state leading the New Partnership for Africa's Development). In any event, the creation of the G20 made up of heads of state largely succeeded in its response to the global financial crisis in that it avoided a complete collapse and the fragmentation of the global economy.[1]

Ready for Action!

Between 2008 and 2010, we lived through an enchanted period when the world had its back to the wall and world leaders finally tackled the financial and macroeconomic cases they had put aside until then: regulation of banking activities, the fight against tax havens and tax base erosion (a project conducted jointly by the OECD and the G20), and even the campaign against financing terrorism. The summits in London and Pittsburgh in 2009 marked the peak of this glorious G20 period when the international community displayed vision, will, and leadership, when it knew it was up to the task and avoided the shipwreck of the 1930s, with the failure of the London conference.[2] Europe itself knew how to act in concert, by completing its very first union in the eurozone: the banking union (a highly improbable prospect 25 years earlier, yet it seemed obvious in 2010–2011!).

Momentum and Leadership, However Welcome

The extraordinary spirit that had animated the international community is deflated today, to say the least. Despite the 2015 rebound and the economic slowdown that occurred, it is now obvious that the G20 has become more and more a "talk shop" where domestic agendas are carried out, as the global crisis is perceived to be less acute and less pressing than before. The G20 is not far from looking like a "G-Zero" where the O-H-I-O strategy reigns. The ineffectiveness is particularly flagrant regarding a matter particularly dear to me, that of infrastructure financing: no progress has been made despite the strength of the evidence, that being the vast amount of global liquidity available compared to the immense need. What are we waiting for?

I hope American readers will forgive a European detour: The European problems, exacerbated by the euro and refugee crises and brought to a boil by the referendum on Brexit and the decision of the British to leave a European Union denounced by populists, should not cause us to disregard the progress made by what we have built together since 1950. Because the European framework is a complicated idea that tends to get separated into technique and superstructure—to the detriment of the original spirit nourished by twin cities and exchanges between schools and students—supporters often find themselves on the defensive, while they should be proud of what they have made. Moreover, these hesitations tend to obscure the important part: Europe has the means to act! If the Brexit crisis revealed one thing, it is that Europe's best chance is the Franco-German pairing: the original alliance of the economic leader (Germany) and the military and diplomatic leader (France), who have now become two powerful engines between east and west, north and south, who can pull up the rest of the EU, enabling it to make its mark on the world stage. The world does not have the luxury of a weak

Europe while fires rage from Ukraine to the Sahel. This continent that dreamed, 20 years ago, of an "ever closer union among the people," embodied a project that became a model for the world: a model of common values, built on democracy, human rights, industry recognition, a laboratory for learning to live together. This project remains a model for the future that we have the duty to protect. If we do not succeed in Europe, what other group of countries could we expect to manage it? We have the tools, the ideas, the institutions. We have the means to achieve our goals. But these tools are worthless if Europe does not find leaders to provide direction, or support from its people to encourage them and move them in the right direction.

France in particular, in light of the election of Emmanuel Macron and the symbol it represents, has a specific responsibility in this in the sense that it still has a chance to exert real—and in truth largely disproportionate with respect to its economic and demographic weight—influence on global governance. Whether it is the IMF with Christine Lagarde, until recently at the ECB with Jean-Claude Trichet, at the WTO with Pascal Lamy, at the World Bank with the position I held, or even from our highly coveted permanent seat on the UN Security Council, France still controls a set of attributes that we can mobilize to make our voice heard within globalization. But this voice will be heard only if it uses Europe as its amplifier. Seen from Washington, Europe is self-evident, just as France is self-evident within the European Union. Let us rise to the occasion! French weakness in Europe explains some of the European weakness in the world, at a time when Europe's need is immense. The French influence is positively, as well as negatively, disproportionate.

I belong to the generation that breathed a united Europe into life. We are not going to be the ones to break the chain. After Brexit, we have to avoid rancor and simplicity. Let's be an example to others! Assume the historic responsibility that is ours to exercise our prerogatives, use our capacity for action to grant new life to a project that, for many of us, has inspired our professional callings and obligations. As I had the chance to say at a conference, half formally and half flippantly: "We've been dating long enough, it's high time we got a room!"[3] It is time to finally take a quantum leap toward a new type of federalism, perhaps in concentric circles, to choose the revolution of the United States of Europe instead of the end of the Roman Empire. In a way, Europe was constructed out of a series of crises and has always, up until now, found the energy to rebound at the last minute. But the fact that it has managed to do so for 60 years is not proof that it can continue to do so for 60 more, and beyond. History has not been written. It is up to us.

What is true for Europe is to a large extent true for the rest of the world. The tools that we use to work together, as imperfect as they are, are crucial. Our current hesitations should not cause us to shun the G20's capacity for action, even if this model of cooperation would be infinitely less integrated and advanced than the European model. In either case, we have the people at the table who have the capacity to make decisions and therefore to get things done. The members of the G20 are majority shareholders of the IMF and the World Bank, as with most international financial institutions. They have a global and regional ability to lead. They are able to influence international financial regulation through the FSB. The weight of their economies confers powerful clout and mobilization on them. This is not nothing and suggests how, by providing precise objectives, these countries and this forum could contribute to advancing the common good.

Making Finance a Global Governance Tool and Not an Agenda Item

The G20, even if it is not perfect, is now the most effective and representative forum for global economic governance available. It is the only globalization location where markets meet institutions. What are we waiting for to make it something more than a place for finance ministers and central bankers to meet three or four times a year or for heads of state to meet once a year—something more than a place for technical discussions on exchange rate policies, banking regulations, or inflation rates? To deal with the real questions that affect the future of humanity?

To make finance something more than a mechanism, an agenda item? To bring to the table the fact that we have the resources to act, and ask ourselves, in practical terms, how do we harness the energy? How do we encourage cooperation between public, private, and community players? What methods of cooperation do we use? How do we adapt regulations? What controls and incentives do we use? What instructions do we give to institutions in which G20 members are majority shareholders, such as the World Bank and the IMF? How do we mobilize all these resources for the 2015 commitments?

I cannot emphasize often enough how perfect the case for dealing with infrastructure is. Separately and all together, G20 members are able to take all the regulatory and financial obstacles into account, mobilize expertise, train talent, and define how to create a new and recognized "infrastructure asset class," able to attract a significant amount of the world's savings under the best conditions, far from zero, or even negative rate investments.

What are we waiting for to make the G20 and its train of international institutions real leadership centers—for shared leadership? To make them decision-making and implementation centers, force mobilization and intelligence mobilization sites? To make them integration and convergence forums, places for practical consideration of expectations and needs? To make them innovation and economic, regulatory, financial, and social centers for testing ideas and defining standards, global laboratories for the painful but profitable public–private cooperation?[4]

A series of satellite organizations around the G20 are just waiting to be better used: the B20 (Business 20) brings together companies from member countries, the L20 (Labor 20) gathers unions, the T20 (Think 20) combines think tanks, not to mention the W20 (Women 20) and the P20 (Public 20). What are we waiting for to make these global gatherings into practical work sites, and not just talk shops and platforms for declarations of principle? These are training centers for the silent revolution with the potential to change the world. Let's lead the system with a vision and a philosophy—that of makers, inventors, builders, drivers, and catalysts—that give it flesh, meaning, substance, heart! This is the best way we currently have to avoid seeing the world shattered by the forces of fragmentation. We have had the intelligence to create the tools; let us grab them and use them.

Choosing an Existing Path

The G20 summit in September 2016 in Hangzhou in southwest China represented an important moment in global economic governance in several respects. Not only was it the first time that China, the second-largest economy in the world, hosted such a summit, but it was also the first time that the G20 foresaw defining an action plan for the application of the SDGs set in the 2030 Agenda for Sustainable

Development. Back in spring 2016, led by China, the G20 published its first declaration by the presidency on climate change. This plants the seeds of a promising future for international cooperation in this effort, which we should encourage. This message was echoed in the speech of President Xi Jinping in Davos in January 2017, when, in the marked absence of US and EU leadership, he celebrated the benefits of globalization.

The G20 is starting to take the full measure of its capacity for action, its obligation to show leadership and mobilization, and its ability to serve as an example. China knows, in part because of its self-interest, that it has an important role to play in encouraging other emerging countries to a shared consensus on international economic cooperation—not necessarily the same policies, as the British economist Jim O'Neill noted recently,[5] but appropriate policies to implement in various parts of the world. In this case, during China's presidency of the G20, they urged all participants of the future summit to include strict application of SDGs in their medium-term to long-term national development goals, aligning domestic efforts precisely with the international agenda. It is engaged in a major development promotion campaign, encouraging leaders to reconnect with their populations. This unique opportunity represents application of the 2030 agenda, refocused on the human element—scientific research, interconnectivity, institutional innovation,[6] improved governance—and facts; participants in the working group ahead of the summit in Hangzhou praised the openness and transparency of China during these preparations. Finally, and most importantly, it has made infrastructure investment a priority (particularly industrialization in Africa and less advanced countries), designed as a pillar of sustainable global growth in the short and long term. I welcome these efforts and give my loud and earnest support for shared and responsible leadership from China and the United States!

Infrastructure: What's the Hold-up?

In Chapter 9, I discussed my view that the issue of financing infrastructure is the best path for humanity to succeed, in practice, in working in concert for a sustainable future. In this field, as with others such as climate change or big data, multilateral development banks (MDBs) and the G20 offer valuable laboratories of planetary consensus.[7] There is no better place in the world to test tools and ideas, to take a few risks, to agree to make mistakes, and to try again another way. But to do this, we need to be capable, as I said in a 2015 interview, "of testing an idea in one country, without a uniform vision." You need to "ask what is specific to each country, understand what can be replicated elsewhere or needs to be adapted. Some companies are more successful than others by encouraging this capacity."[8] MDBs have an essential role to play at the world, regional, and national levels in developing new models and paradigms and forging holistic approaches. Beyond their obligation to innovate, they have been entrusted with a coordination mission that is crucial to encourage the harmonization between the new and old initiatives supporting the SDGs, but also to encourage the exchange of information between all actors of global governance—governments, the private sector, development banks, international organizations, and civil society. That is the beating heart of consensus within humanity.

This historic role of MDBs will be adopted by the establishment of the Global Infrastructure Forum, which launched officially in April 2016 and is set to meet every year. Enrolled by the international community in the Addis Ababa Action Agenda, this forum is co-organized by the MDBs based on a rotating presidency, in partnership with G20, G24, G77, and G7+ representatives, as well as United Nations agencies, among others. Such an association should enable states and development partners to work together to overcome existing shortcomings in infrastructure on the global scale by relying on existing multilateral collaboration mechanisms. As its president noted in a short speech, the forum "will encourage a greater range of voices to be heard, particularly from developing countries"; it will "support country-led approaches to planning, executing, supervising, and evaluating sustainable, resilient, inclusive, and well-prioritized infrastructure programs and robust infrastructure frameworks"; it will "systematically [encourage] the participation of all stakeholders—namely public authorities, users, the private sector and civil society—[in] scheduling, financing for domestic resource mobilization as well as national and international financing, and operating infrastructure services."[9] This type of gathering place is crucial to nourish the spirit of cooperation. It is not a new tool per se but the appropriate coordination of existing ones.

The other major global challenge where the G20, as well as development banks, could be better used is that of financing climate change mitigation. As Mark Carney emphasized in his London speech, "an effective market response to the risks of climate change, as well as technology and policies to confront it, must be based on information transparency" and an improvement of this "on costs, opportunities, and climate change risks." While "there are already close to 400 initiatives aimed at providing this information," such as the Carbon Disclosure Project, which provides investors, businesses, and policy makers with information on the environmental impact of companies, cities, states, and regions at risk of exceeding limits on carbon emissions, the G20 must "do more to publish consistent, comparable, reliable, and clear information concerning the carbon intensity of various assets." Meeting these standards requires "coordination that only organizations like the G20 and Financial Stability Board can implement." Hence, the Task Force on Climate-Related Financial Disclosures was established in January 2016, presided over by Michael Bloomberg, to publish climate information and "to design and propose a voluntary standard for publication of information on carbon producing or emitting companies."[10] First deliverables have been discussed and implemented throughout 2017. While MDBs have a key role to play as an effective catalyst for a reliable and resilient carbon economy, they also have a key mission to ensure coordination on a global scale. This is the aim of the Carbon Pricing Leadership Coalition, created by the World Bank Group—in collaboration with more than 90 companies and 20 governments, among other private and public actors—to respond to the need to accelerate global action on setting a price for carbon.[11] Meeting first in Washington and then in Paris in spring 2016, the Carbon Pricing Leadership Coalition quickly took advantage of the energy created by the Paris climate accord to gather an increasing number of partner countries, promote effective carbon pricing, and distribute information on these mechanisms, via new "principles for effective carbon pricing" in particular.

In terms of collective action, big data is another future field where MDBs have a strategic role to play, as data managers for development. Not only is big data a "common good" that is important to manage as such, appropriately freed from the GAFA monopolies and open to all, but the construction of reliable data, accessible to all, is an essential raw material for establishing effective development policies on a global scale, making suitable decisions, and being accountable. Also in this field, MDBs are committed to developing global consensus on the principles and standards for consolidating development data and continuous improvement in knowledge-sharing methods. Priorities to enable everyone to contribute to solving global development challenges include helping countries obtain measurable results, improving information access, and encouraging use of open-source software and open development. The new World Bank Live platform—which enables Internet users around the world to participate in online discussions—is now an important part of the meetings held with the IMF.

As you can see, there are practical approaches opening up to us at all levels of society and in all countries of the world to make the international commitments of 2015 something more than pious vows and enable the forces of unity to overcome the forces of entropy.

These forums and places are critical places. They are far from perfect, and much needs to be done to improve both legitimacy and effectiveness. They are where we have avoided the sinking of the world by finance. They are where we have acknowledged that we need to regain control over the system and where we have started to move, albeit not as fast and as effectively as one could have wished. They are where a consensus can be built around common good. But they are also where doubts resurfaced in 2017, sometimes in a brutal and direct manner. They are thus where the crossroads we are facing is made visible.

Our responsibility now is to get everyone involved: national and international leaders must lead by example and mobilize while profiting from the best of the institutions they direct and participate in; companies, investors, international organizations, associations, and citizens must use the various instruments and networks available today (every day there are more and more) to help the "silent revolution" grow that will change the world. We are all key players in global governance. If we all consciously consent to act, we will learn to understand one another. Regulatory tools, financial incentives, means of exerting pressure on stakeholders: all the pieces of the puzzle are there. Don't throw them away—these pieces will build our future.

Our future starts with our capacity to finance a sustainable development of our planet, core to common good today, as will be discussed in Part 4.

PART FOUR

Finance Serving the Common Goodand the Sustainable Development of the World

Part 4 discusses financing sustainable development, which can be considered to a certain extent as a proxy for the common good. When we agree to shared objectives, the path to get to those objectives maybe uncertain, but finance can surely be one of the most effective mechanisms to help us achieve them.

The sheer magnitude of the goals we have set (and so desperately need for our world), such as the SDGs, requires us to revisit the basics of finance. We have to establish new ways of operating and working hand in hand. A refreshed approach calls for a combined movement involving the public sector, the private sector, and civil society. This approach requires a genuinely new type of partnership using transparency and honest communications to avoid the bear traps of suspicion. If we can achieve this, then we are going to be well positioned to put in place keystones that will help bring together the main principles of how we work together and maximize the use of the power of finance. The choice is in our hands and setting out some concrete examples of how we can all move now is the best way to make real what we wish for.

Chapter 13 looks at the specific roles of the multilateral development banks and reviews some of the innovations I have led over the past few years; these show that real change is possible and provide tangible examples of how things can be done. Chapter 14 considers the limitation of the model in today's world and how we need to adapt the model and our instruments to finance sustainable development. Chapter 15 highlights the importance of cooperation between the public and private sectors and the challenges they face; it also discusses several instances where progress has been made. Finally, in Chapter 16, I bring it all together to show how we can put all of these principles into action, citing as examples healthcare, education, and the refugee crises. I show that where we have reasserted control over finance and joined all forces, the common good can be served effectively.

CHAPTER 13

The Multilateral Development Banks as a Laboratory?

The multilateral system is a special environment. It offers one of the best laboratories within which to develop and test new ideas. Its different sources and uses of capital and return requirements (ranging from grants or loans at zero percent financial return at market levels), together with the ability and mechanisms to accept input from the whole spectrum of stakeholders (donors to users to investors to civil society organizations), place the system in a unique position.

The experiments I piloted at the World Bank in recent years have only strengthened my conviction that financial innovation can be used for good. Multilateral development banks (MDBs) are institutional proof that controlled finance can contribute to bringing sustainable solutions to questions of development. The innovations that they are capable of introducing can create visible, progressive transformations—let's use them to make a difference and change the world!

Unleashing Billions of Dollars

The first disruptive approach I was able to introduce at the World Bank, IDA+, was a new way to consider the structure of an institution's capital by optimizing and restructuring the World Bank Group's own funds to increase its lending capacity. The International Development Association (IDA) is the concessional financing arm of the World Bank Group,[1] created in 1960.[2] The capital it raises every three years from donor nations is used to allocate grants and concessional loans to beneficiary countries. Loans are repaid to IDA in due time; as such, it is not possible to envision them being returned to the original donors as dividends. IDA holds significant assets—cash or loans—in its accounts without having debt per se: technically, these assets could be considered as constituting its own equity. These funds are considerable—more than $150 billion in 2016.[3] They can be used to support borrowing activities and thus, through leverage, to create a significant capacity for supplemental funding or to supply guarantees for additional loans. In other words, IDA can significantly increase its firepower to benefit the poor. IDA+ follows the same idea of better utilizing the capital base of the MDBs and benefiting from their balance sheet structure. This is a way to demonstrate the opportunities this unique banking model offers to clients and shareholders. Depending on the scenarios, an annual capacity of more than $10 billion can be created. This amount was finally agreed upon in

December 2016 and developed during 2017, after I left. Twenty-five billion dollars will be borrowed against this newly recognized equity and will be lent to the countries in need at very attractive rates and at zero additional cost to donors and shareholders such as the United States.

Insurance: An Obvious Tool but Still Underutilized

The second innovative approach to finance is the use of insurance to protect against natural catastrophes and pandemics. When I arrived at the World Bank, I saw that insurance was underutilized in development finance, although it is an instrument suitable to manage shocks of all kinds and to limit their long-term impact. An earthquake in Nepal, an Ebola outbreak in West Africa, a tropical storm in Vanuatu, or even economic shocks that are faced by emerging and developing economies are severe obstacles to the convergence efforts deployed there. Yet actors in development rarely use this financial product. There are many reasons why: It could be as simple as a bad personal experience leading to lack of confidence in insurers, which they believe will always find a way to minimize liability. Quite often, beneficiaries as well as certain donors believe that once the insurance premium is paid, if the insured event does not happen, it is "lost money," without any visible material impact. Finally, the pricing question is complex, since the majority of the domains explored are new and insurance models are not yet stable (let alone the concerns some people have about excessive profits being grabbed by private insurers).

In truth, insurance always seems more costly before the accident. I certainly considered all these objections when I defended my idea before the World Bank Group, but I also believe in the power of demonstration: as with any innovation, we have to try it out before we can evaluate it and improve it.

The experiment in the Pacific using this insurance-based approach, combined with an approach based on capital markets, was crowned with success. Our pilot project of catastrophe risk insurance came from this fact: the Pacific islands are exposed to a variety of extreme risks (tropical storms, earthquakes, and tsunamis). In the past 60 years, these risks have affected nearly 10 million people. However, given the size of the Pacific Ocean, the correlation risks are not nearly as big as we might think. There are options for diversification, which is why the region is open to an insurance-based solution. Japan is one of the largest donors, and insurers wanted to be involved as long as the World Bank positioned itself as a natural intermediary. In other words, we were able to show off our creativity better in this zone.

Separately, in June 2014, the World Bank Group issued its first "catastrophe bonds" (or cat bonds) related to the risk of earthquakes and tropical cyclones in 16 Caribbean nations. These bonds allowed us to transfer the risk of a natural catastrophe to investors and avoid the issuer having to reimburse the bond capital if a major event occurred. The World Bank notably developed the MultiCat Program, which also provided the possibility of reinsurance through the Caribbean Catastrophe Risk Insurance Facility, to which France and other countries directly contributed. In addition, contingent lines of credit (Catastrophe Deferred Drawdown Options, or Cat DDO) have for several years allowed the emergency provision of immediate liquidity to countries hit by natural disasters. This is how, after tropical storms hit the islands of Tonga in 2014 and the archipelago of Vanuatu in 2015, they could be assisted in the span of just a few weeks.

The Case of Ebola and Pandemics

I followed the same line of thought for Ebola, even though, unlike with natural disasters, it is difficult to precisely identify the moment when a pandemic takes hold and when one is fully eradicated. Also, the damages felt are naturally different and spread over time. But we know that the Ebola crisis had a devastating effect on the economies and development gains in Guinea, Liberia, and Sierra Leone. In April 2015, the World Bank estimated the total GDP loss for these countries at $2.2 billion. The economic and human costs of the next pandemic could be even greater.[4] Although it may be difficult to envision now just how to insure a country against a pandemic—Liberia against Ebola, for instance—it is equally impossible to guarantee that, in the event of an epidemic, we have the financial capacity to rapidly contain the problem and organize a line of defense to prevent the shift from epidemic to pandemic, which would be even deadlier and more costly. With this in mind, the World Bank Group kicked off some brainstorming with the World Health Organization (WHO) and a number of other partners, particularly from the private sector, to refine a global mechanism for emergency funding in the event of pandemics for accredited and pre-approved countries and international responders: with dozens of millions in annual premiums and the availability of a cash element, we would unlock hundreds of millions of dollars in the event of real need. The initiative has been on a fast track, and the first mechanism was launched in June 2017. The participating parties have created parameters for the release mechanism using publicly available and traceable donations to set the insurance payments. The proposed coverage focuses on infectious diseases identified by the WHO as the most likely to cause major epidemics. Japan, which presides over the G7, was the first to commit $50 million in 2016 to kick off the new initiative. Just the fact that the idea could become a plausible model, which insurance companies are considering covering, is a major step forward!

Sharing Risk at the Global Level

The third innovative financial approach also relates to risk management: Exposure Exchange Agreements

(EEAs) rely on the principle of diversification. The idea is to allow MDBs to manage their risk of concentration and thus limit the impact of ratings exposure by exchanging this exposure with other MDBs. The overall risk of the system doesn't change, but it is better distributed among the institutions,[5] which can then free up the capital they need to cover the risks of concentration in specific countries and regions. The World Bank Group first tested this solution internally at the International Bank for Reconstruction and Development (IBRD) and the Multilateral Investment Guarantee Agency (MIGA), freeing up resources for supplemental investments in Brazil and Panama. In December 2015, new agreements were signed between the African Development Bank, the Inter-American Development Bank, and IBRD: for a negligible financial cost to the shareholders of the three institutions, we created a $20 billion funding capacity. Resources are immediately available to achieve the SDGs!

Development Banks: A Key Tool in Our Toolbox

These diverse innovations illustrate the potential stored in financial instruments used properly: they can create financial capacity, better serve the countries and populations in need, and assist with more efficient risk management. These are only a few of the many examples of the financial solutions that MDBs can provide. I am not oversimplifying or being naïve to state that these institutions have much to gain from exploring, testing, and reinventing these fields. I am thinking particularly about the oldest field of various types of guarantees, cofinancing, loss-sharing mechanisms, and the like. There are so many approaches in which public finance holds an eminent role of responsibility. The more we mobilize public and private money together, each in its own environment or comfort zone, within the framework of clear and transparent rules, the more we will reinforce and catalyze them for a significant and noticeable result. MDBs can also cooperate with private actors to establish efficient tools; they can bring their excellent credit ratings, an increasingly rare and precious asset, as well as their intellectual capital and reputation; and they can take risks that others, lacking such advantages, cannot. MDBs could do much more good if they would think of themselves as a system—rather than a collection of institutions that can share tools, harmonize approaches, and spread risks. They have to at least try! If failure is possible, we have to recognize it and analyze it quickly. MDBs can and must play the role of financial laboratories on behalf of all of us.

More broadly, we should encourage all the initiatives, both individual and collective, that are oriented toward the COP21 and the SDGs set by the international community in 2015. Through the multiplication, from every angle, of socially responsible financial innovations, the international system will build the best new foundation. There is no limit to our imagination once we set it to work for the common good. Financial innovators of the world, unite! The past few years have seen an unprecedented coming together of different actors. This special commitment and investment of time and energy has to be protected and nurtured. As discussed earlier, the nationalistic tendencies being seen in different places around the world risk destabilizing the precarious global entente cordiale. Ensuring we work together will benefit all of us. Rolling back commitments, be those on climate or trade or regulation, could jeopardize global cooperation and growth. These mutually beneficial institutions and frameworks are not perfect, far from it. However, they represent our best chance today to get the most important players around the table, including voices for the underrepresented. That is special and worth protecting.

CHAPTER 14

Pushing Back or Extending the Frontiers of Development Finance

All the institutional investors in the world combined will soon manage $100 trillion, so you know that not all of them can invest in negative-yielding sovereign debt. There must be solutions for financing sustainable development, and these solutions have to include more than just official development assistance (ODA) or solely the actions of public institutions. Instead, we must go off the beaten path: mobilize all available forces, put the most diverse players in touch with one another, and use the financial system (its tools and institutions) as a catalyst. MDBs, including bilateral institutions like Agence française de développement (AFD, the French Development Agency) or the US Agency for International Development (USAID), have a historic role to play here—provided that they know how to reinvent themselves. Today, these organizations are being complemented by large philanthropic groups, many of which can move faster and be more targeted than their more bureaucratic cousins. Such philanthropic groups play a valuable role and are powerful and rightfully impatient allies to the MDBs and bilateral agencies.[1]

The Development Bank Model: Still Valid?

Can a few billion dollars in capital make a difference in a global economy that has a GDP of more than $75 trillion, and considering that institutional investors will soon be managing $100 trillion?

The question of the relevance of the model of the development bank paradigm is a recurring one that is doubtless never posed clearly enough. By "relevance," I mean the combination of the fact that it is unique (no one else can offer what you are offering), useful (you are really making a difference), and well adapted (you are acting in an appropriate manner). The question had already been asked before I joined the World Bank Group.[2] Now, almost two years after my departure, I still hear it. The idea kept me busy throughout 2015, because the three conferences, in Addis Ababa, New York, and Paris as discussed in Chapter 4, were meant to redefine the framework and terms of development financing.

Some people might still be tempted to ignore this question of relevance by pointing to 70 years of continuous expansion, in a world that has profoundly changed, at a level sufficiently high to prove the efficacy of the model. We can also argue that the recent establishment of the New Development Bank (also known as the BRICS Development Bank) and the China-led Asian Infrastructure Investment Bank (AIIB) confirms that this tool is still right, since newcomers are seemingly copying it with only a few adjustments. The relevance of the model is rightly regularly questioned. Whether it is relevant is still to be determined and requires constant adaptation to changes in the world.

Obsolescence is a risk, one that is more tangible today given the many changes that have occurred since the last significant readjustment of the model at the end of the 1990s, before the adoption of the MDGs. As we have already explored in some detail, the world underwent multiple shocks during the new century's first decade that should have affected the development bank's model.

The transformation of the world's economic map caused by the great strides made by the emerging economies raises some financial and governance questions. The needs of these economies have changed as their expectations have grown more sophisticated and their demands for funds have increased. The slowdown in global growth also shows how these economies are increasingly interdependent, with spillover and spillback effects.[3] These new phenomena demand the construction of a worldwide network of secure financial networks as well as broader risk sharing, involving a readjustment in the way development banks operate.

Readjustment is even more necessary because South–South cooperation is emerging in parallel. In the 1990s, the World Bank alone committed to half of all multilateral development finance, which is no longer the case today: the establishment of the AIIB and New Development Bank in 2014 clearly signaled a change in the competitive landscape. This is a positive change because competition is beneficial in general, because it strengthens the multilateral approach to cooperation after years of criticism directed toward China for its individualism, and because it can help solve the problems that we have not been able to handle alone. An additional capacity of $10 billion or even $20 billion per year, in a world where the needs are in the trillions of dollars, leaves plenty of room for everyone to contribute. There is no need to take offense at the creation of new lenders of regional and multilateral funds.

Regulatory Changes of Private Sector Banks and the Need for the MDBs to Step Up Their Game

Another structural upheaval for those active in development has been the transformation of the traditional role of banks in the financing of the economy following the global financial crisis. Because of regulatory changes and market expectations, it has become more costly and less attractive for a commercial bank to finance complex, risky, and exotic projects over the long term, in other words, far from the domestic market and its natural habitat. This is particularly clear for infrastructure, but it also rings true for health and education. The capacity for financial action is now found more often in the hands of institutional investors. Yet although these actors may be taking a central role in financing the economy, they are still not fully able to invest in emerging and developing economies. It must be recognized that they do not operate like banks. Their margins are lower.[4] They do not have branches or employees in different countries, and, for the most part, they do not really understand these economies. Add to that the fact that they have their own regulatory constraints (the most commonly known being Solvency II for insurers). Under these conditions, the MDBs clearly have a role to play as intermediaries between the immense needs identified and the many investors in search of yield and purpose, to make sure that funds are injected into attractive projects that will definitely create jobs and be profitable, under an appropriate framework. The MDBs need to have skin in the game and with that be a true catalyst for private funds, giving them the comfort to join in.

This role for the MDBs is even clearer because the private sector is now recognized as key for development. As we have seen, that is probably the biggest, and least visible, change since 2000 and the adoption of the MDGs. In the meantime, although public development aid has nearly doubled, it has declined relative to other financing sources such as direct foreign investment, transfers of funds, and, more generally, the North–South flow of private investment. Far from being a source of dirty financing, this private money is indispensable and welcome. Remember that the market financed a large share of the infrastructure produced in industrialized countries over the past two centuries, which has been satisfactory overall, whether the operators were public or private.

Let's not deprive ourselves of any of these resources. Domestic public resources, which were used in the 19th century, along with savings, to equip the Industrial Revolution, are central to the financing of economies and must be increased today with a higher, more evenly balanced tax.[5] But is it not equally relevant to draw from the enormous reservoir of private savings that globalization has made available to the planet as effectively as possible? And could we not draw on public transfers to create a leverage effect? In a world where the new agenda is to go from "billions to trillions" to finance the sustainable development of our planet, the SDGs as well as the COP21 objectives demand that we tap the potential from all financing sources and capabilities available worldwide.[6] Nevertheless, these resources must be channeled so they can be directed to projects that make sense, to work for inclusive growth and shared prosperity that benefits the poorest first. This is where the need comes in to implement the necessary means for effective "intermediation," by using all types of instruments that can distribute risks, particularly the key instrument—guarantees.[7] These instruments can be of different kinds (including credit, foreign exchange, and political risk) and are one of the most powerful engines to mitigate risks and mobilize resources for social objectives.

The most recent change to affect the MDB model is that of taking into account new shared global concerns such as climate, fragility related to migration and pandemics, and even the equality of men and women. These questions surround and will even go beyond traditional global public goods. Faced with an alarmingly fast increase in losses attributable to natural disasters tied to human impacts on climate, as we have seen, climate financing has become a subject in its own right with new products (green bonds, for example) and new approaches (in terms of types of projects, rating, and even risk management). Fragility is also a case that requires a paradigm shift: it requires mobilizing capital for high-risk projects but also developing new financial instruments to mitigate these risks.

Deciding whether questions like gender, diversity, and minorities need to be taken into account in financing policies starts by acknowledging that the change in thinking has been too slow here. When an institution like the World Bank has to work with Uganda, which has a restrictive vision of some human rights, should it put conditions on its aid? And should it do so without repeating the past mistakes attached to some conditions. Fifteen years ago, no one had really addressed this question. Now is the time.

In the past 15 years, an approach to finance via the prism of gender has slowly spread, based on the idea that finance can help promote women in society. This is a smart bet, particularly in emerging and developing countries, where women prove their determination and initiative every day. I visited Henan, China, where two small and medium-size enterprises were run by Chinese people and supported by the Bank of Luoyang, itself financed by International Finance Corporation (IFC) as part of a program introduced by the World Bank to make it easier for women entrepreneurs to gain access to financing. One of these entrepreneurs was the head of an online commodities trading platform, very focused on the "new economy," and the other was an Ikea supplier, who took me on a brisk tour of the giant hallways where the products with "barbarian names" used by the Swedish furniture maker were lined up. The contrast was startling, but each of these women entrepreneurs had real charisma and the same urge to create.

However, the question of how to approach these global public goods remains to be addressed. For many years, the temptation was to create "global funds," for example, a fund for education, forestry, or the oceans. The approach had its virtues, particularly in terms of visibility, fund-raising, and, in some cases, results, but it did not handle interdependencies between all the questions, which a more integrated financial institution should be able to respond to in a satisfactory manner. We have yet to find the perfect balance. In all of these fields, a development bank clearly has a capacity and specific duty to act where no one else could.

Rebooting the System While Preserving Its Essence

Those involved in development and multilateral institutions, in particular, must learn from these major changes and adapt the ways in which they operate. How do we establish the optimum size for a balance sheet and what incentives do we use to maximize it? How can we ensure that funds are managed productively in a context of tight public budgets and increased public sensitivity to cost effectiveness? How do we promote new financial instruments, including those for green financing, catastrophic risk management, and support for women entrepreneurs? How do we encourage multilateral institutions to integrate private sector partners into their activities? How do we develop the capacity of these banks to mobilize institutional investors and their intermediation? How can we extend and value the key instrument of guarantees? There are so many questions that must be faced squarely in the debate over the revision of the risk category and financing of the World Bank Group and other similar institutions.[8] These questions and how to provide practical answers were at the heart of the few years I spent at the World Bank. I enjoyed success, but I also felt frustrated, and left with one conviction: change is necessary and doable. That is what the following sections are about.

Making the Most out of the Precious Public Money Made Available

When I joined the World Bank in early 2013, I quickly observed that for most teams, the debate over the increase in capital granted in 2009–2010 was over. This debate occurred after the World Bank had made a major effort, reaching a new record of committing over $44 billion, before returning to more modest levels of commitment of around $15 billion per year, where it seemed content to stay. Rebuilding IDA's resources at the end of 2013 was dependent on the tight budgetary resources of larger donors, particularly in Europe, even though the institution was fixed on the ambitious objective of eradicating poverty by 2030. With a total commitment capacity estimated at $50 billion per year for the whole World Bank Group, the general sentiment was that to do more was impossible.[9] The idea of rethinking the levels was not really considered as an option. From a financial point of view, the priority was to ensure that the bank made the most of the resources available.

For my part, I arrived with a few simple ideas in mind. My main conviction was the following: The World Bank Group is not a global development agency, or at least not just that! It is also a bank, and that is precisely the difference between that institution and others that work in the same field. What does it mean to be a bank? First, it has a balance sheet, and therefore has the capacity to project itself into the future and play with time. Next, it has the ability to take risks, measure them, and select the best way in which to manage them. It has access to all types of markets and their associated infrastructures (from ratings to swap agreements and reinsurance contracts). It is able to form and structure partnerships. It does not depend on budgetary support decided on an annual basis, or the ability to make profits and keep them to build and develop its capital. To be named "World Bank" is incredible, if you want to work in such a field. There's really no better name and brand!

These ideas were not obvious to the various World Bank Group stakeholders yet. As one of the people assisting me with financial reform put it, the general understanding of the World Bank's model up to that point was something like "Give me the money so I can spend it."[10] My interpretation had been "I don't know where the money comes from and I don't care, but I know my idea is good and your job is to make sure that my idea or my project is financed correctly." The idea that the institution is a bank first, and thereby offers flexibility as well as interesting opportunities and constitutes a key instrument in the international plan, was not fully appreciated by the system. I was convinced that operating with the banking model and taking full advantage of all of its potential would be the most efficient way. If the economic and financial circumstances that necessitated a restructuring of the system call for the financial capacity and paradigms accepted until now to be reconsidered, they should also preserve its essence. A development bank is, before anything else, a bank, and that is what makes it relevant.

The reform carried out at the World Bank was therefore intended both as a readjustment of traditional approaches and an attempt to adapt to a new global environment. Among the four objectives that I set, reestablishing the financial viability and making the model self-sufficient and sustainable were fundamental: it was a question of both capacity and credibility. In fact, any bank has the obligation to be profitable in order to grow.[11] Profits not distributed are the basis for an increase in capital, which in turn develops financial capacity. The mechanics of this virtuous cycle seems clear, but it is lost sight of too often. In contrast, a vicious cycle is set up when expenses exceed revenues and capital decreases, first in real terms and then in nominal terms. In a bank, revenue and income must be linked: there is no wiggle room like there is with governments, which can use deficits as an option. This is also a question of credibility for an institution that explains to its public and private partners on a daily basis how to manage their financial situations and adjust their accounts. When you are entrusted with public resources, in the form of capital or grants, you have an obligation to show that this money is used in a sustainable manner.

A potential increase in capital will be required only if it is clear that all additional capital will benefit clients and not a system under pressure. It is management's responsibility to ensure that the institution does its homework.

A Useful, Unique, and Well-Adapted Model

The reform conducted by the World Bank was radical and perceived as such. The institution needed it. In fact, it had broadly anticipated the request expressed by the G20 to optimize the MDBs' balance sheets, to restructure and develop over the long term, rather than show off who had the larger balance sheet.

I found myself, quite unexpectedly, recalling these fundamentals while I was traveling in Xiamen, China. During an official banquet, the deputy governor of Fujian Province (one of China's most prosperous provinces and one that is open to private capital), gave a slightly sarcastic toast: "Monsieur Badré, the World Bank is very nice, but if it were a Chinese bank, you would be the 10th largest; you are not that big despite being a 'World Bank'!"

My host had put his finger on the truth, but the implication was not one I let trouble me. I replied, "Certainly, but don't forget that it is easy to make a bank grow: it is harder to make it grow up healthy. It is easy to churn out credit, make a ton of loans. It is harder to make sure that borrowers can repay them. In addition, the size of the balance sheet is not the only thing that counts. The ability to work with others and to foster cooperation is also important—and this is the case with China, for which the World Bank opened up development a lot by working with Deng Xiaoping, in particular.... Beyond the numbers, it is this intangible reality that makes all the difference."

What makes the World Bank useful, unique, and well adapted in this case, and what justifies its existence and role in this new era that has begun? Its relevance will rely on the right combination of the following ingredients:

- Its capital and its knowledge
- The capacity to be public/private and engage in partnerships of all kinds
- Its focus on innovation and implementation
- Its openness
- The full leverage of its global dimension

The World Bank Group is not a consulting firm or a savings bank. It provides both *financial* and *consulting* services. This is what differentiates it from most UN agencies, for example. The other MDBs share this characteristic, even if the relative proportion of finance and advice may vary from one institution to another. This supposes that the World Bank maximizes use of its financial capacity while respecting the restrictions imposed by its rating, and protects its knowledge, making it profitable and accessible in an appropriate, simple, and attractive manner, to all of its clients and partners. The knowledge must be constantly updated and available to the system continuously.

The World Bank Group includes different institutions that have both *public* and *private* clients. People often talk about IFC as the bank's "private arm" and IBRD as its "public arm." This is largely true. But what makes the World Bank unique is its solid foundation with both groups of clients. Most MDBs are oriented toward the public sector. The European Bank for Reconstruction and Development is mostly focused on the private sector. The Inter-American Development Bank in Latin America is continuously expanding its private sector approach with strong support from its shareholders, but none of them yet have the depth or breadth of the World Bank Group, with its potential to unite public and private forces. However, this potential is not enough. This is not only about having the private sector on one side and the public sector on another but about combining these forces when needed. Yet this combining is not always clear, despite the progress in recent years. This is why one of the reform objectives was to make sure that the collaboration with private actors was real, effective, and not artificial, knowing that in a world where suspicion between various actors remains, a new, audacious approach was necessary.

With its central placement and ability to bring all of the actors together ("convening power"), the World

Bank Group has a unique ability to structure all types of *partnerships* from fiduciary funds to working groups by going through coalitions. If partnerships are possible, it is because of the World Bank's banking and operational structure, but also, and perhaps most importantly, because of the entrepreneurial spirit of its teams. The task still remains to better organize and prioritize all these forces based on the priorities suggested by shareholders, and in particular to better structure the capacity of the bank to mobilize capital granted by third parties and not let bureaucracy consume it all.

In the post–financial crisis world, development banks must be as much financing tools as mobilization tools. They need to use their own capital directly, and they also need to use their resources indirectly to mobilize money from others, in particular, from private investors. Clearly, financing is a priority. It provides a voice to attract attention and command respect. That is why it was important to develop the World Bank Group's capacity for engagement. But MDBs also have a major role to play in generating leverage, which in my mind is the only way to obtain capital and innovative products. The *From Billions to Trillions* report was a strong declaration in this sense: "Due to our vast expertise, MDBs and the IMF are drivers of finance for the entire development community, with business models that we authorize not only to provide much needed policy advice, but also to act as a catalyst in mobilizing and obtaining funds from various sources—moving from traditional 'development financing' to a broader and more global 'finance for development' approach."[12]

For a long time, most development banks have mobilized private capital, in the sense that any investment has an exponential effect that can attract additional private investments. At IFC, which is more specific in its accounts, mobilized capital is raised for remuneration via various channels.[13] But MDBs can go even further. They have a specific duty to act as an intermediary with institutional investors, which now are more central to the financing of the economy, to steer their funds to more interesting projects. Over the decades, they have shown that it is possible to generate real yields from emerging and developing markets. They can help overcome the risk perception gap, which discourages actors from investing today in some countries. They have the advantage of being less costly, thanks to their high-quality rating, their instruments, their credit mitigation guarantees, and even their technical assistance. They can, for example, channel appropriate funding via refinancing of local banks. They can also help countries develop solid regulatory frameworks and a business climate likely to attract growing funding streams.[14] They can still contribute to the development of capital markets and local financial markets—these can represent opportunities for domestic savings and stable and sustainable sources of financing for the economy, often key to a country's capacity to support its own development.

Helping Others Help Themselves

I am a staunch supporter of including this last lever. As our water group says, "There are many reasons to encourage local savings and the formation of financial markets in emerging and developing countries: setting up local savings and not seeing it go elsewhere encourages a better job-resources balance and decreases financing costs."[15] MDBs have a crucial role to play in triggering this virtuous cycle. In local capital markets, which "most often only exist in an embryonic state and only handle symbolic business, most often for the purpose of financing the Treasury,"[16] they can use their AAA rating to issue local currency: by drawing the attention of investors and stimulating business, the local market gains in volume and sets an anchor for future developments for the greater benefit of companies and governments. Since 2011 the World Bank has issued over $9 billion in bonds, denominated in two dozen currencies, including, for the first time, Ugandan shillings, Thai baht, and Chinese yuan. For its part, the IFC has issued 14 bonds in national currencies since 2002, in countries where it has often been the first international issuer in the bond market. It issued bonds in Rwanda, and negotiations are ongoing with other developing countries in Africa and Asia, as well as with developing countries in Europe and Latin America. In fact, the mechanism offers opportunities regardless of the level of advancement of the economies. By enabling Rwandan stakeholders to purchase a World Bank Group note in Rwandan francs, for example, the bank provides them the assurance, thanks to the AAA rating, that this is a high-quality note. That gives the market visibility both in terms of price (we know how much a AAA note is worth, so we can invest on this basis) and confidence. Another example is India, which is certainly more advanced, but whose currency is not convertible. At a time when its economy was in chaos on the market, by being able to issue a rupee note "offshore,"[17] it could recycle Indian savings to invest in the national economy. This is a convincing illustration of the usefulness of finance in the service of the public good.

But MDBs can go even further. The tools already at their disposal are valuable and would create even more value if they were multiplied and adapted to meet the specific needs of each country, each partner, each investor—and to meet each global challenge. The objective would always be to create confidence. MDBs, which have long acted as a bridge between the public and private sectors, able to gather a variety of actors around important development questions, have a responsibility to show the way in this field.

In this rapidly changing world, *innovation* is a prerequisite. We have seen how finance has been inventive in this field. The tools used wisely can create financial capacity to better serve clients, or even help manage risks more efficiently. This attractive characteristic of the development bank model is often ignored or overlooked. One of my priorities in the reform led by the World Bank was to emphasize precisely this capacity for innovation that an AAA rating confers on the bank—as well as its staff of several thousand highly skilled employees and its capacity for mobilization—to strive to better adapt themselves to new needs and expectations. People have often reproached me for being a "banker"; I completely understand this criticism. But I sincerely believe that a banker can also contribute to making a difference and helping the most vulnerable. Finance has clearly shown its potential for destroying value: there still is time for it to show its usefulness.

No institution other than the World Bank Group and other MDBs have a real capacity to play the role of financial laboratory for the global community. To have an idea of the underlying force, all you have to do is count its flagship publications, which are widely recognized, or its numerous conferences and meetings that its teams organize every day around the world. Even so, the World Bank is not an academic institution—it cannot be, nor should it be: it must strike the right balance. The World Bank should not be a simple repository of fixed knowledge: it must be the instigator of new ideas, in both finance and development policies. And it must be able to *implement* these ideas in the field. The more than 70 years of experience the World Bank has is irreplaceable, because the capacity to implement is the most important skill and takes the longest time to acquire. This requires fighting constantly against freezing or fossilization of expertise.

The capacity for *openness* is the essential antibody for any bureaucratic institution, whether public or private. Any large group has a tendency to take this path and start to withdraw into itself when clients are too far away. At a time when high-performing organizations are undercapitalized and ultraconnected, the World Bank Group must stay open to the outside world and keep listening for changes in the economic, digital, and academic worlds, and more. In a group so large, with such an extensive workforce, there is a risk of losing contact with the rest of the world and playing a game of "us" against "them." This risk can be limited by making sure that there is always a close connection between the majority of employees and the World Bank's clients. From this point of view, I think that there is a disproportionate number of employees at the headquarters in Washington compared to those in contact with clients in the field. Change should not happen once in a while but should be a state of mind and should be delivered on a continuous basis.

Finally, the World Bank is *doubly global,* and this is what makes it truly unique and different from other development institutions. It has a global presence with offices in more than 100 countries. Its network is a key asset, of which it could make even better use. It is also global because of its access to global decision making, which offers a range of opportunities that are still little understood.

Despite the challenges, including doubts about multilateralism by a number of newly elected governments and increasing competition, the World Bank Group has all the ingredients it needs to stay relevant in today's world. But nothing is permanent: relevance cannot be taken for granted. It must be proven day after day with all the ingredients it has been granted, as described above.

The miracle of Bretton Woods has done well to survive for more than 70 years. It is fragile, but it should stay the course for a few more decades if the model is adapted generation after generation, and if the bank draws on the best part of the banker's intuition of the founders, despite growing pressure against multilateralism (this should be part of an adaptation strategy, not a dismantling). Contrary to how we too often tend to think, finance is not a by-product of the institution but is instead essential to the performance of its mission to end poverty.

If there is a place where the mission of finance is to save the world, it is the World Bank, along with other MDBs. And if there is a laboratory where all the ways to regain control over money to serve common good can be tested, it is the World Bank and other MDBs. This cannot be taken for granted, as we have seen. And the MDBs cannot, and should not, stay on their own and work in isolation. They are part of a broader system whose emergence needs to be encouraged at the confluence of public commitment, private interests, and civil society action.

CHAPTER 15

Using the Financial Cement

Reaching a state of sustainable development requires effective governance. Our working group on water says,

> To understand this connection, is as simple as remembering that the word "sustainable" means more than just "durable," but also acceptable, feasible, viable, livable; in short, it implicitly refers to compromise. The philosophy attached to sustainability (in the sense of viability) suggests that only compromise is lasting. It is not the correctness of a policy that makes it endure, but rather the concessions by which each player gives up something in order for everyone to benefit collectively.[1]

To make it possible for everyone to benefit collectively is the challenge of international cooperation, a cooperation between every level in this world, in which we are all involved; no problem can be solved by acting solo anymore. This is also the whole meaning of a reinvented finance: to learn (or relearn) to work together has never been as vital over the past 70 years as it is today.

There is nothing obvious about this working together in practice. Everyone—in the public, private, or civil sectors—will have a cultural revolution imposed upon them, in which we have to move away from the silo mentality. It's worth the effort. The tool of finance can help us. It can help deliver some early wins to help different constituents embrace the collective approach that, at the same time and critically, is respectful of individual goals and objectives.

No 100 Percent Public or 100 Percent Private Funding

The momentum of 2015 surrounding the SDGs, development finance, and climate finance demonstrated that the global community has been awakened to the need to collaborate on the most complex and essential projects. Coming from all aspects of society, fed as much by governments as by civil society, financial players, multinational corporations, small and medium-size enterprises, consumers, savers, and multilateral institutions, the momentum demonstrated above all that this union of forces was *possible.*

We need to keep this momentum going now during the implementation phase, while we make good on these goals for 2030. Nothing is guaranteed from where we stand, especially with the rise of populism and nationalism. But one thing is certain: no SDG, whether it concerns poverty, education, healthcare, infrastructure, or the climate, can be achieved through 100 percent public or 100 percent private funding.

None of these problems can be resolved through only public, private, or civil action. To work toward inclusive growth, to allow countries like Mauritania to free themselves from the "curse of iron"—that is, an excessive dependence on one resource—and diversify their economies by developing their fishing resources, for example, requires the engagement of all the players on the same course. This is a multistage course including all of the world's levels, from the global to the local.

A Primary Responsibility for Governments

But this is a movement in which governments must be the primary players. The *From Billions to Trillions* report says, "Countries must be in the driver's seat, leading the development process and the construction of nurturing, supportive environments." National leadership, as well as regional, continental, and global leadership, is key to putting countries on a viable trajectory toward development.

One example of effective leadership can be seen in the revival that Côte d'Ivoire is currently experiencing, one of the most interesting stories of modern African history. After the "Ivorian miracle" of the 1960s and 1970s under the presidency of Félix Houphouët-Boigny (the "cocoa king"), the country was plunged into a long and painful civil war. The gains of the preceding decades were largely lost. But the election of President Alassane Ouattara in 2011, confirmed by his first-round reelection in 2015, has given birth to new hope. The pairing of President Ouattara and his former prime minister and now vice president, Daniel Kablan Duncan, is one of the most inspiring that I have ever seen. The partners were able to base their policies on a long-term vision of the future (a vision of making Côte d'Ivoire an emerging economy in just a decade), as well as a detailed understanding of both international mechanisms and local realities. This integrated, clear, and confident leadership, simultaneously demanding and dedicated, ambitious and humble, and in touch with the rest of the world, has contributed hugely to the reconstruction of the country. Whether you look at the political plans for national reconciliation (although the process has not yet been implemented), domestic security with army reform, human rights, the fight against corruption, or the economic plan with the reform of the coffee-cocoa subsidiaries or infrastructure rebuilding, the results are palpable: Côte d'Ivoire has registered nearly 9 percent growth every year for five years. Every time I was assigned to Abidjan, I was shocked by the transformations taking place in the Ivorian capital. Although nothing ever seems to get finished and there are still many pending economic and political issues, the progress has nonetheless been impressive.

Another example is Colombia, which owes much of its current emergence to its leadership team (including Mauricio Cárdenas Santamaría, a brilliant minister of finance, and Sandra Bessudo, an environmental activist, both of whom I am proud to have developed a friendly relationship with). Colombia is one of the most sophisticated countries I have had the opportunity to explore, despite my French prejudices associating the country with the Revolutionary Armed Forces of Colombia (FARC), which kidnapped Íngrid Betancourt, and drug trafficking. It came as no surprise that the Nobel Prize was awarded to President Juan Manuel Santos. Colombia also now has one of the most comprehensive plans to implement the SDGs.

Governments Unable to Do It All Alone

But we cannot expect governments to do everything. We cannot make governments that are already heavily in debt take on the entire responsibility for building physical, social, or even financial infrastructures. The future of sustainable development for our planet requires us to also mobilize private capital, whether that means local savings, investments of all kinds, or migrant transfers, and leverage this capital to mobilize supplemental funds in a healthy and sustainable manner.

We cannot expect the markets to do all the work, either. As our water group says,

> [The market] risks, guided by the exclusive consideration of profitability, [overlook] ever-essential human needs. There are enormous areas the market will never reach. It is in those ... that we must seek the best source from which to draw budgetary resources that advanced

> economies have committed to allocating as official development aid and powerful instruments of cooperation that we have had in place for more than 50 years in the global plan, and more recently within Europe.... That said, we cannot limit the use of public funds to the role of a stopgap where the private sector dares not tread. It is better for them to create, as adeptly as possible, powerful leverage that they can use as a potential catalyst: 100 units of private funds plus 50 units of public funds can create much more than 150 units for the beneficiaries.[2]

But it is important that this public effort "not only not let other actors abstain from or decrease their contributions, but even better, work as a powerful catalyst. Hence the importance of using this aid to facilitate their grants rather than replacing them, by avoiding fully financing these projects or programs through subsidies, which runs the risk of eliminating local initiatives."[3]

In short, the SDGs and COP21 objectives require capturing the potential of all sources of finance available to the world, and thereby leading to the cooperation of all types of players.

Painful but Profitable: A New Way to Mobilize Finance

It goes without saying that this whole operation is easier said than done. Getting players with opposing interests and cultures to work together is complicated. So is "[lifting] the unspoken restrictions of joint use of official development assistance and private funding. There is an old fear that such an approach would introduce a sort of contamination of profit to the pure, supposedly immaculate operations led by the public sector."[4] As comical as this prejudice sounds, it is tenacious and cannot be ignored, any more than we can ignore the suspicions that the private sector holds of the public sector being slow and bureaucratic, unreliable and corrupt, or that civil society holds of the two other points on this triangle. The current crisis of confidence has exacerbated this reciprocal and historical mistrust.

If we are to move past that mistrust, we must tackle these difficulties head on and acknowledge that cultural adaptation is necessary. These conflicts of interest can be real—the mission and goals of the public sector and civil society are not the same as those of the private sector. We have to find concrete solutions—such as the price of carbon—to reconcile the parties with one another. We also have to concede that no one point of the triangle is the keeper of the truth, or the keeper of making an effort to see the situation from the other's point of view in order to better understand expectations. And we must not believe that only developing countries—that are thought to be corrupt by many—are creating the problems. Just look around you: What do you think is the most "honorable" country in the world?

Generally, the answer is Norway, Switzerland, or Singapore. Yet Norway recently saw breaches of a public–private partnership (PPP) on a gas transport project (the tariff, for example, had been changed by the government along the way). By contrast, Senegal was able to successfully complete a roadway project between Dakar and the airport, in collaboration with the World Bank using a PPP that is widely considered as exemplary and is now being expanded. The world is not split between PPPs that succeed in the North and those fail in the South. The reality is much more complex. We must all remember this now, at a moment when the United States is considering a big push to fix infrastructure using the PPP technique. In these highly political and sensitive projects, compromise is everything: public-private cooperation can be demanding and labor intensive. In short, it can be painful.

But the many questions that such cooperation raises should not be an excuse to do nothing, as I have heard too often, any more than they can be considered irrelevant. We should also not create a new Washington consensus on public–private partnerships and impose it in every case, when it is often unsuitable. The PPP cannot be just another silver bullet offered to address every problem. But we must be able to recognize the benefits of collaboration in many complex cases in which partnerships can move things forward. Collaboration may be painful, but it will be profitable!

These projects ask that we find the right regulations, the proper tools, and the appropriate places to resolve conflicts. The ability to collaborate should be maintained with cooperation forums (meetings where public, private, and civil society institutions work together to see how they can better cooperate). Above all, the two parties must be trained to use the multidimensional approach I call "P4C" (painful but profitable public-private cooperation), because it is one of the most promising paths for future development. I found it reassuring to see the record number of registrations in the first massive open online course (MOOC; free, web-based educational courses) on PPPs given in 2015 by the World Bank Group (almost 30,000 people from more than 100 countries).[5]

A Question of Methods

A gap has widened in recent decades, particularly in the aftermath of the financial crisis and whistleblower disclosures, between the Davids and the Goliaths—the common people and the elites, the citizens and the government, consumers and corporations.

Nonetheless, we can patch things up once we emerge from the enlightened dictatorship, in which we put faith in fortuitous men, despise the common man, and divide to conquer. My experiences working with the water group and on international financial innovation to increase solidarity have taught me that even the most different people can have a dialogue, that the most divergent interests can be reconciled, and that the most complex questions can be resolved. What are required are (1) the challenge is great enough or inspiring enough to enrich our intelligence and good will; (2) every person consents in good faith to come together around the table; (3) the respective differences and expectations are stated, acknowledged, and explained to the group; and (4) the timeline can be adjusted and agreed upon.

Breaking the Ice with 20 Experts on Water

I have already described how, after 15 months of discussion, our working group on water came to suggest more than 80 measures to finance access to water for all: these individuals, who at the start were in complete opposition (the first meeting was not just cold—it was glacial), ended up coming to an understanding on the essentials. We have Michel Camdessus's genius to thank for this result and for knowing how to implement a method for negotiation based on commitment, explanation, honesty, coherence, mutual respect, curiosity, inventiveness, goodwill, and good faith.

Unanimous Support for a Tax That Nobody Liked Initially

The reception to the Landau report was an attempt to test the application of this method. President Chirac, at the height of his popularity (particularly because of his opposition to the war in Iraq), hoped to welcome bosses, unions, and civil society in turn before the G8 summit in Évian, France; April 30 was civil society's turn; all the major French and international NGOs headed to the Élysée Palace: Amnesty International, Greenpeace, ATTAC, Doctors without Borders, and more. The meeting was organized for the end of the day with the generally understood intent of it not lasting late on the night before a long weekend. The atmosphere was good natured but also hopeful and proud. It was two and a half months after Dominique de Villepin's speech at the UN.[6] Each NGO in turn took the podium to draw the president's attention to the topic it worked on and that the G8 could help address; these included water, biodiversity, disabilities, human rights, women's rights, and children's rights.

The representative from ATTAC (Association for the Taxation of Financial Transactions and Aid to Citizens) was one of the last to speak: "Mr. President, you are aware of our strong beliefs, and we hope that you establish a tax on international financial transactions in order to finance development."

Jacques Chirac responded, "You know what I think? I am not in favor of that tax.... And yet you pose a real question: We must find a way to finance global solidarity. We will do something, and I will include you in it."

The meeting was ending, or more like dissolving given the great number of people slipping away to start their weekend (an imperative that was manifestly more important than the agenda for the French president, too!). Maurice Gourdault-Montagne, chief diplomatic adviser and sherpa for the G8, asked the president, "But what is it we will do?" The president's commitment to ATTAC had been totally unexpected.

"Sort it out, Maurice, I kicked off the idea."

Maurice then turned to Jérôme Bonnafont, the adviser in charge of globalization, and me: "Your turn, kiddos!"

That was how I ended up suggesting to the table of experts from all areas, skill sets, and the most diverse interests, the mission to find a sensible solution to a fundamental question. The working group, led by Jean-Pierre Landau, was composed of managers from ATTAC, Agence française de développement (AFD), Oxfam, the IMF, employer groups, ministries of finance, and large corporations.[7] These individuals were not in agreement about the tax idea beforehand—the British, in particular, tended to think it was a truly *French* idea. And as far as figuring out *what* to tax—that took more than six months of work. In the end, though, the method paid off: the members of the Landau commission unanimously supported the final report, and all took part in the press conference to present what could become a promising financial invention of the 21st century: a tiny levy—raised in different countries on a product or service—that, thanks to its sheer volume, can help mobilize significant resources to finance a global public good.

Michel Camdessus and I had a similar experience in 2005 when we edited *Le sursaut—Vers une nouvelle croissance pour la France* (The wake-up call—a new French expansion), a report commissioned by Nicolas Sarkozy, then minister of the economy, finance, and industry.[8] The mission given to our working group was to "contribute to the clarification for the French people and their national representatives of the forthcoming economic and budgetary choices to encourage growth." I gathered around the table with other experts from the academic, NGO, corporate, and union fields. Upfront, consensus was unlikely, but the participants spent time together, tried to bring out the best of all of us, joined forces, and asked one another, "I get where you're coming from, so how would you manage this issue yourself?" In the end, we got definite results. The discussions I am currently having with Gordon Brown on education, and with Jean Todt on road safety, are continuing in the same spirit. How can we mobilize resources to finance these common goods?

Reforming the World Bank: Joy, Pride, and Frustration

The financial reforms enacted between 2013 and 2015 at the World Bank allowed me to further refine the method, in the sense that the resistance I encountered taught me a few lessons. The first and most important lesson is that when we want to force a change, we first must have a plan—a credible plan with a set deadline. Only with this condition in place (credibility) will people be prepared to grant you credit. You can never lose this group perspective. If one reform is made through compromise, with as many advantages as disadvantages, then you run the risk of losing sight of your goal if you do not keep the overall picture in mind. This does not mean that negotiation is impossible, but it has to maintain a sense of overall balance. The second lesson is that when there is urgency, it is better to abandon points that specific parties find unacceptable and move forward rather than discussing things ad nauseam. The third lesson is that you must ensure that all participants understand the particulars of the reform, and that each side understands the opposite point of view. You need to make an effort to clarify ambiguities and not take for granted that everyone understands you. In the case of the reforms at the World Bank, I probably overestimated the general understanding of the financial model of the World Bank, as well as the financial literacy of participants. We should have spent more time explaining the why, rather than the how—we probably don't talk enough about these things. Sometimes being chatty is a good thing! Finally, I learned that you have to leave room for dreams and enthusiasm, which is the role of innovation. But you also then have to be able to quickly show results.

I had an equally instructive and surprising conversation in this vein with two cardinals and with Jean-Baptiste de Franssu, director of the Institute for the Works of Religion, commonly known as the Vatican Bank. We found many similarities among our respective institutions' finances, and beyond that, between the Vatican and the World Bank, which were both going through a time of reform: the same complexity of global organizations, the same problems of communication and goal sharing, and more. I never would have dared make such a parallel before that conversation.

These organizations, particularly the MDBs, are commonly misunderstood to be opaque, secretive groups. The reality is more that they are dogged by bureaucracies, which have received fresh coats of bureaucracy at regular intervals without scraping off the old, defunct policies and processes. They often require a shock to the system and a reenergizing of the resources that drive them. When we get those factors aligned, then the results can be spectacular.

CHAPTER 16

The Principle Put into Action

Even if they still have strides to make in their cultural adaptation, development banks have a major role to play to promote a P4C cooperative approach and to help dispel suspicions that the public and private sectors harbor about each other. From my perspective, they must act like true orchestral conductors of global development finance. As I've said before, the development of the private sector and the cooperation with these players must become a central point of MDBs' operational model, with sincere commitment beyond the financing and mobilization of capital.

The Role of Multilateral Development Banks as Engines

MDBs can finance only a fraction of the total cost of a project; the rest comes from mobilizing supplemental investors through syndication and other structures of group funding.[1] This financial commitment, as well as its structure, advice, and accompanying distribution of risks, must help bring together additional sources of funding and create, in the case of unexplored fields or endangered environments, a significant demonstration that can attract new projects and investors. But this mechanism benefits even more from liquidity. Private investors generally tell me they expect the MDBs to provide three things beyond the traditional instruments for risk sharing: (1) a selection of well-designed, prioritized projects prepared on their behalf; (2) an implementation that follows the strictest standards, as no investor wants to endanger their reputation; and (3) the capability to manage potential conflicts with public authorities during execution of the project.

From Billions to Trillions: *How to Walk the Talk*

MDBs got the message. In the report *From Billions to Trillions,* the MDBs committed to redoubling their efforts "to build a reserve of viable and attractive projects for investors from the private sector" through their project preparation facilities. They also intended to collaborate

> to find the means to mobilize activity and investment from the private sector in a more systematic way than case-by-case: (i) by exploring effective solutions to manage risks by establishing individual or common mechanisms to offer guarantees, risk insurance, mixed funding, and other measures to distribute risk (for example, structured financing); (ii) by exploring the possibilities for structuring common mechanisms or co-investment platforms at the national, regional, or multilateral level to reduce individual costs for the investor in terms of project preparation and execution; and (iii) by offering a

> credit increase, allowing risk sharing with official entities.[2]

MDBs could also simplify and standardize their operations. The system has a tendency to reinvent the wheel with each project, and everyone wants to promote their own instruments, which causes excessive financial and administrative costs for the system as a whole. It has a tendency to restrict private investors to a backup or subsidiary funder role, although they participate in the project at the same level as other players. They should be present from the start, and development banks must understand that they have a need to facilitate this, because sometimes the gap that needs filling is more cultural than budgetary. Private players cannot just be called at the last minute and expected to accept everything that has been agreed to ahead of time.

The Case of Infrastructure Finance

The adaptations discussed are behind the creation of the Global Infrastructure Facility (GIF). The platform

> coordinates and integrates the initiatives of multilateral development banks, investors and funding backers from the private sector, and countries interested in infrastructure investments in emerging markets and developing economies—supporting collaboration and collective action on complex projects that no single institution can finance. The private sector partners

> that have joined the platform alone manage over 12 trillion dollars in assets, with the purpose of diversifying through profitable investments that offer distributions that reflect the risks. By building a global reserve of investments projects for sustainable development, structured to respond to users' needs and investors' appetites, GIF has the potential to unleash billions of dollars to promote infrastructure in developing nations.[3]

In developing nations, the challenge of infrastructure is not only to make funding available; it is also to correct the lack of viable projects in which to invest.

> GIF went operational in 2015, with an initial capital of 100 million dollars. Its first three years constitute its pilot phase, during which the idea of the platform, its activities, and its partnership model will be tested. In this phase, at least 10 to 12 support activities for projects will be supported, which will allow us to examine the model in diverse sectors, geographic zones, and national environments and in diverse project types. At the same time, the idea of a future flexible financing window will be refined and tested in order to mobilize supplemental resources, as needed.[4]

All the ingredients are there: clear cooperation between governments, MDBs, and private investors; focus on real projects with the goal of carrying them out; a pilot phase to allow for later adjustments; and distribution of the various roles according to the abilities and predilections of each player.

The collective impetus to face the challenges of infrastructure is even more valuable knowing—in a context in which money, budget, and structural policies seem to have become incapable of stimulating growth—that investment in infrastructure will be a pillar of economic policy, a real game changer to stimulate growth in the short-term to create stable jobs, as well as to raise the potential for growth in the long term. While GIF can seem quite modest with respect to the billions of dollars needed for global infrastructure, this potential can be amplified and connected to other related initiatives—like the Global Infrastructure Hub created by the G20 in 2014,[5] the funding mechanism for preparing infrastructure projects at the New Partnership for Africa's Development, or the Sustainable Development Investment Platform I have presided over since 2016.[6] The idea is to demonstrate options for investment, alignment, and coordination between players in order to free up infrastructure project capacity, and to create a new ecosystem in which the MDBs keep their central financing role while also deploying a huge mobilization effort in parallel.

The challenge of creating investment ecosystems goes far beyond the problem of funding infrastructure. Development banks could assist the multinational organizations that develop interesting pilot projects to create shared value in a more structured way, such as the seminal initiative from Coca-Cola in Brazil, Coletivo,[7] by duplicating them elsewhere to create a mass effect and gain visible results in development. This is the same spirit that carried the Danone Communities project, a *social businesses* network that aimed to reduce poverty and malnutrition.[8] In practical terms, the MDBs could create relationships between these innovative companies and socially responsible shareholders, or philanthropic organizations and on-the-ground NGOs. The "scale for good" principle seemed promising to me for deploying impact investments on a large scale and making a new, globalized financial system that would make a difference. This virtuous mechanism relies on the P4C idea, and it is to this goal that I dedicate myself personally and professionally above any other: mobilizing global private savings for positive purposes while respecting investors' expectations of returns. The head of a large insurance company recently told me that purchasing German debt at a negative interest rate was of no interest for Germany or his clients, and likely not for the world, either, and if he could invest under good terms in housing, healthcare, or agriculture in India or Peru, "that would clearly be useful at all levels!"

We can also encourage networks like the Sustainable Banking Network, launched in 2012 and headed by the IFC: this singular community in the world brings together regulatory agencies of the financial sector and banking associations from emerging markets to advance sustainable finance by facilitating collective learning of international best practices and the creation of pilot programs in member states.[9]

Financing Action to Defeat Climate Change When Consensus Might Falter

The other great world challenge for which cooperation is crucial and development banks play a key role is that of financing the effort to curb climate change. MDBs are expected to assist in the transformation of government resources and official development aid into much larger private investments that can support a low-carbon, resilient economy.[10] Here, too, they must work together and in complementary fashion to do the most effective work, for instance, as executive agents of Global Environment Fund (GEF), Climate Investment Funds, and Green Climate Fund; as partners in global initiatives like Sustainable Energy for All, led by my former colleague, Rachel Kyte; and through a harmonized, transparent, and rigorous approach to following measures supporting the climate and financing. The World Bank is also committed, along with others, to assisting the international community in the effort to set a carbon tax, without taking part in any specific incentivizing measure (carbon markets, taxes, or standards): in every country, and in each national or municipal government, the best option depends on local circumstances. Nonetheless, after the Paris climate accord, the World

Bank launched the Carbon Pricing Leadership Coalition to bring together the global public and private sectors on this topic. As another example, the Partnership for Market Readiness is a fiduciary fund for multidonor grants on a world scale that supports collective innovation and the piloting of various instruments for carbon taxation; many countries, from China to Morocco, benefit from individualized support through this organization. We must support these initiatives and encourage a stronger coordination, especially at a moment when the consensus on climate change is under threat.

The complexity of this jungle of acronyms is of little importance. It would make you laugh if it didn't reveal so clearly the stand being taken on climate change. Naturally, the idea isn't to give you an exhaustive list of everything involved, or to arbitrarily highlight this or that initiative. Instead, I want to emphasize the reality of the energy being expended on this. This is not fantasy or pious wishes. This is a world on the move.

P4C, the Key to an Economy with Purpose

Beyond the challenges of infrastructure and the climate, and in addition to helping developing nations, many diverse issues would benefit from a partnership approach. If we can sprinkle P4C around the globe like a new miracle ingredient, certain complex topics would benefit from an effort to establish a painful but profitable public-private cooperation.

Road Safety

Road safety draws simultaneously on legislation (we need laws to prohibit excessive driving speeds, drunk driving, or driving while using a cell phone), enforcement (we need police officers and radar), education (we must educate citizens about traffic codes, best practices for driving, and potentially dangerous behaviors), and infrastructure construction (we need well-built, well-maintained roads). Public authorities cannot address every aspect of this multidimensional issue. They have to get everyone involved, beginning with the private sector. Knowing that Coca-Cola has a fleet of more than 100,000 vehicles worldwide, we see that a multinational company of this size has a role to play in road safety. It is not just a matter of finding innovative funding: we will succeed only with an effective coalition to address the issue on a global scale.

Global Health

Healthcare and humanitarian aid can also benefit from innovative financial cooperation. The Global Financing Facility (GFF) was created in support of an initiative close to my heart, Every Woman, Every Child. This partnership combines the efforts of Canada, Norway, the Bill and Melinda Gates Foundation, and other partners under the aegis of the UN secretary-general. It pioneers a style of finance that connects foreign and domestic sources of funding through a sustainability lens to eradicate the problem of avoidable deaths among mothers, newborns, infants, and children, and to improve the healthcare, nutrition, and quality of life of these women and children by 2030. While the five-year investment plan remains under the helm of national governments, the implementation of an international financial facility allows us to guarantee ahead of time the anticipated funding of transfers expected for a certain period. Some $2.6 billion must be mobilized to allow the GFF funds to supply an initial grant to 63 eligible countries, including Ethiopia, Kenya, the Democratic Republic of the Congo, and Tanzania. These funds will allow us to leverage public and private funds for the Reproductive, Maternal, Newborn, Child and Adolescent Health program. This is a novel approach because of the partnership format and the flexibility of the instruments envisioned.

Education

We could follow the same logic in education financing. In both healthcare and education, the goal is to establish a plan and national priorities that account for the entire menu of philanthropic finance tools available, public and private, to recognize where they dovetail, to avoid duplication and competition, and to connect efforts and results, while being prepared to adjust the aim if the first shot fails. Education cannot be addressed with a national education plan alone but must also mobilize all kinds of public and private structures, and physical and virtual education tracks. For instance, we must not ignore the modern assets of teaching media such as MOOCs or the Khan Academy, which provide an opportunity for everyone to gain access to knowledge. As with healthcare, education is a complex subject that affords major social returns (an educated, healthy population works better and longer), but the economic benefits are not immediately measurable. Hence, the idea is to get governments in a sampling of volunteer countries to commit to ambitious goals (such as universal access to quality primary education). In return, we would solicit aid from donor countries as well as the private capital and capacity for financing and mobilization of international organizations such as the World Bank to translate these national plans into action. This is the whole idea behind outcome-based funding: money connected to results. By getting various actors around the table, we can agree on shared funding for a number of countries to have quality education. This is the purpose of the International Facility for Education (IFFEd), led by Gordon Brown and to which I have contributed since its inception. It was mentioned at the G20 in Hamburg in July 2017 and should be discussed in more detail in 2018.

Refugees

Work is being done to develop partnership financing to accommodate refugees in the Middle East. If all the sources of funding are used to address the need, countries like Jordan and Lebanon will not have access to the lowest-cost loans, since they are not classified as developing countries. One vision, which I contributed to, is to use the World Bank balance sheet and those of other multilateral institutions to request that countries like the members of the G7 or the Gulf Cooperation Council "subsidize" such loans by lowering interest rates, or better still by offering collateral on direct investments. In any case, providing funding means getting national private and public sectors and multilaterals to work hand in hand to meet the financial challenges that too often create snags because of lack of cooperation.

Pandemics

Another case in which the P4C approach could play a decisive role is in preventing pandemics. If we had used this logic when Ebola reached its peak, we could have saved many lives and limited the terrible damage done in Guinea, Liberia, and Sierra Leone. The crisis was poorly managed. We lost time, and funds were mobilized too late. Although the establishment of insurance mechanisms is an essential response to allow the rapid release of funds in the event of this type of epidemic, it is not enough on its own. On the ground, we need a collaborative approach. In the case of Ebola, we lacked hygiene products, for instance; Unilever could have easily contributed soap. We lacked satellite telephones; Vodafone could have provided them. We lacked airplanes; UPS and FedEx could have made them available. We did not think, or thought too late, to solicit help from actors already deeply entrenched in the area who had the necessary products and distribution networks. The public sector did not naturally think to call on the private sector when help was needed. What a waste! But what if, instead of reinventing the wheel at every crisis, we created a reflex for collective, systemic, transverse response? Until now, we have had a vertical picture of health, specialized disease by disease. The Ebola crisis demonstrated the limits of this conception: without a nurse or community health worker in every village, we could not set up a health watch, and the epidemic was detected too late. Still, we recognize that we cannot speak about healthcare without talking about ideas for systems like education, transportation, and communications. These are ideas I promoted and continue to promote as cochair of the Global Future Council on International Governance, Public–Private Cooperation and Sustainable Development, under the framework of the World Economic Forum, which organizes the Davos summit. We created a spot to share stories and lessons about cooperation efforts. The best defense against pandemics is a transversal, integrated, and collaborative healthcare system, which remains to be developed.

Promoting Decentralized Cooperation

The case of Ebola demonstrates how the terrain is often already gridded with networks, initiatives, and actors who work in their own domains, whereas cooperation on a number of issues could be fruitful.

Water is one such issue. Our working group realized, or rather rediscovered, that water, while a global problem, is first and foremost a local topic:

> Water is a territorialized resource. In terms of water, we come from a river basin before being of a country. Above all, water is managed locally. Services related to water are local services. Everywhere, the ultimate responsibility for water is municipal or broken down by village community. It is therefore within this reality that we must act, and we must bring our attention closer to this position. We have to understand that it is not so much a money issue as one of governance.[11]

If you invert the perspective and improve governance, then you can find funding to meet the full challenge. This assumes

> putting the local at the heart of the system, meaning organizing governance starting on the ground, closer to city needs and village women; from the river basins to the United Nations, and not the opposite.... Financially, this does not mean that a global fund [is] spraying its benefits around the earth in a mist, with the serious risk of evaporation related to that, but rather proper funding brought to municipalities and villages and

> projects themselves, relying also on dynamic local savings, specific protections brought to funds invested to account for the specific risks of water.[12]

To national, massive, and inefficient centralized cooperation, we must therefore add, "without taking anything away from the latter, a decentralized cooperation that links many communities at the smallest level: municipalities and villages, movements, and opinion campaigns."[13] Religious organizations, whether they be Christian, Buddhist, Jewish, or Muslim, as long as they manage prayer centers, schools, hospitals, or artisanal structures also play an essential role in cohesion, mediation, and coordination on the ground. We lose much by ignoring them, or worse, hampering their actions.

While this diverse, decentralized cooperation is less important financially, at its own level, it is likely more efficient, with "the major advantage of creating personal, living, and mutually enriching connections between civil societies all around."[14] In poverty zones, where the inhabitants often feel abandoned by the authorities, this mobilization of local, active forces, a distinctive element of on-the-ground NGOs, constitutes an indispensable asset for the success of operations: "The arrival of a business, whatever it is, with the goal of carrying out work of a type, location, and volume that has not been discussed with the population, provokes a justified fear and principled opposition. A local, dynamic NGO can save the day. The intermediary role of NGOs between the local population and the steamroller of administrations and modern companies is irreplaceable."[15]

My experience with the complex water issue has convinced me that an institution like the World Bank—along with all the regional development banks and the national aid agencies—with its unique presence across the four corners of the world, has an eminent role to play in using centralized cooperation to increase decentralized cooperation. With offices in more than 100 countries, it holds its own compared to the largest multinational corporations. It has contacts everywhere. This network is an essential asset that the World Bank could use even better by strengthening the connections between the headquarters in Washington and the teams on location, organizing a more fluid line of communications and harmonious exchanges between the various offices, in order for each to have access to the useful information from every country.

Recipe Tested in the Jungle

This ability to react in the most remote locations of the world can create small miracles of development. For example, consider the action taken in recent years in the Solomon Islands, in the Pacific east of Papua New Guinea.[16] I visited these islands, covered in tropical forests cut through here and there by summits reaching over 6,500 feet, which were the highlight of a voyage—even though it quickly became apparent that with such high heat and impenetrable jungles, this is not a place in which someone would normally want to invest. However, the approaches to the archipelagos are some of the richest fishing waters in the world, particularly for tuna. Over years, this fishing ground had been pillaged by intruders of all kinds who profited from the absence of a navy, and therefore absence of control, on the part of the small island state.[17]

A change occurred when 18 Pacific nations, with the cooperation of the Australian, Japanese, French, and American navies, set up a water surveillance system by satellite, which allowed them to organize their fishing rights. This measure not only allowed the islands to stabilize the resource (and thereby also contain the threat to biodiversity), but it also allowed them to receive significant royalties from fishermen (hundreds of millions of dollars, a significant sum for this small country). Because the participating parties were able to be heard, today they reap both environmental and economic rewards: it was a win-win consensus. So much so that it allowed them to create an even more profitable project: with the assistance of the World Bank, among others,[18] the Solomon Islands has developed a tuna processing plant and created a brand, SolTuna, which exports prepared canned fish with exquisite local spices. Some 1,500 people worked there in 2014 when I visited the factory, of whom 75 percent were women, with the understanding that 500 new jobs were to be created in the next five years. I find this dynamic extraordinary: through international cooperation, we were able to create, in a remote area,[19] a high local added value capable of spreading around the world—even authorized to supply the hyperregulated and demanding Japanese sushi market.

I see in this story the best of finance and of capitalism and globalization, and the best of the potential for cooperation. It confirms that all this is possible. Stories like this need to be broadcast more effectively; the more people see such examples, the more likely they are to trust the system again and see the impact they can have. May all those with goodwill around the globe find inspiration in this example!

CONCLUSION

The Choice Is Ours

Humanity is at a crossroads. Either we let ourselves be carried away by the forces of disintegration, or we take control and stand united. Either we let the "globalization of indifference" and blind finance win, or we tame globalization and domesticate finance so that it benefits everyone. It depends on us all, individually and collectively.

Either we let finance run on its own again, or we regain control of this extraordinary force to serve the common good. Finance is a tool that can make a difference for humanity in the choice we are facing.

Clearly, we cannot rely solely on the will of the people and their representatives—even if, personally, this is my predilection. Realistically, people always have and always will be guided by their own interests.

Despite tensions that have arisen in the past few years, our individual interests have never been in such close alignment. The vital issues of climate, public health, economic inequality and demographic imbalances, access to energy, and big data have come into sharp focus. No country on earth could resolve them alone—certainly not by erecting walls with their neighbors and strengthening borders. Our planet has never been so flat and interconnected,[1] so small and so fragile at the same time. This unprecedented situation induces vertigo, erodes confidence, and exacerbates fears, as the United Kingdom's referendum vote for Brexit demonstrated.

Yet I also see an extraordinary opportunity here.

Humanity has never had so many financial and human resources at its disposal, or so many courses of action. We have at our disposal so much intelligence, energy, money, and so many tools to mobilize them. Humanity, to use an image favored by Michel Camdessus, has the multiple arms of the Hindu god Shiva: his hand is the invisible hand of the market that acts based on incentives; his hand is the hand wielding the justice of the state, the political power that exists to govern and instruct, to prepare for the long term and to correct inequalities; his hand is also, when it wants to be, the outstretched hand of solidarity and charity. Let us serve as all of these hands! We can use them to act together and intelligently, instead of tearing ourselves apart.

Many of us have lost confidence in finance, with ample justification. Finance led us to the brink of ruin—while promising peace and prosperity. But let us not be too quick to banish it. Let us take one more chance to show that, when controlled and used intelligently with benevolence and inventiveness, finance can accomplish great things. It can take us so much further than we ever could have imagined. The silent revolution already in motion in the climate finance sphere is proof that a change of heart is possible; humanity can influence globalization. It is not some blind force that we are powerless to resist. Once harnessed, finance can be an inexhaustible and renewable energy resource, a far cry from the explosions and chain reactions that we have pictured in our minds. We must follow this path and stay the course. We cannot let Shiva lower his arms!

This book is a cry from the heart, a wake-up call.

We cannot fail to act out of weakness and denial. Or even worse, out of a fatalism that thinks that "one of the privileges of the great is to witness catastrophes from a terrace."[2] When the disaster materializes, the balcony collapses, and down with it go the great who thought it was a refuge.

Those who preside over international regulatory bodies within the government, serve at the head of international investment funds, and act as leaders of any stripe have the duty to serve as examples. But we—consumers, investors, citizens, entrepreneurs, association members, all of us—also have the power to press them on this. All of us, wherever we are, hold a piece of the puzzle. What are we waiting for to finally put it together?

This is our world. This is our money. The cement we need to preserve and nurture it is the common good.

We can create this forced solidarity, this "solid reality of the human condition," this "mutual dependence on people obliged to cooperate with one another for the health of all"[3]—a solidarity that is assured, desired, and demanded. Have courage! It will mean regular attendance at shareholders' meetings—we did choose a collective global life, after all. But it is in this effort to form agreements—and it will be an effort—that finance is our best ally. It is without doubt a poor master, but what a wonderful servant!

A lyric from the Broadway musical *Cabaret* says that "Money makes the world go round.... That clanking sound ... of money, money, money..." May the world now make money go straight.

If finance could nearly sink the world, it can also save it, provided we regain control and keep control, provided we decide to join forces, provided we invent the new tools to combine financial capacities of all kinds, and provided we accept our differences.

NOTES

Foreword by Gordon Brown

[1] http://www.un.org/press/en/1999/19990201.sgsm6881.html.

[2] https://www.gmu.edu/centers/publicchoice/faculty%20pages/Tyler/Manila.pdf.

[3] http://www.the-american-interest.com/2016/07/10/when-and-why-nationalism-beats-globalism/.

[4] http://www.huffingtonpost.com/georg-kell/globalization-four-ways-t_b_11081332.html.

Introduction

[1] H.R. McMaster, and Gary Cohn, "America First Doesn't Mean America Alone," *Wall Street Journal,* May 30, 2017.

[2] These innovations are the creation of International Finance Facility for Immunization and Unitaid, as described in Chapter 10.

[3] Created in 1904 by two Catholic laypeople after the exciting publication of *Rerum Novarum,* the encyclical letter by Pope Leo XIII considered to be the foundation for the Church's modern social doctrine, the Semaines Sociales de France is a

watchdog for society and one of the oldest think tanks in France.

[4] Michel Camdessus, Bertrand Badré, Ivan Chéret, Pierre-Frédéric Ténière-Buchot, *Eau* (Robert Laffont: 2004). The present book regularly reflects on this work and what I learned then.

[5] Michel Camdessus, *Le Sursaut. Vers une nouvelle croissance pour la France,* Report of the Minister of the Economy, Finance, and Industry (La Documentation Française, October 2004).

[6] Original translation from Antoine de Saint-Exupéry, *Citadelle* (1948).

Chapter 1

[1] Michel Camdessus et al., *Eau.*

[2] "Official development assistance (ODA) includes all financial transfers for which the 'grant element,' according to the definition given by the OECD Development Assistance Committee (DAC), represents at least 25 percent of the total. In other words, it means aid. Generally, these comprise State-to-State transfers, or bilateral aid. A smaller but no less important aspect is multilateral ODA, by the World Bank, the IMF, concessional funds held by regional development banks, various aid funds from the European Union, and other United Nations agencies such as the United Nations Development

Programme (UNDP), UNICEF, WHO, and FAO. These multilateral development agencies provide loans at close to market rates. Although they do not quite meet the DAC's definition of ODA, these loans are much more attractive offers than what commercial banks and other lenders can give. Other bilateral agencies with development assistance objectives operate in a more commercial manner and offer capital shares, securities, or near-market-rate loans (for example: USAID in the US, KfW in Germany, AFD in France, the CDC in England, or the JBIC in Japan). They share many common features with multilateral financial institutions." Original translation from Camdessus et al., *Eau,* pp.228–29.

[3] United Nations, *The Millennium Development Goals Report* (United Nations, 2015), http://www.un.org/millenniumgoals/2015_MDG_Report/pdf/MDG%202015%20rev%20(July%201).pdf.

[4] United Nations, "Beyond the Millennium Development Goals: The Post-2015 Sustainable Development Agenda" (UN Department of Public Information, September 2013), http://www.un.org/millenniumgoals/pdf/EN_MDG_backgrounder.pdf.

[5] In 2005 the international poverty threshold was $1.25 per day. The World Bank adjusted this figure in 2015 to $1.90 per day.

[6] United Nations, "Beyond the Millennium Development Goals."

[7] United Nations, *The Millennium Development Goals Report 2015* (United Nations, 2015), http://www.un.org/millenniumgoals/2015_MDG_Report/pdf/MDG%202015%20rev%20(July%201).pdf.

[8] United Nations, "Beyond the Millennium Development Goals."

[9] Ranked by the gross domestic product, adjusted for purchasing power parity. "Gross Domestic Product," World Bank, 2014.

[10] Ibid.

[11] United Nations, *The Millennium Development Goals Report 2013* (United Nations, 2013), www.un.org/millenniumgoals/pdf/report-2013/mdg-report-2013-english.pdf.

[12] "China today boasts roughly five workers for every retiree. By 2040, this highly desirable ratio will have collapsed to about 1.6 to 1." Howard W. French, "China's Twilight Years," *The Atlantic,* June 2016.

[13] Richard Dobbs, James Manyika, and Jonathan Woetzel, *No Ordinary Disruption: The Four Global Forces Breaking All the Trends* (Public Affairs, 2016). Reviewed in *Public Affairs,* May 2015.

[14] Luoyang is one of China's historic capitals, located on the Yellow River; it boasts nearly 7 million inhabitants.

[15] United Nations, *The Millennium Development Goals Report 2013.*

[16] Ibid.

[17] Data from the World Bank.

[18] New development data that highlights the success, and sometimes failure, of these policies can be found in the *Doing Business* report published each year by the World Bank.

[19] Original translation from Michel Serres, *Petite Poucette* (Le Pommier: Collection Manifestes, 2012).

[20] Ibid., pp.15–16.

[21] United Nations, "Beyond the Millennium Development Goals."

[22] Salim Ismail, *Exponential Organizations: Why New Organizations Are Ten Times Better, Faster, and Cheaper Than Yours (and What to Do about It)* (Diversion Books, 2014).

[23] Camdessus et al., *Eau,* p.154.

[24] United Nations, *A New Global Partnership: Eradicate Poverty and Transform Economies through Sustainable Development* (United Nations, 2013), https://sustainabledevelopmen

t.un.org/content/documents/8932013–05%20-%20HLP%20Report%20-%20A%20New%20Global%20Partnership.pdf.

Chapter 2

[1] Adair Turner, *Between Debt and the Devil: Money, Credit, and Fixing Global Finance* (Princeton University Press, 2015), p.93.

[2] Percentage of population living in absolute poverty computed by the World Bank. As demonstrated by many, in particular, Amartya Sen, poverty cannot be reduced to a monetary factor. The drop in poverty is, however, real, even if disputed in its measurement.

[3] Turner, *Between Debt and the Devil,* p.1.

[4] Securitization is a financial technique that consists of transforming less liquid assets (loans, receivables, etc.) into financial securities issued by capital markets (bonds, for example) by transferring them to investors.

[5] Even at this time, despite the increase in signs of "irrational exuberance," Alan Greenspan, then president of the US Federal Reserve, was presented as an all-powerful conductor. See Bob Woodward, *Maestro: Greenspan's Fed and the American Boom* (Simon & Schuster, 2001).

[6] For more on shadow banking, see Chapter 8.

[7] Turner, *Between Debt and the Devil,* p.26.

[8] Certification is the confirmation of certain properties, such as of a building, a supertanker, or a toy, for the intended market.

[9] Interestingly, during a discussion we had at the Peterson Institute in June 2016, Neel Kashkari, chair of the Federal Reserve of Minneapolis, noted that the US Treasury had worked up several crisis scenarios, but a fall in real estate prices was not even imagined.

[10] Around $1.5 trillion isn't much at the scale of international finance—but that is still an enormous amount for an individual country.

Chapter 3

[1] François Rabelais, *Pantagruel* (1542): "Science sans conscience n'est que ruine de l'âme" (Science without conscience is but the ruin of the soul).

[2] See Charles P. Kindleberger, *Manias, Panics, and Crashes: A History of Financial Crises* (Wiley, 2000).

[3] See C.M. Reinhart and K.S. Rogoff, *This Time Is Different: Eight Centuries of Financial Folly* (Princeton University Press, 2009).

[4] In particular Gaussian models.

[5] Turner, *Between Debt and the Devil,* p.2. We should also remember the relevance and clear thinking of Raghuram Rajan, chief economist for the IMF, who back in 2005 cautioned against the system's hidden risks and who in 2010 stressed that "hidden fractures still threaten the world economy." See Raghuram Rajan, *Fault Lines: How Hidden Fractures Still Threaten the World Economy* (Princeton University Press, 2011).

[6] Turner, *Between Debt and the Devil,* p.3.

[7] Ibid.

[8] Bertrand Badré, "Un banquier dans la tourment," in Michel Cool, *Pour un capitalisme au service l'homme. Parole de patrons chrétiens* (Capitalism in the service of mankind: Testimonies from Christian managers) (Albin Michel, 2009), p.112.

[9] The LIBOR refers to a series of benchmark money market rates according to various currencies.

[10] Shares would later fall to less than €2.

[11] See John Micklethwait and Adrian Wooldridge, *A Future Perfect: The Challenge and Hidden Promise of Globalization* (Crown Business, 2000).

[12] Alain Peyrefitte, *La société de confiance: Essais sur les origines du développement* (The trust

society: Essays on the origins of development) (Odile Jacob, 2005).

Chapter 4

[1] Development Committee, *From Billions to Trillions: Transforming Development Finance Post-2015 Financing for Development: Multilateral Development Finance* (report prepared through the cooperation of the African Development Bank, the Asian Development Bank, the European Bank for Reconstruction and Development, the European Investment Bank, the Inter-American Development Bank, the World Bank Group, and the International Monetary Fund for the Development Committee meeting held on April 18, 2015).

[2] With a first/second loss mechanism, a public party to the agreement agrees to cover the first/second loss of an investment up to a preagreed amount under certain conditions.

[3] The cost could be up to €450 billion annually by 2050, according to the UN.

[4] Carbon prices signal that carbon consumption includes the cost of externalities.

[5] Camdessus et al., *Eau,* p.107.

[6] Ibid., pp.139–40.

[7] Ibid., p.140.

[8] See, for example, Ibid., p.140–41: "We suspected the industrialists of being interested only in short-term profits and the exploitation of the poor by having them pay too dearly for water from which they dreamed they might some day become completely deprived. The NGOs would prevent us from self-serving business deals.... Private bankers, naturally heartless, would refuse to lend enough money to emerging and developing nations and to projects that might help them develop, halting the machine.... Development agencies and other public bankers are uneasy. On the one hand, they are first in line when it comes to financing development infrastructure. They are the stars, so to speak. But on the other hand, we have to acknowledge that their contributions have steadily declined for years.... It is thus the politicians who are clearly responsible, or irresponsible, since they have never made water their priority, which is at the root of our catastrophe."

[9] Ibid., p.141.

[10] Ibid., p.8.

[11] Ibid., p.9.

Chapter 5

[1] This strong monetary control is exercised by a semifloating exchange system and a central rate

(which was depreciated in August 2015) around which the yuan can change within a range of plus or minus 2 percent.

[2] In purchasing power parity, China is the largest economy in the world.

[3] Marie Charrel, "Les gouvernements doivent agir pour restaurer la croissance" *Le Monde Economie,* January 14, 2016, http://www.lemonde.fr/economie/article/2016/01/14/les-gouvernements-doivent-agir-pour-restaurer-la-croissance_4846974_3234.html. See a similar interview in English here: Dan Weil, "El-Erian: The Global Economy Needs Governments to Step Up," *Yahoo! Finance,* June 7, 2016, http://finance.yahoo.com/news/el-erian-global-economy-needs-101500524.html.

[4] Emmanuel Hache, "Fin de cycle sur les marches de matières premières: un nouvau paradigm économique et géopolitique?" IRIS Analyses, January 25, 2016, http://www.iris-france.org/70347-fin-de-cycle-sur-les-marches-de-matieres-premieres-un-nouveau-paradigme-economique-et-geopolitique/. See a similar article in English: Shelley Goldberg, "The End of the Commodity Super Cycle," *Wall St. Daily,* September 1, 2015, https://www.wallstreetdaily.com/2015/09/01/commodity-prices-super-cycle/.

[5] The uncertainties of 2016 clearly influenced the willingness of the Federal Reserve to increase

rates at a regular interval, adding a new source of uncertainty to all the others.

[6] Mohamed El-Erian, *The Only Game in Town: Central Banks, Instability, and Avoiding the Next Collapse* (Random House, 2016).

[7] Chris Giles, "Fears on Global Downturn are Overdone Say Economists" Financial Times, March 7, 2016. https://www.ft.com/content/ea13c478-e47b-11e5-bc31-138df2ae9ee6.

[8] David Lipton, "Can Globalization Still Deliver? The Challenge of Convergence in the 21st Century" (Sixteenth Annual Stavros Niarchos Foundation Lecture at the Peterson Institute for International Economics, May 24, 2016).

[9] "Number of Conflicts, 1975–2016," Uppsala Conflict Data Program, accessed September 13, 2017, http://ucdp.uu.se/.

[10] Eurovision is an annual pan-European song contest.

[11] Relatively speaking, because at first glance, the decrease in gas prices stimulates less growth than usual, since part of the gain realized is saved by more cautious consumers.

[12] "The Plague of Global Terrorism," *The Economist,* November 18, 2015, http://www.economist.com/blogs/graphicdetail/2015/11/daily-chart-12.

[13] The Schengen Area is made up of 26 European states that have no border controls.

[14] "World Is Locked into about 1.5°C Warming and Risks Are Rising, New Climate Report Finds," World Bank, November 23, 2014, http://www.worldbank.org/en/news/feature/2014/11/23/climate-report-finds-temperature-rise-locked-in-risks-rising.

[15] "Signature de l'Accord de Paris sur le climat: une première étape nécessaire, mais pas suffisante, selon l'ONU," Centre d'actualités de l'ONU, April 21, 2016, http://www.un.org/apps/newsFr/storyF.asp?NewsID=37072#.V0LVFlmMfoc.

[16] Ibid.

Chapter 6

[1] Peter H. Diamandis and Steven Kotler, *Abundance: The Future Is Better Than You Think* (Free Press, 2012).

[2] Antoine de Saint-Exupéry, *Wind, Sand and Stars* (Reynal and Hitchcock, 1939).

[3] Ian Bremmer, "The Absence of Global Leadership Will Shape a Tumultuous 2016," *Time,* December 21, 2015, http://time.com/4154044/geopolitics-2016/.

Chapter 7

[1] Michel Cicurel, "La planète finance danse sur un fil" (The financial world dances on a thread), *La Tribune,* January 30, 2007.

[2] Lipton, "Can Globalization Still Deliver?"

[3] Reference to a quote by Karl Marx: "Those who ignore history are condemned to repeat it." *Communist Party Manifesto,* 1847.

[4] Nassim Nicholas Taleb, *The Black Swan: The Impact of the Highly Improbable* (Random House, 2007).

[5] In 1975 during a referendum to join the European Union, the proponents in the United Kingdom campaigned with the argument "We cannot go it alone in the world." This argument applied so much more in 2016!

[6] Jacques de Chalendar (1920–2015) was special adviser to the director of national safety for unoccupied France in 1942, while at the same time being a member of the Resistance who joined the Inspectorate General of Finances in 1944 He became inspector general in 1973, and was deputy director general of Banque nationale pour le développement économique du Maroc (the National Economic Development Bank of Morocco), 1959–1962, adviser to the cabinet of Edgar Faure, minister of national education,

1968–1969, then president of the Association pour le développement des échanges en technologies économique et financière (Association for the Development of Economic and Financial Technology Exchanges), 1984–1989.

[7] In a conference held May 24, 2016, at the Peterson Institute, David Lipton observed that even if China never provides the boost it has in recent years, it still contributes to the world economy; a country of this size registering 5 percent growth is the equivalent to adding a Poland to the world's wealth every year. India, as well as a dozen other countries such as Vietnam, Bangladesh, Colombia, Peru, and even Ethiopia, also represents enormous potential.

[8] I founded Blue like an Orange Sustainable Capital because I want to devote myself to connecting these needs and resources. As Paul Éluard wrote, the Earth is blue like an orange; it's up to us to take care of it.

[9] Mark Carney, "Breaking the Tragedy of the Horizon—Climate Change and Financial Stability" (speech given at Lloyd's of London, September 29, 2015).

[10] Ibid.

[11] "Seize your luck, hold your happiness tight, and run toward your risk. The more they see

you, the more they will get used to it." René Char, "Mornings' Blush," in *Les Matinaux* (Gallimard, 1950). The name of the resistance poet happens be the same as that for my graduating class at ENA—a sign?

[12] This is one of the beliefs I inherited from Michel Camdessus, during the era of the Semaines sociales de France. We drafted the *Sursaut* (The jolt) report together for the Ministry of the Economy, Finance, and Industry, a report considered to be "ultraliberal" by some members of the Catholic Social movement. In the face of protests, Michel quoted Charles Péguy regarding Kantian morality: "Kantism has clean hands, *but it does not have hands.* But us, we have callused hands, gnarled hands, dry hands, and sometimes, our hands are full." Victor-Marie, comte Hugo, 1910. We cannot change the world without getting our hands a bit dirty. The only maneuvering room we have is to try to keep them dirty instead of filthy, to grapple with what is real while trying not to lose sight of our convictions.

[13] Badré, "Un banquier dans la tourment," p.113.

Chapter 8

[1] Jérôme Kerviel began working for Société Générale in the summer of 2000. He was responsible for the 2008 trading loss of

approximately €4.9 billion and was later convicted of breach of trust, forgery, and unauthorized use of bank computers.

[2] The idea of *reenchantment* was addressed at length by the German sociologist Max Weber.

[3] Jean Boissonat, personal communication with the author.

[4] "Sustainable Energy for All: Sector Results Profile," World Bank, April 9, 2014, http://www.worldbank.org/en/results/2013/04/10/sustainable-energy-for-all-results-profile.

[5] Tier 1 designates the most solid part, the hard kernel, of funds held by financial institutions. After the crisis, regulators differentiated the naming into three sets of funds (T1, T2, T3) to emphasize that they do not all have the same value, and that an institution's true capital, its share capital (Core-T1), should be reinforced.

[6] A clearinghouse is a financial body that acts as an intermediary between buyer and seller to guarantee delivery and receipt in transactions.

[7] Tier 1 designates the most solid part, the hard kernel, of funds held by financial institutions. Going forward, banks must maintain a Tier 1 of 7 percent (instead of the precrisis 4 percent) and a Core-T1 of 4 percent (instead of 2 percent). They must also retain a supplemental buffer of 2.5 percent of their profits during times

of economic prosperity (rather than distributing this as dividends or buying back shares), to which a surcharge is added to institutions systemic in nature.

[8] Total loss-absorbing capacity is a resource buffer made up of debt instruments that can be easily converted to capital in order to protect taxpayers in the event of difficulties.

[9] Transformation is the heart of the banking business. It involves the "transformation" of short-term resources (such as deposits) into long-term uses (loans for housing for infrastructure, for example).

[10] Mark Carney and Bertrand Badré, "Keep Finance Safe but Do Not Shut Out the Vulnerable," *Financial Times,* June 2, 2015.

[11] See, for instance, Ibid.: "When institutions acted as correspondents, they relied on their local 'respondents' to develop systems that prevented the two sides from doing business with criminals or transferring illicit funds. These systems sometimes failed and certain international banks, deliberately or not, provided accounts and money laundering services, facilitating the activities of drug cartels and terrorist groups."

[12] Today, it is no longer possible to transfer money to Somalian refugee camps, which is problematic to say the least.

[13] *Blockchains* are secured, distributed databases that are shared between various users without an intermediary and that contain the history of changes made between these users since its creation. This blockchain system allows each user to guarantee at any given moment the authenticity and individuality of its transactions.

Chapter 9

[1] "Seven Themes of Catholic Social Teaching," United States Conference of Catholic Bishops, accessed September 13, 2017, http://www.usccb.org/beliefs-and-teachings/what-we-believe/catholic-social-teaching/seven-themes-of-catholic-social-teaching.cfm.

[2] Pope Francis, "Pope Francis: Stop the Culture of Waste," OnFaith, accessed September 13, 2017, https://www.onfaith.co/onfaith/2014/04/21/pope-francis-stop-the-culture-of-waste/31766.

[3] Pope Francis, "Address to Global Foundation Roundtable," Vatican Radio, January 14, 2017, http://en.radiovaticana.va/news/2017/01/14/pope_francis_address_to_global_foundation_roundtable/1285625.

[4] The Consumer Classroom, http://www.dolceta.eu/, has also outfitted itself with a valuable tool, lafinancepourtous.com, developed by the Institutpour l'éducation financière du public (Institute for public financial education), a general-interest group approved by the French Ministry of National Education.

[5] Camdessus et al., *Eau,* p.154.

[6] Ibid., pp.155–57.

[7] Badré, "Un banquier dans la tourment."

[8] Carney, "Breaking the Tragedy of the Horizon."

[9] See Larry Fink quoted in Matt Turner, "Here Is the Letter the World's Largest Investor, BlackRock CEO Larry Fink, Just Sent to CEOs Everywhere," *Business Insider,* February 2, 2016, http://www.businessinsider.com/blackrock-ceo-larry-fink-letter-to-sp-500-ceos-2016-2.

[10] Jean Favier, *De l'or et des épices. Naissance de l'homme d'affaires au Moyen Âge* (Gold and spices: The birth of the businessman in the Middle Ages) (Fayard, 1987).

[11] Jean Favier, *Les Grandes Découvertes. D'Alexandre à Magellan* (The Age of Discovery: From Alexander to Magellan) (Fayard, 1991).

Chapter 10

[1] Bruno Roche and Jay Jakub, *Completing Capitalism: Heal Business to Heal the World* (Berrett-Koehler Publishers, 2017).

[2] Rym Ayadi, "Word from IRCCF Director, Professor Rym Ayadi," International Research Centre on Cooperative Finance, accessed September 13, 2017, http://financecoop.hec.ca/en/research/.

[3] Michael E. Porter and Mark R. Kramer, "Creating Shared Value," *Harvard Business Review,* January–February 2011.

[4] Shared Value Initiative, *Banking on Shared Value: How Banks Profit by Rethinking Their Purpose* (Foundation Strategy Group, 2014).

[5] Some 2.5 billion people around the world are still excluded from access to quality banking services. Ibid.

[6] See Social Impact Investment Taskforce, *Impact Investment: The Invisible Heart of Markets. Harnessing the Power of Entrepreneurship, Innovation and Capital for Public Good* (G8 under British leadership, September 15, 2014).

[7] Original translation from Pilot Group on Innovative Funding, *Comment encourager la philanthropie privée au service du développement? Étude sur les modèles*

émergents (Pilot Group on Innovative Funding, May 2012).

[8] See Chapter 16.

[9] Social Impact Investment Taskforce, *Impact Investment.*

[10] "RFF's Decision to Divest," Rockefeller Family Fund, accessed 9/13/2017, http://www.rffund.org/divestment.

[11] Carney, "Breaking the Tragedy of the Horizon."

[12] Ibid.

[13] Original translation from Gérard Mestrallet, "Le prix du carbone, une boussole pour les entreprises," *Le Monde,* April 16, 2015.

[14] Camdessus et al., *Eau,* p.143.

[15] Ibid., pp.194–95.

[16] Groupe de Travail présidé par Jean-Pierre Landau, *Les nouvelles contributions financières internationales* (La documentation Française, n.d.), http://www.ladocumentationfrancaise.fr/var/storage/rapports-publics/044000440.pdf.

[17] Original translation from "Financements innovants du développement: Les grandes étapes de la creation de la taxe de solidarité sur les billets d'avion et d'UNITAID," foundation Chirac, http://www.fondationchirac.eu/wp-content/uploads/Financements-innovants.pdf.

[18] Because of a mutual aid agreement signed by Jacques Chirac and Tony Blair, 10 percent of the proceeds of the Chirac tax went to this project.

[19] Building quality traffic infrastructure is a different kind of problem, which is much more expensive and requires a different funding method. See Chapter 15.

Chapter 11

[1] Nations Unies Assemblée générale, *Nous, les peuples: le role des Nations Unies au XXIe siècle,* Rapport du Secrétaire general (Nations Unies Assemblée general, 2000), http://www.un.org/fr/documents/view_doc.asp?symbol=A/54/2000.

[2] The establishment of the World Bank goes back to the Bretton Woods Agreement, signed in 1944, which simultaneously created the IMF. Both institutions had the common goal of getting the global economy back on its feet, but they are entrusted with distinct roles: the IMF's mission is international financial stability, while the World Bank's mission is to aid development. Since 1944 the World Bank has expanded from a single institution to a group of five closely linked organizations: the International Bank for Reconstruction and Development, initially entrusted with supporting postwar reconstruction

and development (hence its name), whose mandate is now to reduce poverty around the world along with its affiliated institution; the International Development Association; as well as the International Finance Corporation; the Multilateral Investment Guarantee Agency; and the International Centre for Settlement of Investment Disputes. These institutions are administered by the member states of the World Bank Group.

[3] Élysée Palace is the official residence of the president of France and is referred to in much the same way as the White House is in the United States.

[4] United Nations General Assembly, *We the Peoples: The Role of the United Nations in the Twenty-first Century,* Report of the Secretary-General (United Nations General Assembly, 2000), http://www.un.org/fr/documents/view_doc.asp?symbol+A/54/2000.

[5] The G8 was abandoned after the annexation of Crimea by Russia in 2014.

[6] The Brexit referendum may mean rerunning this analysis!

[7] Such is the result of inclusive growth, as I was able to expound on recently during LVMH's (Moët Hennessy Louis Vuitton SE) annual meeting, where I was invited to speak on the unlikely

but ultimately inspiring theme of "Luxury and Development."

[8] See Bertrand Badré, "Quand la Banque mondiale soulève le couvercle des cultures" (When the World Bank lifts the lid off cultures), interview with Alain Henry, *Le Débat* 2015/3, no.185, pp.185–90: "I have never seen an executive board that was as diverse as the one in which I participated today. Never! I was used to executive boards composed of graduates from French Polytechniques and Énarques: in short, white men, from the same schools, raised Catholic—and also with their own universalist bias. The Bank presents real cultural diversity. It is striking to be in the cafeteria here. You have the entire world at your feet. I don't know anywhere else in the world where you could see the same thing."

[9] Ibid.

Chapter 12

[1] A special tribute must be paid here to Gordon Brown, whose leadership at the G20 summit in London in 2009 was decisive.

[2] From June 12 to July 27, 1933, the London Economic Conference gathered representatives from 66 countries determined to restart the global economy that had been seriously damaged

in the 1929 crash and the devaluation of the British pound in 1931. The international agreement broke down on opposition from President Franklin D. Roosevelt, who had not even made the trip, to a currency exchange stabilization agreement, promoted specifically by France. The international monetary system founded on the gold system then collapsed, relaunching the global crisis.

[3] In French "Depuis le temps que nous multiplions les rendez-vous galants, il est temps d'aller conclure au lit!"

[4] I call this "P4C." See Chapter 16.

[5] http://news.xinhuanet.com/english/2016-05/22/c_135377957.htm

[6] One way to monitor implementation of the 2030 Agenda for Sustainable Development would be for the G20 leaders to reconstitute the Development Working Group (DWG) within their sustainable development working group: an embodiment of the universal commitment to SDGs, this institutional innovation would strengthen the existing system for evaluating countries' responsibilities—the G20's Mutual Assessment Process, which tracks the various growth strategies and structural reform programs—by defining a set of priorities and guiding principles, and by relying on a voluntary

statement by the countries of their progress, based on evidence and data.

[7] MDBs include the African Development Bank, Asian Infrastructure Investment Bank, Asian Development Bank, European Bank for Reconstruction and Development, European Investment Bank, Inter-American Development Bank, Islamic Development Bank, New Development Bank, and World Bank Group.

[8] Badré, "Quand la Banque mondiale soulève le couvercle des cultures."

[9] "Chairman's Statement—Global Infrastructure Forum 2016," World Bank, April 16, 2016, http://www.worldbank.org/en/topic/publicprivatepartnerships/brief/chairmans-statement-global-infrastructure-forum-2016.

[10] Carney, "Breaking the Tragedy of the Horizon."

[11] "Carbon Pricing: Building on the Momentum of the Paris Agreement," World Bank, April 15, 2016, http://www.worldbank.org/en/news/feature/2016/04/15/carbon-pricing-building-on-the-momentum-of-the-paris-agreement.

Chapter 13

[1] Concessional lending is a form of finance that is extended at very low rates ("concessional rates") and that is free of the traditional

collateral requirements of commercial banks and other lenders. Concessional loans offer borrowers a number of advantages related to guarantees and interest rates: when the former rates are low, or zero, or when the borrower receives a temporary relief or extension of repayments, the loan contains a "grant" element.

[2] Since the creation of IDA, donor countries have contributed to raising over $250 billion, or close to 20 times the capital contribution of the International Bank for Reconstruction and Development, 100 times that of the International Finance Corporation (IFC), and more than 600 times that of the Multilateral Investment Guarantee Agency.

[3] This number compares to $65 billion for the IFC, International Bank for Reconstruction and Development, and Multilateral Investment Guarantee Agency combined. Even though these funds are not exactly the same in nature, it shows that donors have provided a significant amount in a few decades.

[4] For more on pandemics, see Chapter 5.

[5] All MDBs are rated. One of the key points considered by ratings agencies is the level of concentration of exposure of these institutions in their credit portfolios. By nature, given the limited number of sovereign counterparts, all the MDBs have concentrated portfolios. This is, of

course, not totally comparable to various concentration ratios used by commercial banks, but there are similarities. Coverage methods also cannot be applied in the same manner. Hence the idea is to turn to derivative products and to realize transactions implicating different banks exchanging some of their exposure in a synthetic manner.

Chapter 14

[1] On philanthropic groups, see Matthew Bishop and Michael Green, *Philanthrocapitalism* (Bloomsbury Publishing, 2008).

[2] If I am concentrating on the World Bank Group here, it is because that is where I gained my experience. The analysis could be applied to most MDBs: its model differs due to its cost base (the cost–revenue ratio of the World Bank is substantially higher, in part because the bank must take global public goods into account) or even the relative importance granted to public or private sector engagement, but these institutions have many things in common, in particular their mission and status.

[3] Spillover and spillback effects measure the effects of a decision of one country on the other countries and vice versa.

[4] Their margins are dozens of basis points, or 0.1 percent, compared to hundreds of basis points for the former, or several percent.

[5] See Development Committee, *From Billions to Trillions:* "Domestic Resource Mobilization (DRM) has become more and more key to financing national development plans. Taking positive growth trends into account, the DRM of emerging and developing economies totaled 7.7 trillion dollars in 2012. In other words, the treasuries of developing countries now receive over 6 trillion additional dollars each year, compared with in 2000, thereby helping to reduce their dependence on aid and improving the solvency of many countries."

[6] See Ibid.: "Financing the investments needed to reach SDGs will require the international community to adjust its scale from billions in public development aid to trillions in all kinds of investments: human and material, and using public and private, national and international sourcing. In fact, SDGs require each dollar donated to be used as wisely as possible, starting with the 135 billion dollars in public development aid. But this also concerns individual donations, migrants' remittances, South-South flows, other forms of public aid, and direct foreign investments. To reach the expected levels, two other major financing sources must be mobilized: the internal resources

of each country, as that is where most of the development expenses are, and financing and private investor financing with a real potential to obtain additional funds."

[7] See Camdessus et al., *Eau,* p.205: Guarantees "can take different forms but, ultimately, they are all the same thing: an institution outside a project provides a guarantee that enables the project developers to face a specific risk that exceeds their current financial standing and makes it possible to finance a project or decrease its costs."

[8] The need for adjustment was less pronounced at IFC—which had recently suffered from a more hostile environment, as expected—or at MIGA: from the point of view of the financial model, these institutions were more advanced, in particular because of their closer ties to the private sector.

[9] It has become a self-fulfilling prophecy to IBRD, particularly, which was faced with the risk of seeing its annual commitment of $15 billion start to decline.

[10] Again, this observation applies less to IFC and MIGA.

[11] A bank must be profitable even if your system is made more complex because of instruments such as trust funds.

[12] Development Committee, *From Billions to Trillion.*

[13] This includes syndication of B loans, fund-raising by its Asset Management Company subsidiary (equity), or even Managed Co-Lending Portfolio Program (this relates to debt) loans, more recent and innovative loans, which involve working with external investors. Intelligently combined, both approaches pave the way to a systematic mobilization effort.

[14] See the *Doing Business* report published each year by the World Bank.

[15] See Camdessus et al., *Eau,* p.209.

[16] Ibid: "The establishment of financial markets is not a place for improvisation. It is a field par excellence where the technical assistance of advanced countries saves precious time and avoids initial errors, which can accelerate training of local actors and adoption of operating regulations which have been proven elsewhere in terms of discipline, transparency, liquidity, equality of access, etc."

[17] One way to develop financial markets in emerging countries lies in "offshore" sale of bonds denominated in national currency to national and international investors.

Chapter 15

[1] Camdessus et al., *Eau,* pp.153–54.

[2] Ibid., *Eau,* pp.227–28.

[3] Ibid., p.234.

[4] Ibid., pp.235–36.

[5] https://ppp.worldbank.org/public-private-partnership/library/ppp-massive-open-online-course-how-can-ppps-deliver-better-services

[6] de Villepin's speech on February 14, 2003, addressing the responsibilities and implications of the Iraq crisis, received a standing ovation. Transcript: "Statement by France to Security Council," *New York Times,* February 14, 2003, http://www.nytimes.com/2003/02/14/international/middleeast/statement-by-france-to-security-council.html.

[7] Groupe de Travail présidé par Jean-Pierre Landau, *Les nouvelles contributions financières internationales* (La documentation Française, n.d.), http://www.ladocumentationfrancaise.fr/var/storage/rapports-publics/044000440.pdf.

[8] Camdessus, *Le sursaut.*

Chapter 16

[1] Syndication is a technique that allows a bank to share a loan with other financial institutions and hence diminish the impact on its own balance sheet.

[2] Development Committee, *From Billions to Trillions.*

[3] Ibid.

[4] Ibid.

[5] Established within the support framework of the G20 to the Global Infrastructure Initiative (a multiyear program to improve the quality of public and private investment in infrastructure), the Global Infrastructure Hub, based in Sydney and given a four-year mandate, was conceived as the neutral center for the program. Its goal is to encourage cooperation and information exchange among all actors—governments, the private sector, development banks, and international organizations—in order to improve the function and financing of the infrastructure market.

[6] I am now the honorary chairman of this platform, which is a joint venture between the World Economic Forum and the OECD, sponsored by the Swedish International Development Cooperation Agency and USAID, as well as

Citibank and Sumitomo Mitsui Banking Corporation. It brings together bilateral and multilateral agencies, banks, investors, sponsors, and NGOs, to name a few.

[7] The Coletivo initiative launched by Coca-Cola Brazil is the example par excellence of the shared-value approach. Through this project, designed in collaboration with local NGOs, the company gave two months of sales training to a few thousand troubled teens, giving them a springboard to landing their first jobs. At the same time, these young people contributed to selling more sodas in stores where they did their internships and were asked to reflect on ways to improve stock management, promotions, marketing, and more. The investment yielded a profit within two years. By rigorously measuring these results, the subsidiary was able to convince the parent company to extend the pilot project to more than 150 low-income communities around Brazil. More than 50,000 youths received training through Coletivo, and 30 percent of them landed their first job working for Coca-Cola or its partners.

[8] The Danone Communities initiative had its beginnings in a meeting between Franck Riboud, CEO of Danone, and Muhammad Yunus, president of the Grameen microcredit bank and Nobel Peace Prize recipient in 2006. Strengthened by their common convictions and complementary

skill sets, they decided to join forces to found a new company, Grameen Danone Foods. The goal was to create a yogurt factory in Bangladesh that was profitable enough to stay in business while also contributing to local development. Taking it a step further, Danone decided to fit it out with an innovative financial tool, open to everyone and created to encourage the development of social business initiatives: danone.communities. Launched in 2007, this open-end mutual fund, managed and marketed by Crédit Agricole, had a pathway marked out: to develop Grameen Danone Foods by building other factories in Bangladesh; to aid the development in other parts of the world (in Senegal and Cambodia today, for instance) of other social business enterprises consistent with Danone's mission; to develop partnerships with other local actors or NGOs through the original business model; and to bring together through the Danone Communities all those who contribute to the project, including investors interested in giving a sense of solidarity to their portfolios.

[9] The Sustainable Banking Network launched following the first international forum on green credit (the International Green Credit Forum), organized jointly by the IFC and the China Banking Regulatory Commission in Beijing in May 2012. For more, see, for example, "Sustainable Banking Network," IFC, accessed September 15,

2017, http://www.ifc.org/wps/wcm/connect/Topics_Ext_Content/IFC_External_Corporate_Site/IFC+Sustainability/Partnerships/Susatainable+Banking+Network/.

[10] Development Committee, *From Billions to Trillions:* "In 2013, MDBs committed more than 28 billion dollars to encourage climate action in developing and emerging economies, which brings the total commitments in the last four years to over 100 billion dollars."

[11] Camdessus et al., *Eau,* pp.143–44.

[12] Ibid., pp.147–48.

[13] Ibid., pp.247–48.

[14] Ibid., p.248.

[15] Ibid., pp.187–88.

[16] The main island, Guadalcanal, was the theater of the famous battle in 1942–1943 between the Japanese and Americans, immortalized by Terrence Malick in his 1998 film *The Thin Red Line.*

[17] Having completed my own military service in Polynesia, I remember missions intended to prevent Taiwanese, Korean, and Japanese trawlers from stockpiling fish from French territorial waters.

[18] The tuna packing plant received a loan in 2013 of $10 million backed by the IFC, specifically to finance the acquisition of new equipment (cold chambers, improved housing for employees, etc.). For more, see, for example, "Saving Tuna: IFC Provides $10 Million Loan to Soltuna in Solomon Islands," IFC, accessed September 14, 2017, http://www.ifc.org/wps/wcm/connect/news_ext_content/ifc_external_corporate_site/news+and+events/news/ifc+provides+%2410+million+loan+to+soltuna+in+solomon+islands.

[19] To reach Honiara from Australia, it takes a multi-hour flight, then another two-hour flight, then an hour by car to reach the factory.

Conclusion

[1] For more, see Thomas Friedman, *The World Is Flat* (Farrar, Straus, and Giroux, 2005).

[2] Jean Giraudoux, *Tiger at the Gates,* trans. Christopher Fry (Oxford University Press, 1955).

[3] Camdessus et al., *Eau,* p.115.

ACKNOWLEDGMENTS

I do not want to close this book without thanking those who have helped me on my nearly 30-year voyage in finance.

I think about my different bosses, and the first of them, Philippe Sala, who gave me confidence, as well as teams that I worked with at BFI, the Ministry of Finance, Lazard, Élysée Palace, Crédit Agricole, Société Générale, the World Bank, and Blue like an Orange Sustainable Capital. I am also reminded of the Semaines sociales de France: my thanks to Michel Camdessus.

Thanks to President Emmanuel Macron, with whom I had the privilege and pleasure to discuss in real time most of the topics addressed in this book and who agreed to introduce the English version of this book.

Thanks to Prime Minister Gordon Brown, one of the major architects of the 2008–2009 economic rescue, and a postcrisis thinker who also provided a foreword to the book.

Thanks to my colleagues in the *Eau* (water), Nouvelles contributions financières internationales (New international financial contributions), and *Le sursaut* (The wake-up call) groups, who confirmed for me the value of good faith, goodwill, and the spirit of deliberation to tackle complex problems and find agreement.

Thanks to everyone working in NGOs; directors of international organizations and development institutions, central banks, and business leaders; and the men and women working for the common good who have helped to form my thoughts in recent years, with particular gratitude for Steve Howard and the Global Foundation, with whom I have interacted extensively over the past few years. I have called on the ideas of a number of them in the pages of the book. Thank you for this shared wisdom.

Thanks to all the people who welcomed me into their countries, who helped me to understand the complexity of what we call development, the immensity of the needs, and the infinite possibilities. To these everyday architects of a better world: bravo!

Thanks to Professor Klaus Schwab and the teams at the World Economic Forum, who entrusted me with the position of Cochair of the Global Future Council on International Governance, Public-Private Cooperation and Sustainable Development, and Honorary Chair of the Sustainable Development Investment Partnership. These discussion venues have had a considerable influence on the book.

Thanks to Adam Posen and Olivier Blanchard, who have hosted me at the Peterson Institute for International Economics over several months and pushed me to write down my thoughts. Without them, this book never would have been written. The environment of openness and friendly curiosity that I found with them, at a time that called for good judgment, was an amazing stroke of luck.

Thanks to all who have invested in Blue like an Orange Sustainable Capital with the idea that finance can improve the world, and not just the bottom line.

Thanks to the Blue like an Orange Sustainable Capital team who help me walk the talk of this book. Particular thanks to Amer Baig for his patience and support throughout the editing and review of the English version of the manuscript.

I am also particularly grateful to Jean Guyot, Jean Boissonnat, and Michel Albert, with whom I discussed the questions raised in this book over and over again. They are always at my side.

Finally, I would like to express my appreciation to Emmanuel and Pierre, two uncles I lost too soon, who introduced me to the mysteries of finance and guided my first steps.

ABOUT THE AUTHOR

Bertrand Badré is CEO and Founder of Blue like an Orange Sustainable Capital, an investment fund with the objective to deliver market-level financial returns while at the same time achieving credible, sustainable development outcomes.

Previously, Bertrand was Managing Director and Chief Financial Officer of the World Bank Group, where he led a number of the most important reforms that the group undertook and also represented the group in various international forums, such as the G20 and the Financial Stability Board. Prior to joining the World Bank Group, Bertrand was the Group Chief Financial Officer at Société Générale and before that, at Crédit Agricole, two of the world's leading financial institutions; he helped navigate both banks through the financial crisis. Before joining Crédit Agricole,

Bertrand was a Managing Director of Lazard in Paris and was responsible for the Financial Services Group.

In 2003 Bertrand was invited to join French president Jacques Chirac's diplomatic team and was closely involved in the preparation of the G8 summit in Évian, France. In that capacity, he served as the president's deputy personal representative for Africa and as a spokesman for the working group on new international financial contributions to fight poverty and fund development, which produced the Landau report. In 2002 he was a member of the World Panel on Financing Water Infrastructure, chaired by Michel Camdessus, the former Managing Director of the IMF.

Prior to joining Lazard, Bertrand served in France's Ministry of Finance, where he led a number of control, audit, and consultancy missions for the French National Audit Office. Bertrand began his career in 1989 as Assistant Group Controller for BFI-IBEXSA, a Franco-American company that is now part of Avnet.

Bertrand has served as director on a number of boards, including the supervisory board of private equity firm Eurazeo, the board of manufacturing company Haulotte Group, and various boards of the leading French regional daily newspaper group *Ouest-France.* He represented Crédit Agricole and Société Générale on the boards of a number of their subsidiaries. He is a member of the board of Wealthsimple, a leading Canadian fintech based in Toronto, and nonexecutive chairman of Future Positive

Capital, an impact venture capital technology company based in Europe.

Bertrand is a member of the advisory board of the newly created International Water Bank and of the Paris-based IDDRI (Institute for Sustainable Development and International Relations). He is also a board member of the French-American Foundation, an honorary member of the Cincinnati Society, and a fellow at the German Marshall Fund of the United States. He is Cochair of the World Economic Forum's Global Future Council on International Governance, Public-Private Cooperation and Sustainable Development.

Bertrand has taught in a number of schools and universities and is the author of several books. He is a graduate of ENA (Ecole Nationale d'Administration) and Institut d'Etudes Politiques de Paris. He also studied history at Paris IV University (La Sorbonne) and graduated from HEC Paris (Hautes Etudes Commerciales de Paris) business school. Bertrand is married to Vanessa; they have four children and live in Washington, DC.

Berrett–Koehler
BK Publishers

Berrett-Koehler is an independent publisher dedicated to an ambitious mission: Connecting people and ideas to create a world that works for all.

We believe that the solutions to the world's problems will come from all of us, working at all levels: in our organizations, in our society, and in our own lives. Our BK Business books help people make their organizations more humane, democratic, diverse, and effective (we don't think there's any contradiction there). Our BK Currents books offer pathways to creating a more just, equitable, and sustainable society. Our BK Life books help people create positive change in their lives and align their personal practices with their aspirations for a better world.

All of our books are designed to bring people seeking positive change together around the ideas that empower them to see and shape the world in a new way.

And we strive to practice what we preach. At the core of our approach is Stewardship, a deep sense of responsibility to administer the company for the benefit of all of our stakeholder groups including authors, customers, employees, investors, service providers, and the communities and environment around us. Everything we do is built around this and our other key values of quality, partnership, inclusion, and sustainability.

This is why we are both a B-Corporation and a California Benefit Corporation—a certification and a for-profit legal status that require us to adhere to the highest standards for corporate, social, and environmental performance.

We are grateful to our readers, authors, and other friends of the company who consider themselves to be part of the BK Community. We hope that you, too, will join us in our mission.

A BK Business Book

We hope you enjoy this BK Business book. BK Business books pioneer new leadership and management practices and socially responsible approaches to business. They are designed to provide you with groundbreaking and practical tools to transform your work and organizations while upholding the triple bottom line of people, planet, and profits. High-five!

To find out more, visit www.bkconnection.com.

Dear Reader,

Thank you for picking up this book and joining our worldwide community of Berrett-Koehler readers. We share ideas that bring positive change into people's lives, organizations, and society.

To welcome you, we'd like to offer you a free e-book. You can pick from among twelve of our bestselling books by entering the promotional code **BKP92E** here: http://www.bkconnection.com/welcome.

When you claim your free e-book, we'll also send you a copy of our e-newsletter, the *BK Communiqué*. Although you're free to unsubscribe, there are many benefits to sticking around. In every issue of our newsletter you'll find

- A free e-book
- Tips from famous authors
- Discounts on spotlight titles
- Hilarious insider publishing news
- A chance to win a prize for answering a riddle

Best of all, our readers tell us, "Your newsletter is the only one I actually read." So claim your gift today, and please stay in touch!

Sincerely,

Charlotte Ashlock

Steward of the BK Website

Questions? Comments? Contact me at bkcommunity@bkpub.com.

Certified B Corporation™ bcorporation.net

A

B

C

D

G

H

I

J

K

L

M

S

T

U

V

W

X